LITURGICAL RESOURCES
FOR THE YEAR OF MATTHEW

To Kevin Lyon,
A gift for his Golden Jubilee

Thomas O'Loughlin

Liturgical Resources for the Year of Matthew

ORDINARY TIME, YEAR A OF THE LITURGICAL CYCLE

the columba press

First published in 2007 by
the columba press
55A Spruce Avenue, Stillorgan Industrial Park,
Blackrock, Co Dublin

Cover by Bill Bolger
Cover photo by Kevin Lyon
Origination by The Columba Press
Printed in Ireland by ColourBooks Ltd, Dublin

ISBN 978 1 85607 593 0

Acknowledgement
I would like to acknowledge the help and feedback I have had from so
many people – priests in parishes, musicians, liturgists, scripture schol-
ars, and most importantly many who 'sit in the pews' – to the materials
printed here during the time that I was putting together this collection
of resources. I would also like to thank Dr Francisca Rumsey of the Poor
Clare Monastery in Arkley for proofreading the manuscript.

Table of Contents

Preface

Celebrating the liturgy well is a far more complex task than providing good preaching; yet, right or wrong, preaching is used by many people as their thermometer of what they think about either a particular celebration or president. This may be a symptom of a more profound malaise that 'the rest' of the liturgy is just a fixed formula and it is simply a matter of getting through it as fast and efficiently as possible. However, given that attitude that one can 'judge a priest' by his preaching, I find it very interesting to ask groups of people what do they consider the qualities of 'a good sermon' (most people do not respond to the word 'homily'). The results are predictable. In most discussions three groups emerge. The first I call the 'Penny Catechism lobby' who want instruction and information, often qualified by such adjectives a 'clear' and 'straight forward'. The second group I call the 'Thought for the Day brigade' who want to be inspired and provided with a weekly fill of spiritual insights, while being given a new sense of pleasure/beauty/ happiness. The third group are 'the Advocates of Youthful Relevance': they are not concerned for themselves (being beyond the stage of needing to hear any preaching for their own benefit) but for 'the young people'. These young people, they argue, will listen only if the homily is interesting, relevant, and amusing. And on this note they usually get some support from the other two groups. It is a rather sad picture as one suspects that only half-a-dozen people in the whole history of the church would fit the bill – and that would not include Augustine, Gregory the Great, nor Thomas Aquinas!

Turning from groups of listeners to writers on communications theory, one finds yet another set of demands: in a media-savvy age of politicians more famous for their media skills than their grasp of the implications of policy, the preacher who has only his/her voice and an audience that is only listening to them as part of a larger event is doomed. Anyone who offers skills-

training for 'communication events' when faced with the conditions of a Sunday homily is apt to throw up her/his hands and
declare that 'it is a no-go' in the media-saturated world we live
in.

Turning to writers on liturgy, and formal church pronounce-
ments in particular, one finds yet another set of demands. The
homily – and they are clear it is a homily not a sermon – is to be
linked to the readings (but it is to be more than 'simply' biblical
exegesis), linked to the liturgical event being celebrated, and
linked to the liturgical year.

And, if all that was not enough, there is then the thorny question of time. Most people 'in the pews' believe that preaching
'goes on' far too long (ten minutes seems the ideal for most
preachers; much less for most audiences); and in this perception
they find support from teachers and communications experts
who can demonstrate that the average attention span on any one
topic is much less than ten minutes – a fact we witness in their
love of getting politicians to use 'sound bites'. The preacher is
now someone who is set up to fail: she/he must inform, instruct,
inspire, interpret, interest, influence, and even, amuse in about
five minutes! Good luck! So why tell you all this at the beginning
of a book of liturgical resources: with morale so battered, is there
any purpose in even trying?

The good news is that the above analysis is fundamentally
flawed. It assumes that the activity of the preacher can be understood by analogy (or even, in the opinion of many communications' specialists, by direct comparison) with that of the sales-
person/marketer selling widgets, services, or ideas. This confuses
the action of preaching for a few minutes with the action of a
commercial (or 'infomercial'), a party political broadcast, or a
sales-pitch. In these cases there is a product and an end-result:
acceptance or absorbance of what is being 'pushed'. But while
there may be occasions when Christianity has to engage in such
sales pitches or in 'getting its ideas heard', that is not the activity
of the homily and should never be compared with it. Propagating
religious ideas may have a place in the work-load of the pastor,

but not at the Sunday Eucharist. Indeed, going back over the examples of our Sunday preaching from the very beginning (and we have extant Sunday homilies that are older than our written gospels), selling religious ideas has never (at least, in Catholic and Orthodox preaching) been a major component. Our fundamental assumption is that the community is gathering already formed by the Spirit and animated by the Christ so that it can rejoice and offer praise, thanksgiving, and petition to the Father. It, most decidedly, is not some amorphous throng to be bombarded with ideas they do not yet possess.

So how should we perceive preaching? First, and foremost, it is just one moment in the whole act of memory that is the community's gathering. Just as we remember who we are in the opening rites (our identity or place in the year or our sinfulness), in the readings (our common basic memories that make us the group we are), in the eucharistic rite (when we engage in anamnesis of the paschal work of the Christ) or in eating and drinking as one body, so also, during the preaching, we remember in some *viva voce* thoughts who we are and what we are up to as Christians. Just as at any celebration there is need for 'a few words' to actualise what it is that the gathering is about, so also there is that need at the Eucharist. Which, incidentally, is why 'the few words' must link up with what we are doing, what we have read, and with the time of year. But the key point is that the homily must be just one element in the preparation and good execution of the whole liturgy that involves many ministries in the community apart from that of the preacher. The homily is but an element in what must be a richly prepared whole.

The fact that the homily is neither a lecture nor a sales pitch does not mean that we should ignore the work of communications experts. One can learn many speaking and communicating skills, and one should do so. One should not be boring if one can help it; and if anyone has a talent to amuse then that is one more gift that should be placed at the service of God's people. But, in a media saturated age, we must not forget our primary task. The homily is a spontaneous narration of where we as the community, a unified body made one with Christ in baptism, have come from; a narration of who we are; a narration of where we are going; and a questioning aloud of how we are performing as a pilgrim people. This narration looks backwards (where have we come from, which involves the whole mystery of faith and not just the readings), it looks forward to the vision of the kingdom and the end times, and it looks at today: our identity as the church in the world, and at our performance of our discipleship.

It is to provide ideas in this work of narration, not just for the homily but the whole of the Eucharistic celebration, that these pages have been written.

T.O'L
Lampeter
Pentecost 2007.

Psalm Numbers

In the *Lectionary* and *Missal* the numbers given to the Psalms follow that given in the Latin *Ordo Lectionum* which, being in Latin, naturally follows the Vulgate numeration. The Vulgate numeration followed that of the Old Greek translation ('The Septuagint') as this was seen as 'the Psalter of the Church.' However, most modern books, apart from Catholic liturgical books, follow the numeration of the Hebrew text of the Psalter.

Since this book's primary referents are the books of the Catholic liturgy, the Septuagint number is given first and the Hebrew numeration is then given in (brackets). The same convention as is used in the English translation of the Liturgy of the Hours. See *Breviary*, vol 1, pp 640*-641* for further information.

For example: The Psalm that begins 'My heart is ready' is cited as Ps 107(108).

For convenience here is a concordance of the two numeration systems:

Septuagint	Hebrew
1 – 8	1 - 8
9	9 - 10
10 -112	11 - 113
113	114 - 115
114 - 115	116
116 - 145	117 - 146
146 - 147	147
148 - 150	148 - 150

The Sequence of Gospel Readings:
An Overview

The purpose of this table is to show at a glance the sweep of readings through Matthew in Year A. We must remember, of course, that this sweep is always interrupted by Easter. It also shows at a glance that there is no sequence in the first readings; each being chosen as having some relationship with the gospel of the day.

Sunday	Gospel	First Reading
	Lectionary Unit I	
1 – Baptism	Mt 3:13-7	Isa 42:1-4, 6-7
2	Jn 1:29-34	Isa 49:3, 5-6
	Lectionary Unit II	
3	Mt 4:12-23	Isa 8:23–9:3
4	Mt 5:1-12	Zeph 2:3; 3:12-13
5	Mt 5:13-16	Isa 58:7-10
6	Mt 5:17-37	Sir 15:15-20
7	Mt 5:38-48	Lev 19:1-2, 17-18
8	Mt 6:24-34	Isa 49:14-15
9	Mt 7:21-27	Deut 11:18, 26-28, 32
	Lectionary Unit III	
10	Mt 9:9-13	Hos 6:3-6
11	Mt 9:36–10:8	Ex 19:2-6
12	Mt 10:26-33	Jer 20:10-13
13	Mt 10:37-42	2 Kgs 4:8-11, 14-16
	Lectionary Unit IV	
14	Mt 11:25-30	Zech 9:9-10
15	Mt 13:1-23	Isa 55:10-11
16	Mt 13:24-43	Wis 12:13, 16-19
17	Mt 13:44-52	1 Kgs 3:5, 7-12
Lectionary Unit V		
18	Mt 14:13-21	Isa 55:1-3
19	Mt 14:22-33	1 Kgs 19:9, 11-13

Sunday	Gospel	First Reading
20	Mt 15:21-28	Isa 56:1, 6-7
21	Mt 16:13-20	Isa 22:19-23
22	Mt 16:21-27	Jer 20:7-9
23	Mt 18:15-20	Ezek 33:7-9
24	Mt 18:21-35	Sir 27:30-28:7
	Lectionary Unit VI	
25	Mt 20:1-16	Isa 55:6-9
26	Mt 21:28-32	Ezek 18:25-28
27	Mt 21:33-43	Isa 5:1-7
28	Mt 22:1-14	Isa 25:6-10
29	Mt 22:15-21	Isa 45:1, 4-6
30	Mt 22:34-40	Ex 22:20-26
31	Mt 23:1-12	Mal 1:14-2:2, 8-10
32	Mt 25:1-13	Wis 6:12-16
33	Mt 25:14-30	Prov 31:10-31 (bits)
	Lectionary Unit VII	
34 – Christ the King	Mt 25:31-46	Ezek 34:11-12, 15-17

The Sequence of Second Readings:
An Overview

The purpose of this table is to show at a glance the sweep of readings through the epistles in Year A. We must remember, of course, that this sweep is always interrupted by Easter.

Sunday	Second Reading
1 – Baptism	Acts 10:34-38
2	1 Cor 1:1-3
3	1 Cor 1:10-13, 17
4	1 Cor 1:26-31
5	1 Cor 2:1-5
6	1 Cor 2:6-10
7	1 Cor 3:16-23
8	1 Cor 4:1-5
9	Rom 3:21-25, 28
10	Rom 4:18-25
11	Rom 5:6-11
12	Rom 5:12-15
13	Rom 6:3-4, 8-11
14	Rom 8:9, 11-13
15	Rom 8:18-23
16	Rom 8:26-27
17	Rom 8:28-30
18	Rom 8:35, 37-39
19	Rom 9:1-5
20	Rom 11:13-15, 29-32
21	Rom 11:33-36
22	Rom 12:1-2
23	Rom 13:8-10
24	Rom 14:7-9
25	Phil 1:20-24, 27
26	Phil 2:1-11

Sunday

The church celebrates the paschal mystery on the first day of the week, known as the Lord's Day or Sunday. This follows a tradition handed down from the apostles, which took its origin from the day of Christ's resurrection. Thus Sunday should be considered the original feast day.

General Norms for the Liturgical Year and Calendar, n 4

Lectionary Unit I

An Overarching Theme

The Year of Matthew is envisaged by the Lectionary as comprising seven units ranging in length from one Sunday (Unit VII) to nine Sundays (Unit VI) (see *Lectionary*, vol I, pp xlviii-xlix).

The core of the year is the five great 'sermons' that go to make up Matthew's gospel, and these form Units II, III, IV, V, and VI; preceded by Unit I on the figure of Jesus the Christ; and concluded by the last Sunday of the year focusing on the fulfilment of God's kingdom (Unit VII).

In this year each Unit is made up of two types of text: some narrative (over one or more Sundays), then some discourse (always over more than one Sunday).

The five sermons are:

The Sermon on the Mount (Sundays 4-9);

The Mission Sermon (Sundays 11-13);

The Parable Sermon (Sundays 15-17);

The Community Sermon (Sundays 23-24); and

The Final Sermon (Sundays 32-33).

As with schematic divisions of the gospels, it is neater to look at in the abstract than in terms of actual lections chosen. However, it is worth bearing in mind the lectionary's desire to respect, in so far as it can, the five-sermon structure of Matthew, as it often helps us to appreciate the rationale behind making the junctions occur where they do, and the choice of accompanying first reading, which often functions as a lens highlighting a particular aspect of the gospel on a particular Sunday.

The First Unit

This consists of just two Sundays and focuses on The Figure of Jesus the Messiah.

The question, who is the Christ, is then explored with the story of Jesus's baptism (Sunday 1) and the witness of John the Baptist (Sunday 2).

The Baptism of our Lord

CELEBRANT'S GUIDE

Note

This feast's history really begins in 1970 when it was chosen as the last moment of the Christmas cycle. It has no conceptual link with Christmas except, it could be argued, that in the eastern rites it is part of Epiphany and so could be seen as an extension of Epiphany (and it is so linked in the current western Liturgy of the Hours). However, that is not how it is presented in the eucharistic liturgy where it is celebrated as a distinct 'event' in the life of Jesus. So how should we approach this feast?

First, it is now approaching mid-January and for everyone in the congregation, the president included, Christmas is long in the past, people have been back at work for weeks, schools have re-opened, people are already thinking of a 'Spring Break', and even chatter about the New Year seems a little dated. So looking back to Christmas or referring to this as the close of Christmas is just adding noise to the communication.

Second, this is about the baptism of the Christ by John, it is not a celebration of baptism as a sacrament or even the concept of baptism within the Paschal Mystery. Such thoughts belong to Easter, and the Easter Vigil in particular, not to this day. So this is not a day for having a baptism during the Eucharist. Such a celebration just confuses the understanding of what is being re-called and fills the understanding with muddle. Indeed, if it is the community's practice to celebrate the baptism of new members of the gathering during the Eucharist, then this is one of those Sundays which should not be used for baptisms.

Third, when we look at the position of the baptism of Jesus within the gospel kerygma we note that it is the public announcement of the beginning of the work of the Messiah. It marks a beginning of a period, not a conclusion. The basic structure can be seen in Mark (after the opening of the gospel comes the work of John which comes to its conclusion in his baptism of Jesus and the glorious theophany of approbation): 'Thou art my beloved Son: with thee I am well pleased' (Mk 1:1-11). The other synoptics maintain this structure except that they add the prelude of the Infancy Narratives, while in Jn 1:29-34 the testimony of John the Baptist is concluded by his reference to the theophany of the Spirit descending on Jesus like a dove. In all the gospels, this 'event' is then followed by the messianic ministry (what we often refer to as the 'public life'). So the baptism of the Lord by John had a distinct place in the preaching of the church, it marked the 'visible' anointing by the Father in the Spirit for his work. It is the great beginning.

Fourth, the baptism of Jesus now has a definite place in the liturgy of the church, it is now a moment in our common memory and celebration of the Lord. So it would be appropriate to look on it as the beginning of Ordinary Time and, in particular, a celebration of Jesus as 'the Messiah', 'the Anointed One', 'the Christ'. So the tone of these notes is that of beginnings, not of conclusions.

Introduction to the Celebration
Today we celebrate our faith in Jesus: he is the Beloved of the Father, the Anointed One, and the one on whom the Spirit rests. During the coming months we will be recalling each Sunday his works and preaching as the Chosen One of the Father, but Christians have always begun the retelling of the gospel of Jesus by reminding ourselves who Jesus is. The gospels tell us this by recalling that he was baptised by John the Baptist in the Jordan and at that moment the Father's voice was heard and the Spirit appeared in the form of a dove.

Let us pause and reflect that we are here because we believe that Jesus is 'the Anointed One', 'the Christ', 'the Messiah', 'the One who does the Father's will'.

The Asperges
Use Option A (the Rite of Blessing and Sprinkling Holy Water)

and then the first form of the opening prayer; if you choose
Option B (a rite of penance) then these kyrie-verses pick up the
words of the gospel:

Lord Jesus, you are the Son of the Father. Lord have mercy.

Lord Jesus, upon you the Spirit descended in the form of a
dove. Christ have mercy.

Lord Jesus, you are the Beloved of the Father. Lord have
mercy.

Headings for Readings
First Reading

The Lord's Anointed is the servant who does the will of the
Father; he is the Chosen One, the one in whom God's soul delights.

Second Reading

Today we celebrate the beginning of Jesus's work as 'the
Messiah', which means he is 'the Anointed One', 'the Christ'. In
this reading we hear that Jesus is the one who is anointed,
marked out, with the Holy Spirit. He is the one who brings healing to all who are suffering under the power of evil

Gospel

Jesus is identified as the Christ by earth and heaven: John testi-
fied he is the One whom Israel awaited; the Father's voice testi-
fied that he is the beloved Son.

Prayer of the Faithful
President

Friends, the work of the Messiah was to gather scattered individuals and make them a single people, a people of God, and a
priestly people able to stand in the presence of the Father inter-
ceding for ourselves and all humanity. So now let us stand and,
as a priestly people united with the Christ, ask the Father for our
needs.

Reader (s)

1. That whenever during the coming year we hear the Word of God in the liturgy, we will hear it in our hearts. Lord hear us.

2. That during the coming year we will respond to the Lord's call to care for the poor, the suffering, and the oppressed. Lord hear us.

3. That during the coming year there will be a new recognition that the world is God's creation. Lord hear us.

4. That during the coming year those who are leaders in our society will follow the ways of truth and integrity. Lord hear us.

5. That during the coming year we will grow closer together as a community. Lord hear us.

6. That during the coming year we will grow more attentive as a community to ways to bear testimony to the Christ. Lord hear us.

7. That during the coming year we will be given new courage to confess that Jesus is the Christ, the beloved Son of the Father. Lord hear us.

President

Father, you anointed Jesus with the Holy Spirit and with power as our Saviour. Hear our prayers to you and grant what we ask through your beloved Son, our Lord. Amen.

Eucharistic Prayer

Preface of the Baptism of the Lord (P7), (Missal, p 410). Use either Eucharistic Prayer 2 or 3 which mention the working of the Spirit in the mission of the Christ.

Invitation to the Our Father

The beloved Son was acclaimed from heaven when the Father's voice was heard; now let us raise our voices to our Father in heaven:

Sign of Peace

When the Lord set out from the Jordan to preach, he announced a message of peace and called men and women to form the new people of God. Let us celebrate this new relationship he proclaimed by offering each other a sign of peace.

Invitation to Communion
Behold the Lamb of God, behold him upon whom the Spirit descended like a dove, blessed are we who are called to have a
share in his supper.

Communion Reflection
The hymn given in the Breviary, 'When Jesus comes to be baptised' (vol I, p 371), for Evening Prayer I of this feast is appropriate as a reflection today.

Conclusion
Solemn Blessing 3 for the Beginning of the New Year (Missal, p
368) is still appropriate – we should within our eucharistic assembly formally ask God's blessings on the coming year – and
we have been celebrating one of the great beginning moments of
the church's kerygma.

COMMENTARY

First Reading: Isa 42: 1-4. 6-7
This is taken from the first of the four Songs of the Suffering
Servant found in Deutero-Isaiah. Its significance within the text
of Isaiah is not relevant to this liturgical use, where it functions
to identify in prophecy several of the themes heard in the 'voice
from heaven' in the gospel. The servant is the Lord's, i.e. the
Father's, 'chosen one', 'the one who delights the Father's soul',
and 'upon whom he has put' his 'spirit'.

Second Reading: Acts 10:34-38
This is one of the great set-piece speeches in Acts in which Luke
presents his view of the fundamental kerygma of the church by
expressing it in perfectly formed homilies. This speech is set immediately after the crucial encounter with Cornelius when the
difficulties in bringing the gospel to the nations is, for Luke's
readers, finally settled. This is the ideal second reading for today
for it is the only reference outside the gospels to the relationship
between the work of John the Baptist and the beginning of the
work of Jesus, in effect, the mystery we celebrate today.

It is clear from the gospels that the baptism by John the Baptist was one of the key fixed points in telling the story of Jesus. Indeed it appears to have been the defining point in the narrative. Here we see that narrative retold in summary form and the 'baptism event' retains that marker position at the start of the messianic work. Luke takes the trinitarian format of his account in Lk 3:22, refashions it without the narrative form, and presents it as an interpretation of the name 'Jesus Christ' or 'Jesus the Christ'. Jesus is 'the anointed one', 'the christ', but what does that mean. God (the Father, not mentioned in the Lk 3 but only heard) anoints Jesus with the Spirit. But this now means that Jesus acts in a unique way in the Spirit: that God has set upon him the Spirit and power in a way that is not found among all the others – the Christians – who have received the Spirit. In summary we could say that Luke's preaching here is 'God gets Jesus to act in the Spirit' and that phrase is equivalent to saying 'Jesus is the Christ'.

First Reading > Gospel Links
The link between Isa 40 and the gospel is one of prophecy and fulfillment. The passage in Isaiah is read as text from the past pointing to a particular moment in the future (time of service ended, the work of the one who prepares) which has now come with John the Baptist and Jesus, and indeed that moment is now the past and the background of the church.

Gospel: Mt 3:13-17
The simplest form of the baptism event is that found in Mk 1:9-11 and the almost identical Lk 3:21-22. Matthew makes two changes. First, he adds vv 14-15 stressing John the Baptist's hesitancy over baptising Jesus – this insertion may be his caution lest it be unclear that Jesus was not in need of baptism by John. The second significant difference is that here the heavenly voice – which the hearer is expected to identify as that of the Father – does not address Jesus as in Mark and Luke, but the assembly: 'This is my beloved Son …'

However, the key to the scene is not in its details but in its overall impact: the human and divine worlds, heaven and earth, the history of Israel and the eternity of God's inner life, all come together in an unforgettable image. This is a mighty event that is fitting to act as the marker of the commencement of the work of the Christ. And so, it is one of the most explicitly theological scenes in the gospel narrative: the Father identifies Jesus as his Son and the Spirit is seen. Here lies the whole of later christology presented not as propositions but as something that the imagination can work with, while still not giving the false notion of 'seeing' God. We see the Christ, the Son acclaimed as such by the voice from heaven which is heard and not seen, while the Spirit is seen 'descending like (*hosei*) a dove.'

Scenes such as this have become victims of two types of exegetical confusion during the twentieth century. The first was the product of a materialist notion of truth. It began with the materialist question: 'If I were there that day what would my TV camera have recorded?' Then when the exegete said 'nothing', it seemed as if the scene was false and so the whole thing was a concoction to be avoided. We have to realise that this scene is sacramental and placed within a narrative precisely so our human imaginations can handle the mystery: to ask the 'TV camera' question is not to get at the Truth but to commit the blasphemy of Wisdom 15 and imply 'god' as referring to another object, a thing, in our universe. The second confusion is that of assuming that 'theology' is an obscurity overlaid on the 'simple message of Jesus'. The confusion runs like this: Jesus was a loving guy who spoke about God and captured hearts; then came the boffins who made everything complicated with notions of the incarnation, the trinity, and what not, but you can by-pass this and get to the 'heart of the matter'. It's a lovely picture and one that still wins adherents, but there is no evidence for such a 'simple time'. By the time that Mark began preaching his gospel – in the sixties – we see in the baptism-event a fully developed Christian doctrine of God, and it is this that we read again today in the liturgy.

HOMILY NOTES

1. This is a good opportunity to give a simple catechetical homily whose aim is to impart some simple linguistic clarity in order to help people reflect on the gospel's image more fruitfully.

2. We use the words 'Jesus Christ' over and over again. Indeed, we use these two words so often side-by-side that we forget that they have any meaning. Sometimes, we almost think that the word 'Christ' is just a surname tacked on as if one needed to distinguish several people called 'Jesus'. Most Christians use the words interchangeably. I have seen history books with the index entry: 'Christ, J.' followed by page numbers. When I asked a student what was the significance that her essay kept varying between using 'Jesus said' and 'Christ said', her answer was that she changed the usage simply to make it sound less repetitive. So this is a phrase whose significance we cannot take for granted.

3. But our confession of faith is that 'Jesus is the Christ.' The word *christos* means the marked one, the one who has been smeared with oil. But why use this as a description of Jesus? The people of Israel looked forward to the new David, the new king who would institute the Day of the Lord and his victory. David had been marked out as the chosen one of the Lord: 'Then Samuel took the horn of oil, and anointed him in the midst of his brothers; and the Spirit of the Lord came mightily upon David from that day forward' (1 Sam 16:13). 'To be marked out with oil' is the same as 'being the anointed one' or, if one uses Hebrew, 'the messiah' or, if one uses Greek, 'the Christ' or to say 'He is the chosen one of the Father.'

4. Jesus was not literally anointed with oil to mark him out as 'the anointed one', but in the gospels he is shown as being marked out by the Father's voice and by the descent of the Spirit upon him. To say 'Jesus is the Christ' is to say he is the one who is uniquely the Son of the Father, and uniquely the bearer of the Spirit.

5. To say 'Jesus is the Christ' is to utter a basic creed which only

makes sense when we imagine that statement within the
scene we have just read in the gospel. To say 'You, O Jesus
are the Christ' is to offer praise through the beloved Son to
the Father in the Holy Spirit.

Second Sunday of Ordinary Time

CELEBRANT'S GUIDE

Introduction to the Celebration
We gather here each Sunday to encounter one another and to encounter the Chosen One of the Father. We are, as St Paul tells us,
'the holy people of Jesus Christ, who are called to take their
place among all the saints everywhere who pray to our Lord
Jesus Christ'. So let us reflect on who we are as a group and on
how we have become this holy people through our baptism.

Rite of Penance
Given the baptismal story in today's gospel, this is a day when
the *Asperges* option is particularly appropriate.
    Lord Jesus, you are the Chosen One of God. Lord have mercy.
    Lord Jesus, you are the man on whom the Spirit has come
    down and rests. Christ have mercy.
    Lord Jesus, you are the Lamb of God who takes away the sin
    of the world. Lord have mercy.

Headings for Readings
First Reading
The prophet speaks of the Servant of the Lord who will gather a
scattered people and bring God's light to all people right out to
the ends of the earth. We see in Jesus the fulfillment of this act of
obedience to the Father's loving plan for all humanity.

Second Reading
Note: Announce the lection as: 'The Beginning of the first letter
of St Paul to the Corinthians.'
    This is the opening greeting of Paul to one of the churches he
founded. He calls the members of the church 'the saints' because
they have been made holy through becoming one body in Christ
through sharing the one loaf and the one cup at the eucharistic
meal.

Gospel

Jesus our Lord is the Lamb of God, the bearer of the Spirit, the Chosen One of the Father: him we praise and him we witness.

Prayer of the Faithful
President

The Spirit comes down and rests upon us when we gather in the Lord's Anointed for this holy meal; now empowered by the Spirit as a priestly people, let us intercede with the Father.
Reader(s)

1. For all Christians, that we will witness that Jesus is the Chosen One of God. Lord hear us.

2. For all women and men, that we will respect the universe God has given us. Lord hear us.

3. For all who are suffering due to the sin of the world, that they may receive new life. Lord hear us.

4. For all who are seeking the ways of wisdom, that the Spirit will enlighten their searchings. Lord hear us.

5. Specific local needs and topics of the day.

6. For all who have died, that they may share in the heavenly banquet. Lord hear us.
President

Father, you sent your Son among us to take away the sin of the world and to show us the path to you, listen to us and the needs we place before you for ourselves and our sisters and brothers, for we place these prayers before you in union with your Chosen One, who lives with you and the Holy Spirit, one God, for ever and ever. Amen.

Eucharistic Prayer

Given that today's gospel is John's presentation of the baptism event, the Preface of the Baptism of the Lord (P7), (Missal, p 410) is again suitable for today. Use either Eucharistic Prayer 2 or 3, which mention the working of the Spirit in the mission of the Christ.

Invitation to the Our Father
The Spirit gathers us in the Chosen One and makes us his People, so now in the Spirit's power let us pray to the Father:

Sign of Peace
The Lamb of God has taken away sin and division and offered us the possibility of a new life of peace; let us express our willingness to begin that new life with one another.

Invitation to Communion
Today we recalled John the Baptist's announcement 'Look, there is the Lamb of God who takes away the sin of the world'; today we too can behold in this meal the Lamb of God who takes away the sin of the world.

Communion Reflection
Over the Christmas period the liturgy has been very full in terms of words: hymns, prayers, announcements, carols. Now is a good time to create a structured silence. Begin this with an opening such as: 'We shall now reflect in silence for a few moments on being the Body of Christ because we have shared in the one loaf and the one cup.' Then measure the passing of two minutes and conclude the silence by standing and saying: 'Let us pray.'

Conclusion
Solemn Blessing 10: Ordinary Time I (Missal, p 372).

Notes
1. Since last Sunday we read Matthew's account of the baptism of Jesus for that feast, getting John's account today seems like too much of a good thing. There are differences between the synoptic accounts and John's of the baptism, but they are not such that an average congregation can appreciate these differences when the two readings are a week apart. Equally, the baptism event at the beginning of all four gospels is itself a significant

pointer to its place in the early church's understanding of Jesus, and so it is good that we read all four versions of the story; but again, the average congregation are not likely to note this when read on separate Sundays. So, in effect, we have entered into Ordinary Time and the Year of Matthew, yet today we have readings that are more suited to the explicit theme of last Sunday. This means that the liturgy today is either a continuation of last Sunday, if the focus is on the First Reading – Gospel; or else one concentrates on the Second Reading.

2. The pneumatology of today's gospel, the Spirit descends upon the Son of God and remains on him, is that which is reflected in the Nicene Creed. This is therefore not a Sunday to use the (so-called) Apostle's Creed option.

COMMENTARY

First Reading: Isa 49: 3, 5-6
This lection is made up of three verses of the section of Deutero-Isaiah that is the commissioning of the Servant-Prophet who will comfort Zion. The whole section is 49:1-7. As edited here only the divine voice is heard, not the servant's reply, and this enables the text to be read as the Father addressing the Christ. This particular christological reading of Isaiah has been in use in the church since the earliest times. We see verses 5-6 echoed in the Song of Simeon (Lk 2:32).

Psalm: 39 (40)
The liturgy today interprets the speaker as the Servant of the Lord and then invites us to identify this with Jesus who delights in the Law of God and does the Father's will.

Second Reading: 1 Cor 1:1-3
This is the opening greeting of the letter and as such it introduces a text that will be read, in bits, over seven Sundays. Since the next Pauline greeting will be heard on the Twenty-ninth Sunday, it is worth examining the theology that is inherent in Paul's greeting.

In most religious views of the universe there is an assumption that sinfulness, impurity, and pollution are contagious: hence dietary laws, laws forbidding contact with the impure, and the widespread notion that people, objects and places become defiled. On the other hand, holiness is that which is found in limited amounts and has to be carefully guarded. It is as if holiness and purity are fragile and always threatened unless they are defended by high walls – often literally high walls as those built around enclosed convents – and legal safeguards. In this vision, sinfulness is the norm and holiness the exception. And, indeed, unless checked that worldliness will contaminate and spread everywhere until holiness has been corrupted and is expunged. This has been noticed by anthropologists of religion in religions far and wide. It is true of most Christians as well and can be seen to operate in Christian theology since the fourth century, with the rise of specific holy places (as distinct from the rest of the world: the ordinary places, the places that are not of any particular sacred worth) and in the rise of sacred persons. For instance, the regulations of the Council of Elvira, AD 306, that any presbyter who had sexual intercourse with his wife could not preside at the Eucharist on the following day. In this case, the earthiness of sexuality was threatening the holy and so could not come into contact with it; the converse notion that the marriage bed of the presbyter and his wife was sanctified by their contact with the Body of the Lord in the Eucharist was not even considered. This alternative might seem far-fetched, but this same notion of holiness by contact can be found in Paul (see 1 Cor 7:14).

In stark contrast to such notions we have the early Christian notion of holiness which lies behind this greeting. Here the basic notion is that in the Father sending his Son into the world, it is holiness that has become contagious and is communicated from the Christ to every one and every situation he comes in contact with, and then it is communicated further – until it spreads right across the earth – by his people, his holy body. This notion that it is holiness that is spreading, and that is threatening the darkness and has the darkness retreat before it can be found right through early Christian literature: here in Paul, in the synoptics (e.g. Mt 23), in Acts (e.g. 10:13), and in John (e.g. 1:5). Let us examine it here, and then see some of its wider implications.

The church of Corinth is 'the holy people of Jesus Christ.' They have become holy through entering into his life and adhering to him. It is not that they have individually become saintly people, but by being joined with Jesus they have received, shared in, absorbed his holiness. They are now, because of Jesus, the daughters and sons of God. This holiness that they have caught is transforming them and so they stand not as a little group of devotees, like the cultish group of some guru, but as part of the whole company of the saints: they are part of the new movement of holiness that is spreading over the world from the Son of the heavenly Father. This new people knows no bounds, and are not dependent on the law to keep holiness safe and wickedness at bay, for that church in Corinth, in union will all the other groups, are calling on Jesus as Lord.

Holiness is spreading over the earth and is expansive and contagious, and each little church is the means of this spread. The arrival of holiness makes the earth holy, every bit of it. In the older vision the Temple was holy, and within it was the Holy of Holies, and then as one moved outwards the level of holiness kept decreasing. Finally, one came to the edge of the land of Israel – a notion Christians later re-invented as the notion of the Holy Land – beyond which there was just land, raw matter untouched by holiness, far from the sacred, a sort of hinterland threatening the holy region. This is the notion that the earth is just there to be exploited as if it does not matter. This is the attitude that has contributed to the global ecological crisis, and then wonders why Christianity has so little to say about the matter! The reality of the Son coming among us is that holiness now belongs in the world, not in the temple. His entry is changing everything through us who have come into contact with him. The earth is not raw material to be used, abused and discarded, but the place into which holiness, and goodness, and beauty must spread. Paul's greeting is deceptively simple, yet it is a glimpse into a forgotten theology. However, if that theology is ever to be dusted off and brought back into service, it will mean dumping such an amount of our notions of sacred people, places and things that many will find the nostalgia and inertia more attractive than that of Jesus being the communication of the Father's holiness to the creation.

First Reading > Gospel Links
While at first glance this might appear a relationship of promise and fulfilment (the promise that there will be a servant, then the Father acknowledging the coming of Jesus); that is not how the liturgy presents it. The first reading is God, whom we are to identify as the Father, speaking to his servant who will re-gather the scattered flock, and bring light and salvation to the nations (and this is confirmed in the Son's response in the psalm). Then in the gospel the Father looks upon his servant and had John the Baptist witness to him as the Chosen One. Thus the relationship is one of the continuity of the two testaments: what the Father was saying in Isaiah, he is still saying in the gospel.

Gospel: Jn 1:29-34
This is the Johannine account of the baptism of Jesus by John the Baptist; and the following points are worth bearing in mind.

1. The 1981 English lectionary uses the Jerusalem Version which has in verse 30 'he is the Chosen One of God'. This is a variant found only in a minority of the manuscripts and it is a symptom of how the JB reflected some of the idiosyncratic notions of the 1960s that it opted for this reading. The Greek text, as edited in Nestle-Aland 27 and following the majority of the manuscripts, reads *ho huios tou theou*; and this has been followed by the Neo-Vulgate with *hic est Filius Dei* and the NRSV with 'this is the Son of God.' This reading brings out John's christology even more clearly, but one can make a case for just leaving it as it is in that it introduces the hearers to yet one more genuine christological title (cf Lk 23:35).

2. In the synoptics we all see the Spirit descend and are all hearers of the divine voice speaking of the Son. In John, no one except John the Baptist sees the Spirit or hears the Father's voice. We do not live by sight for John the Evangelist but by faith in accepting the witness of John the Baptist. He hears the Father, he bears witness to him, and through him we come to know the true and full identity of Jesus.

3. In the synoptics the Spirit descends on Jesus, but in John he descends and remains on him. The Spirit dwells in the Son and gives him life. This is the relationship of the Spirit to the Son we confess in the Nicaeo-constantinopolitan Creed. The Son sets out on his work of words and signs with the Spirit remaining upon him.

4. 'Behold the Lamb of God' is a phrase which originates in John, here and at 1:36, and this lamb takes away 'the sin of the world' (i.e. that which sets the creation and the Creator at odds). Since the notion of atonement is not a significant theme in John, this taking away the sin of the world was probably intended as being the establishment of the reign of peace through the coming of the Son of God into the world. Read in this way, there is an overlap, by accident, with the second reading: both John and Paul see holiness spreading out over the earth as a result of the Son of God's coming among us.

HOMILY NOTES

1. Every day we hear of further research into global warming and of new symptoms of the ecological crisis of the planet. This often provokes a cry that religion has little to offer on this problem or that it is a matter that little interests the churches. It is as well to acknowledge this criticism in that there has been a tradition of exploitation of the planet in the industry-driven west – the slash and burn mentality – that has taken Gen 1:28 ('fill the earth and subdue it') literally. Equally, many traditions of Christianity have been so centered on the spiritual life of the human being that they have neglected the creation, the environment, and even our bodily

material natures. There are plenty of examples of dualist spiritualities that saw humans as souls trapped and held down by matter. And, there are indeed many forms of Evangelical Christianity that sees the message of Jesus so restrictedly in terms of the salvation of individuals or the rescuing of an elect prior to an apocalyptic crunch that they think care for the planet is a waste of time. This produced a certain kind of mechanistic providence: if God wants us to survive, we'll survive!

2. However, a healthy theology of the incarnation and a healthy ecology should go hand in hand. If God is the creator of all that is, seen and unseen, and has entered the creation as a creature, the man Jesus of Nazareth, then his love for the creation can know no bounds and should set the standard for our properly ordered interaction with all creatures: visible and invisible, rational or non-rational, animate or inanimate. But the challenge is to have both a healthy christology and a healthy ecology, and have the two interfacing one another.

3. In the second reading and gospel today – and it is worth pointing out that such occasional overlaps are accidental – we have a theology of incarnation which presents the holiness of God entering the creation and then being contagious, spreading out to all nations, out to the very ends of the earth. We tend to think of the earth as just there, raw earth, and then there are distinct special holy places and holy people. But to those who believe in Jesus as the Son of God who comes from the Father and upon whom the Spirit remains, such limited notions of holiness are now inadequate. Jesus challenges us to a have a whole new way of looking at the world: holiness is now contagious, and everywhere can be a sacred place and everyone can be a saint. We have encountered the Christ, and this challenges us to transform all our relationships. Everyone who is in Christ is a holy person and can spread holiness, everywhere can be a place where we can encounter the presence of God.

4. We must respect each other and the environment as a gift

from God and react appropriately to its God-given nature. We cannot see it as just something that we can selfishly hijack as if it were just there. We tend to live in dualist universes: there is the sacred and the secular; the spiritual and the material; the holy and the unholy; the pure and the impure; the saints and the sinners. The love and holiness of God that became part of the creation in Jesus overcame all these dualisms and division. Holiness is contagious, goodness is diffusive, and care for the planet, care for the poor and oppressed, and care for self cannot be separated.

5. John the Baptist had the task of bearing witness to the incarnate Son among humanity; we have the task of bearing witness to its implications for how we treat the environment.

Lectionary Unit II

This unit comprises Sundays 3-9, and its focus is on Christ's design for life in God's kingdom.

There is one Sunday devoted to narrative: Sunday 3 which highlights the call of the first disciples.

The remaining Sundays' gospels are seen as discourse, which together make up the Sermon on the Mount.

Third Sunday of Ordinary Time

CELEBRANT'S GUIDE

Introduction to the Celebration

Gathering around the Lord's table each week we celebrate the fact that we are the People of God, his chosen ones, those whom he has called to be his hands and voice within the creation. To help us live this life we listen each week to the Word of God giving us a glimpse of the world God intends for us, and challenging us to live up to our calling, and each week we are strengthened with the food of life to enable us to be disciples. Today we hear the story of the beginning of Jesus's ministry: he came proclaiming the good news; he came healing the sick; he came and called people by name to be his followers. If we wanted to think of the life of Jesus in a sound-bite, it would be these tasks: proclaiming, healing, calling.

Now, let us reflect in silence on who we are, why we have gathered, and ask pardon for our failures as children of God.

Rite of Penance

Lord Jesus, you call us to repentance. Lord have mercy.
Lord Jesus, you proclaim the kingdom is at hand. Christ have mercy.
Lord Jesus, you call us to be your followers. Lord have mercy.

Headings for Readings
First Reading

The prophet looks forward to a time when among a suffering people a new light would dawn which would bring joy and happiness.

Second Reading

Every gathering of Christians tends to have factions: one wants things done this way; another group want things done the other way. These squabbles not only are divisive, but also show that we are not listening to the call to be united in Christ and act as his body. Such divisions were a problem in the church in Corinth, and Paul takes issue with their divisive behaviour.

Gospel
We see the Lord's anointed engaged in his three characteristic works: he is proclaiming the kingdom; he is bringing healing; and he is calling people to become his disciples.

Prayer of the Faithful
President
Having heard the good news that Jesus proclaimed, having been forgiven and healed, and having heard his call to follow him, we now stand here as his priestly people, and so we now call on the Father.
Reader(s)
1. For the church of God across the world, that we will continue to proclaim the good news to all people. Lord hear us.
2. For this church gathered here, that we will continue to proclaim the good news to those we meet. Lord hear us.
3. For the church of God across the world, that we will be a force for healing and reconciliation in the world. Lord hear us.
4. For this church gathered here, that we will work for healing among for those in need in this society. Lord hear us.
5. For the church of God across the world, that we will grow in our awareness of our calling. Lord hear us.
6. For this church gathered here, that we will renew our commitment to act together as a people called by name. Lord hear us.
President
Father, your Son proclaimed the kingdom, healed the sick, and called a people to follow him; hear us for we seek to be that people and so we make these prayers through Christ Jesus, our Lord. Amen.

Eucharistic Prayer
Preface of Sundays in Ordinary Time VIII (P36) has the theme
the Son bringing forgiveness and gathering people into the
church.

Invitation to the Our Father
As the people called by the Son of God, let us address the Father
in prayer:

Sign of Peace
If we have heard the good news and accepted forgiveness and
healing from God, then we must begin the new life of seeking to
heal divisions and being prepared to offer and accept forgiveness. Let us express that willingness now towards one another.

Invitation to Communion
He comes among us proclaiming the kingdom, bringing us healing, and calling us to gather at his supper.

Communion Reflection
    Father,
    Your Son has gathered us into your church,
    To be one as you, Father, are one
    With your Son and the Holy Spirit.
    You call us to be your people
    And to praise your wisdom in all your works.
    You have made us the body of Christ
    And the dwelling place of the Holy Spirit.
    Amen.
    (Adapted from Psalm 36)

Conclusion
The Lord Jesus proclaimed the kingdom: may that good news be
a light to your steps during the coming week. Amen.
The Lord Jesus brought healing and forgiveness to those he met:

may you bear his healing and forgiveness to those in need in the coming days. Amen.

The Lord Jesus called you to be his disciples: may you follow his way in all that you do this week. Amen.

Notes

1. Although there is a shorter version of today's gospel, there is no good reason to use it. We have a piece of narrative that invites the hearers to follow the whole passage as a sequence of events and understand it as such. The shorter version has the additional difficulty in that it reduces the narrative to a prophesy with a rather complex background and a sharp slogan 'Repent, for the kingdom ...' and this is harder for a listener to understand than from the whole passage where the sequence gives a sense of context.

2. Although in all the translations the activity of Jesus is described using parts of the verb 'to preach' (*kérussein* at v 17) I have tried to avoid the word in these resources. Why? Think of the popular uses of 'to preach': 'He kept on preaching!' (= he was droning on as a bore); 'They weren't speaking they were preaching' (= it was an irrational rant); 'Please! don't preach!' (in this case 'preaching' is seen as up-braiding, criticising, disapproving). Like it or not, the verb 'to preach' has become so corrupt in meaning in actual usage that it can no longer be used in real preaching!

So what de we do? The verb *kérussein* is related to *kérux* (a herald, a messenger) and *kerugma* (the good news itself, what is proclaimed). So we can render it as 'announcing' or 'proclaiming' and we avoid the negative images attached to 'preaching' in English (the Greek verb *kérussein* does not carry such negative images in the gospels).

3. It is better to read 1 Cor 1:10-17 in its entirety. The omission of 3 verses in the lectionary text makes the text less fluent.

COMMENTARY

First Reading: Isa 8:23-9:3

This is the Prince of Peace oracle which forms a central plank of the Advent liturgy (the oracle runs to 9:6 but the last verses are omitted as (1) they liturgically belong to Advent, and (2) they are unnecessary for the text to act as the background to today's gospel. This situation in which Isaiah writes is in the aftermath of a military crisis and he promises hope to a defeated people; the liturgical situation of this text in the church is determined by its use in Mt 4 (which we will read). The prophet's promise is of new divinely-given light to deliver the people from an existence of darkness and shadow (presented as the human situation) rather than from some specific moment of national humiliation. There are few passages in the whole of the Old Testament we, Christians, read so exclusively in terms of a fore-announcement of the Christ-event.

Psalm: 26 (27)

This is chosen as it is seen to continue the theme of waiting for deliverance promised by God: 'I am sure I shall see the Lord's goodness in the land of the living.'

Second Reading: 1 Cor 1:10-13; 17

In contrast to the general image of the early churches as all being happy, almost perfect communities (an image that was developed from Acts), here we see the reality that religious groups tend to be faction-ridden and prone to splits, in-fighting, and more absorbed in their squabbles than in the task they set themselves. Paul objects to this not only as it is counter-productive, but because it is at odds with the identity of the new type of group that has come into existence through baptism.

The passage is important not only because of its enduring message – Christianity is, for a complex of reasons, one of the more division prone religions – but because it is the rationale for Paul's writing the letter to them. It has come back to him what is happening, and the letter is Paul's attempt to preach to them at a distance telling them what he thinks. The argument as he lays it out begins with v 10 and ends with v 17, so this is a well-rounded lection. However, the omission of verses 14, 15, and 16 makes v 17 seem ill fitted to what has gone before. The omission is inexplicable unless the desire was to save circa 20 seconds or the belief that names of early Christians would distract people! If one reads the whole passage, its final point is far easier to appreciate.

First Reading > Gospel Links

The relationship is established in the gospel: in the activity of Jesus 'The prophecy of Isaiah was fulfilled.' We are intended to recall the first reading as speaking in terms of the future, the gospel as speaking of an event which has occurred. In this gospel passage we see one of the key ways the early Christian generations related their belief to what has happened in the history of Israel.

Gospel: Mt 4:12-23 (shorter form 4:12-17)

This is Matthew's account of the first preaching of Jesus in Galilee. Matthew alone, however, presents this action by Jesus as the fulfillment of a prophecy; and this profoundly changes how we are to see this activity: Jesus sets out on this work as the Prince of Peace, the one sent by God to announce the arrival of the good times, the time of happiness, the time of God's favour. Hence the way we read this in the Advent-Christmas cycle: Rejoice, the good times have come, the Prince of Peace has come.

That manner of reading may seem obvious, but down the centuries this text has been read in a very different way and continued to be so read today by many of a fundamentalist hue. The problem concerns two matters. First, the opening word of Jesus's message: *Metanoeite*. This command was put into Latin as *Penitentiam agite!* (Do penance!) and so led to a whole spirituality: that the life of the Christian was to be one of acts of penitence. This was rejected at the Reformation as 'pelagian' and an attempt to work one's way into heaven and replace with 'be penitent' – having an attitude of knowing 'you are a sinner' even if you can do nothing about it. The whole debate ignores Matthew's point: the coming of the Lord is about change, it could be rendered 'change now' for the time has come, realise the moment of the Lord is at hand, have a new vision, start to live the new live. The second problem concerns how the command *metanoeite* (however it is translated) related to 'the kingdom being at hand'. Is it, on the one hand, hurry to repent/ change, but God is about to come and catch you (the 'last chance saloon' scenario), which is certainly how the fire and brimstone preachers read it. Or is it, now you can change because the kingdom of God has come among you, the prince of peace has arrived, now you have light to show you the way out of darkness? It is clear that Matthew intended the second reading or he would not have quoted Isaiah's oracle.

But what is really interesting is the context in which Matthew did so, which has to do with the difference between the messages of John the Baptist and Jesus. John was proclaiming the closeness of the day of the Lord and repentance because when the Lord came it would be to punish those who had not taken advantage of the last change: the Lord is about to come and it is fearsome. Jesus, on the other hand, is preaching that the Day of the Lord has come, therefore one should begin a new life, and the day of the Lord is the day of the Prince of Peace. Matthew is making this difference explicit, but without offering any direct criticism of John the Baptist. This is a tightrope that Matthew walks in that he wants to make sure his hearers do not confuse the eschatology of Jesus with John, but he wants to present them without drawing any direct light on to just how radically distinct they were. This balancing act reaches its high point in Mt 11:11: 'Truly, I say to you, among those born of women there has risen no one greater than John the Baptist; yet he who is least in the kingdom of heaven is greater than he.'

HOMILY NOTES

1. The gospel passage presents us with picture of Jesus continuously engaged in three activities: Proclaiming, Healing,

Gathering. We can look at it as a snapshot of the work of Jesus, and of his identity as the Messiah ('the anointed one'/ 'the Christ').

2. Jesus is the one who announces the gospel in the town of Capernaum, in the countryside, in the synagogues, all through Galilee. His call is for people to change, change ways of living with one another, change the way we think about the world, others, self. And know that God is close to us, loving and caring: 'The kingdom is at hand.'

3. The coming of Jesus brings forgiveness, healing, renewal, and wholeness. He calls on us to change lives and minds, and he brings us God's pardon. He invites us to a new life and he empowers us to set out to live that new life. The God who is close is the God who is gentle and forgiving.

4. He gathers around him, calling each person by name, a people. We are no longer isolated individuals but part of his new people. We change, start over, and seek to follow him as part of the community who has heard his call and received forgiveness through him.

5. We often forget how these gospel pictures can show us the essential dynamics of being a Christian in clear, strong images – and such is the case today – so let the images speak clearly and do not cloud them with many words.

Fourth Sunday of Ordinary Time

Introduction to the Celebration

When Jesus came among us he proclaimed the good news for the poor, the sorrowful, the hungry, the oppressed, and the persecuted. In his kingdom these sufferings have no place, and he gathered a people around him to begin the work of establishing that new lifestyle of the kingdom: caring for the sick, building a world of justice, those who would live and work with an attitude of responsibility, fairness and gentleness towards other people and towards the whole creation. We are that people and as we gather and hear that message again in today's gospel, let us ask pardon for the times we have ignored that call, and ask for help to hear it more profoundly today.

Rite of Penance

Lord Jesus, you come bringing us good news. Lord have mercy.

Lord Jesus, you come bringing us forgiveness. Christ have mercy.

Lord Jesus, you come bringing us peace. Lord have mercy.

Headings for Readings

First Reading

The Lord's people are called to live lives of integrity, humility, and honesty.

Second Reading

The standards that humans use to determine values are very different to those of God.

Gospel

Have no heading; use the symbols of a procession, lights, and incense instead.

Prayer of the Faithful
President
We are a people who have been given many gifts and called to use them to build the kingdom. Let us now ask the Father to bless all these endeavours in our community.
Reader(s)
Make a list of all the various groups that work in the community (e.g. the St Vincent de Paul Society), then have as many petitions as there are groups. For each group us this formula: 'For those of us who work with the ... ... ; that the Lord may bless this endeavour. Lord hear us.'
President
Father, you have sent your Spirit among us to enliven our hearts to respond to the good news your Son announced among us. Look upon our doings, help us, strengthen us, and unite us in Jesus Christ, our Lord. Amen.

Eucharistic Prayer
Eucharistic Prayer for Masses of Reconciliation II fits with the theme of the Beatitudes.

Invitation to the Our Father
Gathered here, let us pray for the coming of the kingdom: Our Father:

Sign of Peace
'Blessed are the peacemakers: they shall be called the daughters and sons of God.' So let us express our willingness to take up the vocation to be peacemakers.

Invitation to Communion
We are a blessed and happy people, for the Lord has come among us and calls us to share in his banquet.

Communion Reflection
The ability to cope with silence does not come naturally to most

people today. Silence is not 'a blessed quiet' but simply an absence: 'What is wrong?' 'Everything has gone silent!' 'Get it fixed!' 'Let's get some background noise!' 'Music, mindless humming, whatever, but let's not just simply have nothing!' In contrast to this desire for background noise our tradition tells us that without silence it is almost impossible to learn to pray, to reflect, to try to make out the way of wisdom. So this time needs to be taken seriously with a structured silence for prayer in silence in a group.

Conclusion

The Lord blesses the poor in spirit, those who are gentle, and those who mourn. May you receive the inheritance he has promised. Amen.

The Lord blesses those who hunger and thirst for what is right and those who are merciful. May you receive mercy and the sight of God. Amen.

The Lord blesses the pure in heart, the peacemakers, and those persecuted in the cause of right. May you one day rejoice in the kingdom of heaven. Amen.

Notes

The Gospel

Matthew presents the beginning of his 'Sermon on the Mount' with verbal panoply: here is the solemn beginning of Jesus's preaching as the new Moses. Today's announcement of the gospel must convey that solemnity and mark this as a special moment in the whole of our celebration of the kerygma over the course of the Sundays of the Year of Matthew. This is a day when if you do not have a formal procession with the Book of the Gospels, then it would be a good idea to institute one. Moreover, this is the day to use the traditional symbols which were intended to draw attention to the presence of the Christ in the liturgical proclamation (i.e. that moment when gospel = text becomes gospel = good news): incense and acolytes carrying lights.

COMMENTARY

First Reading: Zeph 2:3; 3:12-13

This lection is made up of two separate items of text whose only relationship is that they come from the same work. The first item (2:3 is half the lection) has the form of an exhortation, but its exact meaning is unclear and it seems to be ironic: act as you should and perhaps you will be spared! The second item concerns the moral behaviour that will characterise the remnant who live after the time of the divine chastisement: they will know the importance of right living.

However, as read together, these verses take on the character of stressing the moral values of the People of God who are conscious that there is a day of reckoning referred to as 'the day of the anger of the Lord.'

Psalm: 145 (146)

The combination of the Psalm with a response from the gospel brings out that the Lord is faithful in all his promises.

Second Reading: 1 Cor 1:26-31

Paul wants to bring out the difference between God's standards and human wisdom. The community he is addressing is a case in point: would it be those the Corinthians think as wise that God has chosen? No, God has different standards and in the Christ these people have their reason for boasting.

First Reading > Gospel Links

The first reading has been put together specifically to create an Old Testament echo for this gospel; and so the relationship is one of continuity of teaching. However, the first reading as we read it presents those values (strikingly similar to those in the gospel) as being adopted under the shadow of the 'the day of the Lord's anger'; whereas in the gospel these values are seen as being those which bring the Lord's blessing. Thereby, the relationship of imperfect revelation and perfect revelation is also at work between these readings.

Gospel: Mt 5:1-12

This is the opening of the first of Matthew's great discourses, the Sermon on the Mount, and hence it has the formal opening of six separate elements to draw attention to its importance: (1) seeing the crowds; (2) going up the hill – the revelatory symbolic place from which the Law comes; (3) sitting – the formal pose of a master teaching; (4) being flanked by the disciples – the group who wait on the Lord and indicate that this is beginning of a great event; (5) opening his mouth – this is the revelatory formula indicating that it is coming from God (the Jerusalem Bible's 'he began to speak' is simply sloppy translation and should be changed); and (6) he taught them – Jesus is the one sent to be 'the teacher in Israel'.

HOMILY NOTES

1. Today's section of Matthew is so often used in the liturgy (e.g. at funerals) that it has become hackneyed: it flows over most heads without making any impression; it just sounds lovely and we are in favour of it. However, whenever a politician, a manager or a trade union official, or a bishop is reminded of the way of meekness, it quickly becomes clear that this is not seen as a manner in which one can get things done! Few texts in the gospels elicit such a paradox: suppliant, virtually uncritical acceptance at the notional level and intellectually; coupled with almost total disbelief and outright rejection at the existential level and in action. One task of preaching this good news (is it really such for us?) is to try to explore this paradox.

2. However, if the Beatitudes cause such difficulties in perception, there is the fact that the Spirit moving in the hearts of the faithful continues to bring forth the very fruits mentioned in this gospel.

3. So in the community are there groups concerned with:
   • Mt 5:3 'Blessed are the poor in spirit, for theirs is the kingdom of heaven'; i.e. those working for the practical alleviation of poverty in the local area (e.g. the St Vincent de Paul

Society)? Is there a group dealing with global poverty or poverty as a matter of faith and justice (e.g. fair trade for the Third World)?

• Mt 5:4 'Blessed are those who mourn, for they shall be comforted'; i.e. a group working with the bereaved?

• Mt 5:5 'Blessed are the meek, for they shall inherit the earth'; i.e. people concerned with the earth and its resources (e.g. environmental action groups)?

• Mt 5:6 'Blessed are those who hunger and thirst for righteousness, for they shall be satisfied'; i.e. groups working for those who are unjustly treated in our society (e.g. immigrant workers, the homeless, other disadvantaged groups)?

• Mt 5:7 'Blessed are the merciful, for they shall obtain mercy' and Mt 5:8 'Blessed are the pure in heart, for they shall see God'; i.e. groups who engage in the activities linked to specific spiritualities (e.g. prayer groups, reflection groups, those working for ecumenical understanding, groups working for particular developments in the church)?

• Mt 5:9 'Blessed are the peacemakers, for they shall be called sons of God'; those who work for peace in the world (e.g. on the one hand this could be an anti-war movement, or the other it could be those who have taken part in peace-keeping with the armed forces, or those who have worked for reconciliation in divided societies)?

4. The task would be to use today to let these groups be seen by the whole community and so become aware of what they are doing, could do, and could do better if they thought of themselves as different limbs of the body of Christ.

5. Some of these groups may very readily identify themselves, and be recognised by others, as linked to the church's agenda to build the kingdom (e.g. a prayer group). But others might be quite surprised to have their work so considered (e.g. someone working on concerns about the environment who may be one of those who think that Christianity is either silent or antagonistic to such concerns). The again, some will be surprised that some work of another group should be

placed in the same camp of legitimate concerns as their own. For example, sociologists note that there is a high correlation between those who attend religious ceremonies regularly and social conservatism. Therefore, sociologists are not surprised that many congregations are non-welcoming to strangers or have a high proportion of those who feel 'foreigners should not get our jobs'. So having some people from the social justice groups seen as part of the Lord's kingdom building exercise may be rather discomforting to some. Such discomfort is part of the kerygma.

6. Rather than preach, organise it that these various groups – and it is the glory of the Spirit that there will always be more than one already knows – to 'show-case' their work briefly, and invite them to consider how they can see themselves as parts of the Lord's 'project.'

Fifth Sunday of Ordinary Time

CELEBRANT'S GUIDE

Introduction to the Celebration
My friends, we have gathered here because we have heard and answered the invitation of Jesus, the Anointed One. Gathered we become his people, his body, his presence in the world. We are called to act in the world like salt: giving flavour through its presence. We are called to be a light to those around us. We are called to reflect the goodness of our heavenly Father. So let us begin our gathering by recalling our identity as the community of the baptised.

Rite of Penance
Replace this with the *Asperges* option; making sure to include the blessing of the salt (Missal, p 389).

Headings for Readings
First Reading
The prophet calls the People of God to bring help, comfort and freedom to those they encounter.

Second Reading
Paul reminds the church in Corinth that our faith is a community's relationship with the crucified Christ.

Gospel
The Lord calls us, as the People of God, to show a new vision of life to those we encounter.

Prayer of the Faithful
President
My friends, let us pray for the gifts and skills we need to be the salt of the earth, the light on a lamp-stand, those whose good works will help others to give praise to our Father in heaven.

Reader(s)
1. Let us pray for ourselves as a church that we learn, with the Spirit's help, to be salt in our society. Lord hear us.
2. Let us pray for ourselves as a church that we learn, with the Spirit's help, to be light to the world. Lord hear us.
3. Let us pray for ourselves as a church that we learn, with the Spirit's help, to be a group whose good works shine out before our society. Lord hear us.
4. Let us pray for ourselves as a church that we learn, with the Spirit's help, to guide our neighbours to give praise to our Father in heaven. Lord hear us.

President
Father, you have made us your children of adoption. Hear us now and enable us to fulfill our calling in Christ Jesus, our Lord. Amen.

Eucharistic Prayer
Preface of Sundays in Ordinary Time I (P29) makes explicit our vocation as the community which is the church.

Invitation to the Our Father
Let us now give praise to our Father in heaven:

Sign of Peace
In a world torn by violence, may our commitment to peace shine before all as the way of the Lord. Let us offer each other a sign of that commitment.

Invitation to Communion
The Lord Jesus has called us to be his witnesses in the world, and he calls us now to be sharers in his supper.

Communion Reflection
Lord Jesus, you called us to be disciples.
You formed us to be your body with you as head.
You gathered us from many places and gave us a place at your table.

Now, Lord Jesus, help us to hear your call afresh.

Form us anew, and reform us, so that we can manifest you in our world.

Send us from this table strengthened by this holy food. May it sustain us during the coming week and be the taster for us being gathered with all the saints at the heavenly banquet. Amen.

Conclusion

Prayer over the People 20 can be adapted as a solemn blessing, thus:

May God bless you with every good gift from on high. Amen.

May God keep you pure and holy in his sight at all times. Amen.

May God bestow the riches of his grace upon you and fill you with love for all people. Amen.

COMMENTARY

First Reading: Isa 58:7-10

This is an excerpt from a discourse on the differences between true and false fasting (58:1-14) that forms part of Third-Isaiah. The key to true fasting is that it involves service and care for fellow human beings (*note:* true fasting involves this service, it is not that the actual act of fasting is replaced by it or can be substituted with it). When fasting – which is an appeal to God to be heard – involves this larger service, then it is true prayer, and also worship.

As extracted here, it is offered to be read as an absolute obligation on the servant of God to be of service to the human beings around him. While this is a legitimate message to draw, by where one edits, from these verses, the whole unit is a far richer piece of theological wisdom.

Psalm: 111 (112)

Not a good choice as the gospel is concerned with the church's witness, while this psalm concentrates on an individual. The psalm's emphasis on 'the upright man' (in both the text and the response) can add a note of tension to the liturgy. The solution is to replace this with a hymn or other musical item or, at the very least, use 'Alleluia' as the response.

Second Reading: 1 Cor 2:1-5
This little bit of text forms a unit within the letter: it is Paul's statement of the authority of his preaching, and therefore of his authority to reprove the Corinthians regarding the disputes and dissensions that have arisen in their church. The content of that appeal is that they should observe how Paul behaved among them and note how different that was to the normal lifestyle of itinerant philosophers. He only spoke about a crucified one, and not some wonderful 'wisdom'. This difference in style should indicate to the Corinthians the unexpected nature of the Saviour (in comparison with the human expectations from whatever source) that is the crucified-anointed one, Jesus.

First Reading > Gospel Links
Continuity of teaching on the example called for from God's people in both covenants. Both use the image of the example of the people being a light to those surrounding them.

Gospel: Mt 5:13-16
In content, this gospel is also found in Luke so can be said to be part of that body of sayings (referred to as 'Q') which was so influential in shaping the first communities' perception of their role as the continuance of the presence of Jesus in the world. Within Matthew, however, it has a far more precise role: it marks the conclusion of the opening section of the Sermon on the Mount. It is a well formed unit, two interconnected parables (hence the unit's common name: 'The Parables of Salt and Light') that function together, with the latter parable relating to light showing signs of having gathered more detail in the process of tradition: it is not just a lamp on a stand, but the lamp is itself like a shining city on hill. Its power as a set of images can be gauged from the fact that all three images have passed into common expression: 'X is great, he's the salt of the earth'; 'Y was

the shining light in that movement'; and in the USA many Christian groups who think of their country as God's ideal society like to refer to America as 'the shining city on the hill' borrowing directly from this parable.

Within the Sermon, Matthew appears to be thinking of salt as a metaphor for teaching: teaching must be pure if it is to have its effect. Light refers to the kerygma, it must be spread to have its effect. The same themes are found at the end of the gospel as a whole (28:16-20) where the disciples are charged to teach the nations so that they can 'obey all that I have commanded you.' This common element is, traditionally, referred to in a 'missionary' context; while this is correct, it obscures for many – who might be sitting in a church building that is a century or more in age – a more basic component of Matthew's thinking. He imagines the church as a group within, and much smaller than, the society around it. It is to this larger group, with which the community brushes shoulders when they leave the common meal, that they must be 'salt' and 'light'. The phrase 'missionary work' carries with it an undercurrent of work done 'over there' (and such undercurrents within language are not easily eradicated), while the social situation of Matthew (and most communities today) is that their ministry is to those 'just outside'. It is better not to think of it as 'missionary work,' but as 'everyday work' (i.e. belonging to the day when they are not gathering for the Eucharist: on that day they rub shoulders with fellow Christians; on the ordinary days of the rest of the week they rub shoulders with a larger society to whom they must be bearers of light, having already become as pure as salt themselves).

HOMILY NOTES

1. 'Salt', 'light', a 'shining city on a hill': three wonderful metaphors for the relationship of each community of Christians to the larger society in which it finds itself. It is a relationship whereby the Christian community is distinct within the larger society and offers it a service it may not even know it needs and might be unwilling to declare that it

wants. Our society is fine, one can hear people say, and it does not need a group of Christians thinking that they have the light or that they are a model of what our society should be. For our part, many of us Christians would rather keep our heads down, point out that it makes no difference that we are Christians to what we are like as neighbours, employees, or officials.

2. This situation of Christians being a small, identifiable group within a larger society was taken for granted at the time the gospel was written, and indeed survived until well into the fifth century. Then, for more than a millennium, the situation that Christians experienced was radically different: the community and the Christian community became virtually co-terminous. Indeed, the distinction between Christians/non-Christians was often replaced by the distinction of 'church' (meaning the clergy, sometimes formally established as an estate)/state or the distinction of altar/crown. Now, with the occasional exception, that identification of church community and larger society has disappeared. We still hear people referring to 'Christian countries' but they just mean background culture, while we as Christians should be quick to deny that simply belonging to a country can be seen as being part of the body of Christ.

3. However, we are left with a few conundrums. First, we have little experience of being a sub-group within society; and we are often far happier thinking of ourselves as the group that gives form to society. Second, we have many mechanisms/practices in our communal behaviour/pastoral strategies that served us well when we as the Christian community and we as a secular society were almost identical; but little by way of experience in being a servant of the larger society.

4. Just noting this new, or relatively new, situation, and helping people to recognise it as a factor in how they think of themselves, is a first step today.

5. Only when we can think of ourselves as having many 'belongings' can we think of how we, in a particular community,

can be of service. We have to learn to steer between three sets of rocks. First, the Christians cannot separate themselves out from society at large as if they are an elect sect, 'the saved'. This is an option that many sects have taken over the centuries, but it ignored the fact that the whole universe is the creation of the Father. The Christ's love and forgiveness reached out to all, and we are called help the society give praise to the Father, not to abandon it. The second danger is to imagine that there is no distinction between the values of the larger society and that of the community of the church; life is simple if the Christians just disappear and adopt the current trends. We have a distinctive vision that the universe is good, it is loved by the Father, and there is the good news that can transform how we view life. The third set of rocks is to imagine that we can only relate to a society that signs up in detail to our vision. We must work with all people of good will, knowing that the Spirit is always at work before us, beyond our reach, and in ways we cannot see.

6. We are called today – in every place in the developed world – to learn an aspect of being Christians that, for the most part, never even bothered our parents or grandparents. But part of the good news is that in every learning curve there is the Spirit's presence to be called upon to bring light in our darkness.

Sixth Sunday of Ordinary Time

CELEBRANT'S GUIDE

Introduction to the Celebration

The word 'religion' conjures up for most people, and indeed for us Christians also, two great images. The first is that there is a system of moral 'do-s and don't-s' – and that we have such an image is true whether one thinks such rules are a good or a bad thing. The second is that there are various religious activities that have to be followed: like the rule that we have to go to Mass on Sundays. But the message of Jesus, brought out in today's gospel, is that we must go beyond these appearances: our actions must not just be following rules but must be inspired by love; our religious observances cannot be merely formalities, but must open us to mystery of love that is greater that the universe yet which enters every detail of the creation.

Rite of Penance

    Lord Jesus, you came as the fulfilment of the Law and the Prophets. Lord have mercy.

    Lord Jesus, you came as the mercy of the Father. Christ have mercy.

    Lord Jesus, you came as announcing the Spirit of love and truth. Lord have mercy.

Headings for Readings

First Reading

The commandments are not given to us as a test to try to catch us out: they are the expression of God's wisdom, and God watches over us with loving care.

Second Reading

Our faith is not a set of abstract ideas but is based on the actual love of God for us – a love demonstrated in the crucifixion of the Lord of Glory.

Gospel
This gospel is taken from the Sermon on the Mount: Jesus calling us to lives of integrity; and acting with integrity is more demanding that simply keeping rules.

Prayer of the Faithful
Sample Formula 10 (Ordinary Time II), Missal, p 1002, is suitable.

Eucharistic Prayer
There is no preface or Eucharistic Prayer that is particularly suitable for today.

Invitation to the Our Father
The Lord Jesus showed us the fullness of God's love, and made us children of the Father; so in union with him we pray:

Sign of Peace
Love must animate this community, and love manifests itself in peace. Let us express our love of one another as sisters and brothers in Jesus Christ.

Invitation to Communion
The Lord welcomes us to this table now, and so promises us a place at the banquet in the kingdom.

Communion Reflection
Confusing celebrating with uttering words is a constant danger. So, have a structured silence. Begin it, when seated, with some formula such as 'Let us now reflect for one minute in silence on what we are celebrating'; then measure the minute on your watch, and conclude the silence with 'Amen' before standing up for the final collect.

Conclusion
Solemn Blessing 11 (Ordinary Time II), Missal p 372, is appropriate.

Notes

Shorter Form of today's gospel reduces the Matthean preaching to sound bites; it makes a mockery of the idea of relying on the apostolic preaching as a fundamental part of our memory as the church.

COMMENTARY

First Reading: Sir 15:15-20

This is part of a section of the book devoted to the topic of free will and sin, which runs from 15:11 to 16:23. Normally, the treatises that make up Sirach are well-fashioned arguments addressing a problem systematically, but this treatment is the exception: the author makes a number of points without linking them harmoniously to one another. This can be seen in today's lection. First, (vv 15-6) there is a clear statement of a position on sin that is offensive to many western theological ears: the human being is able not to sin, and this is within the power of the human being (this is the position challenged in many older textbooks on grace as *posse non peccare* – and one can immediately see why Luther excluded this book from the canon). Second, (vv 17-8) a statement of 'the two ways' of life and death which was a common theme in some strands of Second-Temple Judaism, and became part of early Christian moral formation in the Didache. Third, (vv 19-20) one has a statement of the divine omniscience in the form of God as all-seeing, and as the overseer of the deeds of his children. This text is often presented as the scriptural basis for the image of the all-seeing divine eye, an eye in a triangle at the zenith of the creation.

Psalm: 118 (119)

These verses pick up the theme of it being wisdom to follow the Law which is expressed in the first reading and so they form a bridge towards the understanding of the Law presented in the Sermon on the Mount.

Second Reading: 1 Cor 2:6-10
This is Paul's exposition of what he considers to be true wisdom
and the true language of love. The section runs from 2:6 to 3:4,
and in the passage read today Paul's argument is seeking to
show that although the cross only occurred a few years previ-
ously, this is an ancient wisdom (i.e. not a 'new-fangled idea')
because it is founded in the very mystery of God. We must remember that one of the standard criticisms of Judaism was that
it was a relatively new religion in imagining a universe that was
only a few thousand years old in contrast to the cycles of 36,000
years that Greek culture spoke of; how must more difficult was
it for Christians to have a claim to wisdom when one of its essential characteristics in the Hellenistic world was that 'wisdom is
ancient'. Here the true wisdom is the cross of the Lord of Glory
which was an event that happened less than two decades earlier;
but it is also a wisdom hidden since before the ages began.

First Reading > Gospel Links
Just as the gospel text stresses the continuity between the times
of both covenants, so the first reading is an earlier expression of
what is found in the gospel.

Gospel: Mt 5:17-37
The dominant memory of the church of the relationship of Jesus
and the Law, the Old and New Covenants, is one of Jesus replacing the Law, abolishing the Law, purifying the Law, or replacing
'letter' with 'spirit'. That this is the dominant way of viewing the
question comes from the way Paul presented the issue (or, at
least, was understood as presenting the issue) and from the anti-
Jewish polemics of the later first century. This is not only the
dominant memory, but has given rise to the notion that there
was a single, coherent, and consistent early Christian view of
this question. There was no single position on this in the first
century, as this part of the Sermon on the Mount makes clear.

Matthew, having finished the preliminaries (5:1-16), now has
the New Moses present the New Law and his first concern is the

relationship of Jesus to the Law of Israel (his presentation of this theme runs from 5:17 to 5:48, most of which we read today). Matthew clearly wants to combat, and eagerly oppose, the views of those who have heard Paul – or preachers like him – and who suggest that the New replaces the Old, or that Jesus abrogates, abolishes or changes the Law. Once we are not trying to reconcile Matthew's position with either Paul or the generic memory, this passage becomes clear and straightforward.

The Law of Moses will endure and continue in effect until the end of the world when all is accomplished (v 18). Other positions, such as that of Paul, are in Matthew's preaching simply untrue to the memory of Jesus. This leaves one gaping question: if Jesus does not abolish or change the Law, what difference does he make? For Matthew it is a case that the Law is now complete: Jesus is the fulfilment of the Law, its perfect expression, and, so also, he is the perfect expression of the Father's wisdom. However, given the general perception of the memory of the relationship of Jesus to the Law – even in such phrases as the Old and New Covenants – it is virtually impossible to preach on this text without veering towards the very replacement notion that Matthew was preaching against.

HOMILY NOTES

1. We tend to think of the contents of today's gospel as a series of little pieces: a rule on this, a rule on that, a bit of theology on some other point. Apart from the fact that this 'chop it into sentences' approach to the gospels is not good exegesis but a variant type of fundamentalism, this approach misses the whole point of the sermon by Jesus. The central point is that the message of the gospel is greater than the sum of its parts. It is not a new rule about this, a change in the rules about something else, and so forth; rather, the message is that God's love is greater than all, and we are called to respond to that love in a complete loving way, not simply by a formalistic fulfilment of regulations. Love always must go beyond 'box ticking' or it is not love.

2. This has an effect on how we preach: if we turn the gospel into a series of new regulations, and preach them as such, our preaching is reversing the very point of today's gospel. This is also the fundamental reason why the shorter form of today's gospel supplied in the lectionary is so inappropriate.

3. So how can we reflect on the message that love and faith are more than 'box ticking'?

4. The first point is to state just that: love and faith are more than 'box ticking.' We can keep all the rules, but if our lives have not got that spark of love and laughter, then we are not following the God of love but the 'great policeman in the sky'.

5. That sparkle of love is what makes the difference between the saint and the intense rule-keeping boor. That sparkle is the ability to see beyond the rules, to glimpse a mystery that is greater than the universe, to glimpse the love of God beckoning us.

6. But while attention to detail and discipline can train us in keeping the rules, we can only discover how to love through forgiving those who have hurt us irrespective of whether they ask for forgiveness or not, or are repentant or not. We can only discover how to love by helping those in need, whether they 'deserve' help or not. We can only discover how to love by standing with those who are oppressed even if it is dangerous for us. We can only discover how to love by asking the Holy Spirit to enlighten our minds with wisdom.

7. Love is the sparkle of the good news, the joy of being a disciple, but it is never the easy option.

Seventh Sunday of Ordinary Time

Introduction to the Celebration

Friends in Christ, we – as the community of the baptised – are called by God to provide the world with an example of a different way of living life. Around us we hear every day of people waging war or getting ready to wage war or waging war to make peace or waging war to prevent war. We often hear the same language in our businesses and in our workplaces. The motto seems to be: grab, grasp, exploit. But we are called to wage peace. We are called not just to be peaceful, but to actively work in a way that builds up peace, honesty, respect for other and the creation. To say we are Christians is to say that we have volunteered to wage peace in our homes, in our work, and in our world.

Rite of Penance

For those times when we have failed to turn the other cheek, Lord have mercy.

For those times when we have failed to love our enemies, Christ have mercy.

For those times when we have failed to pray for those who persecute us, Lord have mercy.

Headings for Readings

First Reading

The Way of the Lord is to reject hatred, to reject vengeance, and to love our neighbours as ourselves.

Second Reading

Paul asks the church in Corinth about how they imagine themselves: do they not realise that they are God's Temple and the Spirit lives among them?

Gospel

We have a distinctive vision of how life should be lived: we see forgiveness, reconciliation, and peace making as the way to happiness.

Prayer of the Faithful

President

We are called by our Teacher to become the community that prays for its persecutors; now in union with Christ let us carry out that command.

Reader(s)

1. That we may grow as a community of disciples. Lord hear us.

2. That we may learn to forgive those who harm us. Lord hear us.

3. That we may be moved to love our enemies. Lord hear us.

4. That we may be willing to recall now in prayer those who have troubled us, harassed us, annoyed us, or persecuted us:

pause

Lord hear us.

5. Specific local needs and topics of the day.

6. That we may work for peace and reconciliation in our world. Lord hear us.

President

Father, your Son has called us to be a group who forgive any who trespass against us, who forgive those who hurt us, who love our enemies, and who pray for those who persecute us. Hear us now as we pray for our enemies, those who hurt us, and those who persecute us; and gather us and all humanity into your love in Christ Jesus, our Lord. Amen.

Eucharistic Prayer

The best expression of 'the kingdom of justice, peace and love' that is flagged up in the gospel is the Preface of Christ the King (P51); and Eucharistic Prayer III invokes the image of the world making a perfect offering from east to west (which is an expression also found in today's psalm).

Invitation to the Our Father
The Lord has told us to love our enemies and pray for those who persecute us. Now let us pray that we will be forgiven our trespasses as we have forgive those who have trespassed against us:

Sign of Peace
Jesus said: 'If you salute only your brethren, what more are you doing than others? Do not even the Gentiles do the same?' Now let us salute each other to declare our willingness to greet everyone we meet with a word of peace and forgiveness.

Invitation to Communion
The Lord calls us to love each other, and to love our neighbours, and calls us to share now in this feast of his love.

Communion Reflection
Peace demands reflection: have a solemn silence.

Conclusion
Solemn Blessing 14 (Ordinary Time V), Missal p 373, is appropriate.

Notes
One of the great strengths of Catholic 'Social Teaching' has been to recognise that the links between peace, justice, reconciliation, and development are not simply accidental but intrinsic – summed by in the lapidary phrase of Paul VI: 'Development is the new word for peace.' In every community there are various groups that take on parts of this agenda. These groups often feel (1) that their global concerns are not intimately linked with the liturgy (except for some 'special celebration') and imagine that their activity belongs to the world of action, while liturgy belongs to the world of piety – this is a false dichotomy; or worse (2) that their concerns for peace and justice are not espoused by the 'official' church. Today is a day where such groups can be shown to be fully part of the Body of Christ in its perfection.

The first point to note is that the activity of gathering for the eucharistic meal is intrinsically linked to the agenda of peace and reconciliation. Before it was known as 'The Eucharist,' some simply referred to the gathering as 'the love' – to share this meal was to establish the new vision of the world and society: love reigning between people without barriers of class, dignity or worth. Meanwhile, the peace and reconciliation that Christians promote is founded on that established by Christ which we celebrate in this gathering.

However, the liturgy is not a set of ideas but a set of actions and signs: so the labour for these groups working for peace, development, and reconciliation must be visible within the liturgy. This is a day when they could be invited to showcase their works at the assembly or speak to the assembly about their missions; or, very simply, representatives from such groups could be invited to read, help distribute communion, or perform other tasks in the liturgy.

COMMENTARY

First Reading: Lev 19:1-2, 17-18
This whole chapter is a miscellany of bits and pieces of legislation and moral teaching on worship, social justice, charity, and sexuality. The various elements all pre-existed within Israelite tradition prior to their codification in the final form of the book where they were arranged in roughly the same order that the topics are mentioned in the Decalogue. Because the whole chapter is a work of cut-and-paste, nothing has been lost in the editing that produced today's reading.

Psalm: Ps 102 (103)
While the first reading and gospel stress the love that must exist between people, this psalm stresses the relationship of love between God and humanity. As a reflection it complements the other readings by stressing that the origin of love is in God. The fourth verse uses the same expression for the expanse of God's love and reconciliation as Eucharistic Prayer III uses for the perfect (reconciling) sacrifice.

Second Reading: 1 Cor 3:16-23

This and next Sunday's reading come from the section of the
epistle where Paul is concerned with the attitude that should
exist in the church in Corinth between the community and its
leaders/pastors (the whole section comprises 1 Cor 3:5 to 4:5).
However, it is clear that while the Corinthians are the target at
hand, Paul is thinking of all the churches he has founded. Paul is
stressing that there is no room for factions or divisions in the
church. However, what is most interesting is not his statement
but the structure of his argument. He does not argue for unity
for moral reasons (e.g. it is uncharitable to have divisions) nor
for empirical reasons (e.g. it uses energy in fighting one another
that should be used for spreading the gospel), rather there
should be unity because of what they are as an assembly: the
temple in which the Spirit dwells. In this we have the kernel of
Paul's ecclesiology.

First Reading > Gospel Links

Continuity of teaching between both covenants. Note that the
juxtaposition of these two texts gives the lie to such preaching as
'the Old Testament was justice and vengeance; the New is love
and forgiveness' or worse 'The Old Testament God was fear and
retribution, the God of Jesus is forgiveness and peace.' Such simple slogans (whose only theological basis is the logical trick used
to sell washing powders: 'Your old powder left stains on your
clothes; our improved formula even takes out chocolate stains')
had done enormous damage over the centuries in Jewish-
Christian relations, and also in how people read and appreciate
the pre-Christian scriptures.

Gospel: Mt 5:38-48

This is the fourth installment of the Sermon on the Mount which
forms the second lectionary unit in the Year of Matthew. Jesus,
as the fulfillment of the Law, takes unto himself, for the sake of
the people who will form his kingdom, the Law of Moses on
retaliation and love of enemies.

HOMILY NOTES

1. This gospel provokes a curious range of reactions.

2. There are many who would be prepared to lose their lives as martyrs for some aspect of the doctrinal content of Christianity, or a particular version of it, but who consider this call to break with the world's way of power to be simply rubbish. In short, Jesus may be the divine Son of God as the creed professes, but this stuff about 'loving enemies' just has to be ignored.

3. Politicians have made a habit in recent years about 'going the extra mile for peace' (how many people realise that the image is derived from this gospel?) and congratulate themselves that they are doing this; but they do so only in that they delay the threat of war! To go the extra mile for peace means foregoing the war option altogether, not simply giving an extension to an ultimatum. Yet such politicians often wear their Christianity very publicly.

4. During the First World War chaplains with the British Army were ordered to provide extra services for troops as they were recognised as helping to build morale. However, they were forbidden to use New Testament passages such as this in the services lest it would undermine the will to fight and retaliate. But these were seen as Christian services nonetheless. It seems you can take Jesus, but skip this bit of the message.

5. Many people say that they cannot accept Christianity because they cannot 'take the divinity of Christ' or they cannot believe the gospel because 'they cannot take the miracle stories' or they cannot accept the church because of this or that doctrine which they find 'repugnant,' and in each case these may be deeply felt and held difficulties. However, there are far fewer who find this vision of Christian behaviour to be their stumbling block – yet it is as much part of the gospel as any other teaching.

6. This gospel reminds us that Jesus's teaching is not just some set of moral guidelines, but a wholly different view of the

world. The call to conversion is to change our whole way of viewing life, not just to add or alter a few attitudes on this or that.

7. Peace, a world of peace, seems often to be a distant illusion – an impossible dream. But peace is not some state that just happens: it has to be established. We know that wars have to be waged, vendettas have to be pursued, acts of retaliation have to be inflicted and prosecuted. These are all active verbs: waging war. And in every case there is a massive investment of resources: human and material. But peace also needs investment of time, energy, emotions, money, skills. If you want peace, justice, development, reconciliation; then these campaigns have to be waged and actively prosecuted. Whatever world we build, a world of warfare and conflict or a world of development and reconciliation, it is going to cost us. It is one's vision of the whole creation that decides which is the correct choice.

8. Here is a little slogan: Christians are called to wage peace with as much energy as others wage war.

Trinity Sunday

This feast is unique in that the focus of our celebration is not an aspect of the history of salvation, but reflection on the nature of God as we believe it has been revealed to us as Christians. Thus every Sunday is the Sunday of the Trinity, every feast, every action has a trinitarian dimension, and should any prayer be uttered or homily preached which does not include that core of faith – at least tacitly with a conclusion such as 'through Christ our Lord' – then we are apostates, and have ceased to be Christians and become some sort of vague deists or unitarians who value the 'message of Jesus'. At the outset of the celebration it is worth reflecting that today's focus is the very essence of Christian identity. We begin every liturgy by stating that we are acting 'In the name of the Father ...' and that is a declaration of our basic faith, not just an opening formula. Our aim in today's liturgy should be to become more sensitive to the trinitarian cues that run right through our religion.

Introduction to the Celebration
We have just blessed ourselves and declared that we are gathering in the name of the Father, Son, and Holy Spirit. I have just wished you welcome by wishing you 'the grace of Jesus Christ'; then wishing you 'the love of God' the Father; and then wishing you 'the fellowship of the Holy Spirit'. Whenever we gather or pray we are talking about the Father, the Son, and the Spirit. It is this mystery that God is Father, Son, and Spirit that we are called on to reflect on today. As we move through today's celebration, listen out for just how often we will call on 'Father,' 'Son,' and 'Spirit.'

Rite of Penance (but see the Notes section below)
> Lord Jesus, you have shown us the way to the Father. Lord have mercy.
> Lord Jesus, you are Son of God and Son of Mary. Christ have mercy.
> Lord Jesus, you have sent the Spirit among to give us life. Lord have mercy.

Headings for Readings
First Reading
The Lord our God is God indeed: God is before all creation, God is after all creation, God is above all creation, God is beneath all creation; and we are God's children.

Second Reading
All we as Christian do and pray is related to the Father, the Son, and the Spirit: here Paul gives a final blessing to the Corinthians using a little phrase they were already familiar with from the liturgy, and which we still use: 'The grace of our Lord Jesus Christ, and the love of God and the fellowship of the Holy Spirit be with you all.'

Gospel
The Father has sent us the Son, and through the Son we have come to know the Father.

Prayer of the Faithful
President
Gathered into the Son, our Lord Jesus Christ, by the Spirit, let us petition the Father.
Reader(s)
1. That we may seek the way to the Father. Lord in your mercy, hear our prayer.
2. That we may bear witness to his Son, Jesus Christ, in our lives. Lord in your mercy, hear our prayer.

3. That we may rejoice in the strength of the Holy Spirit. Lord in your mercy, hear our prayer.

4. That all who seek the truth will find it. Lord in your mercy, hear our prayer.

5. That all who seek justice shall be satisfied. Lord in your mercy, hear our prayer.

6. That all the dead may find joy in the Father's house. Lord in your mercy, hear our prayer.

President

Father, hear your people's prayers for we ask them in the power of your Holy Spirit, and in the name of Christ Jesus, our Lord. Amen.

Eucharistic Prayer

Preface of the Holy Trinity (P43) (Missal, p 446); Eucharistic Prayer 2 is ideal for today as it presents the trinitarian pattern of all prayer in its two opening sentences which taken together are among the most elegant, and concise, statements of trinitarian faith in the whole of the Latin liturgy: 'Lord you are holy indeed, the fountain of all holiness. Let your Spirit come upon these gifts … that they may become for us the body and blood of our Lord, Jesus Christ.'

However, it is worth noting that while P43 is directed to be used today, many people find it a cold statement of doctrine. If you want a preface that is equally explicit in its statement of trinitarian faith, but which expresses the mystery in terms of the history of salvation – what is sometimes referred to as 'the economic trinity' – then look at Preface of Sunday in Ordinary Time VIII [P36] (Missal, p 439).

Invitation to the Our Father

In the power of the Spirit and the words of the Son, let us pray to the Father.

Sign of Peace
We have been baptised into the life of the Father, Son, and Spirit.
Here strife and ill-will have no place. Let us express our desire to
become more God-like in our lives by exchanging a sign of
peace with one another.

Invitation to Communion
Through sharing in this meal we have a share in the divine banquet. Blessed are we who are called to this supper.

Communion Reflection
Our God is the God of all humans.
The God of heaven and earth.
The God of the sea and the rivers.
The God of the sun and moon.
The God of all the heavenly bodies.
The God of the lofty mountains.
The God of the lowly valleys.
God is above the heavens;
and he is in the heavens;
and he is beneath the heavens.
Heaven and earth and sea,
and everything that is in them,
such he has as his abode.
He inspires all things,
he gives life to all things,
he stands above all things,
and he stands beneath all things.
He enlightens the light of the sun,
he strengthens the light of the night and the stars,
he makes wells in the arid land and dry islands in the sea,
and he places the stars in the service of the greater lights.
He has a Son who is co-eternal with himself,
and similar in all respects to himself;
and neither is the Son younger than the Father,
nor is the Father older than the Son;

and the Holy Spirit breathes in them.
And the Father and the Son and Holy Spirit are inseparable.
Amen.
Bishop Tírechán, c. 700

Dismissal
Every good gift comes from the Father of light.
May he fill you with his blessings. Amen.
The Redeemer has given you lasting freeedom.
May you inherit his everlasting life. Amen.
The Spirit inspired different tongues to proclaim one faith.
May he strengthen you in faith, hope and love. Amen.
May almighty God bless you … .

Notes
1. We encounter God, Father, Son, Spirit, in our baptism, therefore this is a good day to begin with the Rite of Blessing and
Sprinkling with Holy Water (Missal, p 387). However, if you
have used this rite regularly during Eastertide, then perhaps
today is the day to simply use the *Kyrie eleison* Rite of Penance.
2. There is no day in the year when the mystery of faith can be so
easily betrayed by making it into a conundrum than today. So if
you hear yourself using numbers ('three in one, one in three') in
your words, then stop. If you hear yourself saying something
like 'to understand the trinity', 'it can be explained like …', then
stop. If you find yourself mentioning triangles, or shamrocks, or
Möbius strips, then stop at once.
3. In the face of the mystery of God we often try to cope by using
more and more words: if there is one day of the year to keep it
simple and have few words, it is today.

COMMENTARY

First Reading: Ex 34:4-6, 8-9
Second Reading: 2 Cor 13:11-13
Gospel: Jn 3:16-18

1. All three readings
The Christian belief about God is an all-embracing confession
whose ramifications only emerged over many centuries in the
life of the church as it recalled, prayed, celebrated, reflected,
taught new generations, and saw off various false prophets. This
is the phenomenon of the development of doctrine by which the
understanding that exists within the tradition (i.e. the living
mind of the church as it believes now and teaches, while looking
back through its life right to the time when the documents such
as today's readings were written) is always greater than any
particular moment or text. Thus what we believe is not 'based'
upon a collection of texts, rather each text is a testimony (to a
greater or lesser extent) to the faith of the church which is a
whole, a unity. Given this, if one wanted to read our trinitarian
faith into these readings we would destroy their integrity as
texts; while to read them as if they 'justified trinitarianism' or
'supported' it, would be to deny the integrity of the tradition of
which texts are only particular expressions. Moreover, the latter
approach would be theologically perverse as it would imply a
fundamentalism that 'everything is in "The Bible"', and that that
book *is* the revelation.

This means that for this Sunday the usual skills of the exegete
are of little value, and so to offer here a commentary on these
texts would be inappropriate.

2. The Second Reading
Only the second reading can be linked in any, more or less, direct way with the mystery we are reflecting upon, and this is
noted in the homily notes below.

3. The Gospel
Lastly, it is best to steer wide of this passage from John in comment and to read it quickly and without any ceremonial. This

passage is John's clearest expression of Christian exclusivness: only those who accept the Son are saved, and so everyone else, including the Jews who refuse to accept Jesus, stands condemned and excluded from eternal life. This is one of those passages, written towards the end of the first century which was a time of bitter polemic when the two religions were each establishing themselves by mutual separation and recrimination, which has been problematic down the centuries and, in almost every generation, caused some to adopt a similarly exclusivist version of God's mercy. On this day we are expected to read it as showing the intimacy of the Father and the Son in the *operatio ad extra* of the world's salvation; however, by the simple fact of using this passage (and there is no way that an adequate exegesis of it, along with health warnings, can be provided in a liturgical setting) we can be sure someone will go away having heard its exclusivness and then, either, rejects it with the shrug: so much for the Christian gospels; or, accepts it and proceeds to have a notion that only those who are baptised will be 'saved'. It would be better if the lectionary planners had taken account of such unintended consequences (and such effects have a life of their own and do not depend on what people 'ought on a particular occasion' to take from a lection), and simply omitted this passage from lectionary use.

If you believe this passage will cause offence (e.g. many people in the congregation are married to non-Christians or non-believers) or could lead to tension (e.g. a community which has a bible group with fundamentalist leanings), then it is best to avoid this reading altogether and chose the reading from Year B: Mt 28:16-20. It is a pity, given that this is the Year of Matthew, the lectionary planners did not do so originally.

First Reading > Gospel Links
The two readings without any intrinsic connection as readings. They are linked within a larger theological framework where they are assumed to be wholly consistent.

HOMILY NOTES

1. Go back through the second reading and note how Paul's relationship with Jesus – Jesus is Lord – leads him to adopt a way of speaking of God as Father which Jesus had taught his followers. Moreover, Jesus had spoken of sending the Spirit and so the Spirit too is spoken of as 'Lord'.

2. Paul is adopting a formula already in use within the churches, it is a formula that speaks of the relationship we Christians have with God: we live and move and have our being in God the Father, God the Son our Lord Jesus Christ, and God the Spirit.

3. We do not accept 'the trinity' within our minds in the way we accept other religious notions such as 'God loves us.' The mystery of the Father, Son and Spirit is the mystery of God and as such cannot be comprehended by a created mind. Rather, we accept this as part of the gracious revelation of God and respond in the way of Jesus: him we address as Lord; with him we call on the Father; from him we accept the Spirit.

The Body and Blood of Christ
(Corpus Christi)

CELEBRANT'S GUIDE

Introduction to the Celebration

Since the very first days of the church – before St Paul had set out on his journeys or any of the gospels were written – our brothers and sisters have been gathering every week for this sacred meal. But when we routinely do anything, we often lose sight of just how wonderful it is. So today we are reflecting on just how wonderful it is to be called by the Lord to gather in his presence, to be his guests at his table, and to eat and drink from his wonderful bounty. In this banquet we become one with Christ, and are transformed into being his Body, and his Blood flows in all our community's veins, giving us the strength to be his witnesses in the world and to inherit the life that never ends.

Rite of Penance

Lord Jesus, you invite us to your table. Lord have mercy.
Lord Jesus, you share your loaf with us. Christ have mercy.
Lord Jesus, you share your cup with us. Lord have mercy.

Headings for Readings
First Reading

The Lord sustained his people with manna on their journey of discipleship; now he sustains us with the Eucharist on our journey of discipleship during which we must learn that we do not live on bread alone but on everything that comes from the mouth of the Lord.

Second Reading

St Paul is here explaining to the community in Corinth the significance of their gathering each week for the Lord's Supper: when they shared the common loaf, they were sharing in the common life of Christ.

Sequence
The *Lauda Zion* (optional) is a theological gem; but conveying it in such a way that it is more than just verbiage is a practical challenge.

Gospel
John reminds us that unless we share in the Eucharist we do not share in the life of Jesus our Lord. It is our sharing in the common cup that enables his life blood to circulate through us as a community.

Prayer of the Faithful
President
We have gathered for the Lord's banquet. Now as his priestly people let us present our needs to the Father.
Reader(s)
1. For ourselves gathered at this holy meal. Lord hear us.
2. For friends absent from this meal. Lord hear us.
3. For all Christians, may we be united around the Lord's table. Lord hear us.
4. For all who are hungry. Lord hear us.
5. For all who are excluded from the world's riches. Lord hear us.
6. For the dead, that they may share the banquet whose foretaste we now celebrate. Lord hear us.
President
Father, in this holy meal we encounter your Son and recall his passion. Fill us with your grace, and grant our needs through that same Christ, our Lord. Amen.

Eucharistic Prayer
Preface of the Holy Eucharist II (P48) has a narrative quality that makes it more accessible than P47; moreover, the emphasis of P48 is more on the actual celebration than P47 and therefore is more suitable for today.

The Our Father
Gathered as the body of Christ around this table, let us pray to
our common Father: Our Father ...

Sign of Peace
In Christ we are united into his body around this table; dishar-
mony and strife have no place here. Let us show this now to one
another.

Invitation to Communion
We are his people when we recognise him in this breaking of the
loaf. Happy are we who are called to this supper.

Communion Reflection
They knew it was the Lord, Alleluia;
In the breaking up of the loaf, Alleluia.
The loaf we break is the body of Jesus Christ, our Lord, Alleluia;
The cup we bless is the blood of Jesus Christ, our Lord, Alleluia;
For the remission of sins, Alleluia.
Lord, let your mercy rest upon us, Alleluia;
Who put all our confidence in you, Alleluia.
They knew it was the Lord, Alleluia;
In the breaking of the loaf, Alleluia.

O Lord, we believe that in this breaking of your body and pour-
ing out of your blood we become your redeemed people;
We confess that in taking the gifts of this pledge here, we lay
hold in hope of enjoying its true fruits in the heavenly places.
*(From an early medieval hymn for during the fraction found in an
eighth-century Mass book from Ireland)*

Conclusion
Prayer over the People 18 (Missal, p 382) is suitable.

Notes
The focus of this feast
This used to be one of the most colourful days of the year, its

focal point being the great procession. Its emphasis was the divine presence in the Blessed Sacrament: a King entitled to public acknowledgement and adoration. The Mass became a thanksgiving for the Blessed Sacrament: the Mass was a doing (the 'sacrifice') and the 'sacrament' was the precious possession which we were so glad to have. While this emphasis, and the attendant confusing theology, have been abandoned, it tends to resurface today where the Blessed Sacrament is approached as if it were a primary part of Christ's gift to the church, rather than as the sequel to our encounter with him in the actual banquet in which we break the one loaf and share the one cup.

Our focus today should be to hold a mirror up to our weekly assembly: a day of reflection on why we gather for the Eucharistic Meal each week, and our aim must be that we depart from this assembly with an enriched awareness of the significance of encountering the body of Christ in the assembled community, in the shared memory, and in the loaf and cup.

It is worth noting that this feast is, since 1970, *Corpus et Sanguis Christi*. This change in name is significant as our gaze has shifted from the monstrance as the key image of this day, to the table prepared for us around which we gather.

COMMENTARY

First Reading: Deut 8:2-3, 14-16
The Book of Deuteronomy looks back to the time in the desert as a time when Israel was purified by having to depend on God alone. As such it it seen as the time of ideal innocence: depending on God they learned and believed those things that a disciple should learn in time of training. There God both taught and purified, but also provided. There they learned the true values. There also they learned to remember the mighty works of God's goodness (the *magnalia Dei*) which were the basis of faith in God: delivery from slavery, preservation in the desert, and care from on high.

This recollection (*anamnesis*) of the 'original' Paschal event makes it inherently appropriate to be part of our recollection of the Paschal event of the Christ which is the Eucharist. The lection's self-reference to the location of its reading (i.e. at a Eucharist) is somehow analogous to the self-reference of today's feast: celebrating the Eucharist to rejoice that we have the Eucharist to celebrate.

Psalm: Ps 147:12-15 (147:1-3)
This psalm has nothing to do with either the first reading (to which it is supposed to be a response) nor the gospel (to which it is supposed to be a meditative preparation). This psalm was chosen for today because of its opening line in Latin (in the Gallicanum translation, which is different to the Neo-Vulgate): *lauda Hierusalem Dominum, lauda Deum tuum Sion.* This line set the headline for the sequence (*Lauda Sion*) and therefore became eucharistic, and so was used as a basic processional psalm in Corpus Christi processions for centuries where it was the call of those processing to the whole of their city to come out and praise their Lord who was then moving through their streets. Its use here is sanctioned by tradition of long usage, but whether it makes any sense in multi-cultural societies where such processions are a rarity, and in a liturgy that is the action of the Eucharist rather than a para-liturgy celebrating the Real Presence of the Blessed Sacrament, is a serious question.

In a revision of the lectionary it should be replaced by text from Ps 78 (focused on verse 24) as found in the Septuagint and appropriated by John, as this verse stands directly behind Jn 6:31 whose explication is today's gospel. However, until such a revision takes place we are stuck with Ps 147 and it makes no sense whatsoever for today's feast. So what should we do? Take advantage of the fact that when a psalm is not sung, it can be omitted; so do not sing it and omit it! If you believe there is a need for something between the readings today, then use the sequence.

Second Reading: 1 Cor 10:16-17
This passage, along with 1 Cor 11:17-35, form our earliest surviving theology of the Eucharist. Its key is the very obvious real-

ity of what it means to share a common loaf, an experience we are still familiar with in the desire to have a piece of the wedding cake or of the birthday cake. The translation of *artos* as 'loaf' in this passage is a strength of the JB version and has now been followed by the NRSV for all eucharistic occurances of *artos* in the New Testament. It is noteworthy that when Paul uses the word *artos*, as here, he is referring to leavened ordinary bread. The basic symbolism that is the basis of Paul's theology, i.e. a theology which follows from what is actually done, is opaque to Latin Christians since the tenth century when unleavened bread began to be used for the liturgy (much to the disgust of the Orthodox) and is virtually invisible to most Roman Cathoics where the basic experience is limitied to pre-cut glossy, individual rondels of a flour-based substance (to use the word 'bread' for these little plastic-like tokens when one uses the same word for a lovely, warm, sweet-smelling freshly baked loaf that one would eat as one carries it home seems to be an abuse of language).

First Reading > Gospel Links
Deuteronomy identifies the care of God for the people with the manna, the bread which came down from heaven; Jesus himself, in John, is identified with this bread. So the two readings are connected in that the content of the first reading is an ante-type of the future which is fulfilled in the gospel. But this relation, which is founded in the gospel itself, and John's way of reading the scriptures is absorbed into a different dynamic of reading when these two lections are adopted by the litugy today. For centuries, the church has read both these readings in terms of the Eucharist. The old versicle at Benediction based on Jn 6:31-2 (*Panem de caelo praestitisti eos [et] omne delectamentum in se habentem*) holds the key to the link: the People of God have always been fed from heaven, the first manna was for this life, the second for the life to come. Jn 6:31 makes this explicit, it underlies the theology of this feast in St Thomas's hymns, and it governs the selection today.

Gospel: Jn 6:51-58

Of the many different eucharistic theologies that survive from the first century, none is more complex than that found in John's gospel: and we have an important section of it as today's gospel. This complexity has several roots. First, although the single longest section of John is his account of the meal on the eve of the crucifixion (the whole of 5 chapters: Jn 13-17), there is no account of the institution of the Eucharist. There has been much speculation as to why this is omitted, and the most likely reason is that he was trying to balance the emphasis found in the other gospels which linked the on-going weekly meal of the church (which in John's theology is necessary as continual sustenance for the church) with the annual paschal meal. Second, John's theology is made up of a 'sign' (Jn 6:1-15), then a discourse (Jn 6:22-40), and then a dispute (Jn 6:41-59) which itself breaks into several sub-sections, just one of which we are reading today. Third, the dispute is framed within John's larger theme of the opposition to Jesus by the mob (*ochlos*) of 'the Jews'; and in the aftermath of centuries of anti-Jewish prejudice by Christians that make preaching this material very difficult (one has to abstract what is of value while rejecting anything that could incite bitterness). The basic point to remember is that John was preaching in the late first century when groups were forming themselves up into two distinct religions, namely the fore-runner of the religion we call Judaism and the fore-runner of the religion we call Christianity, and establishing their identities, in part, by mutual differentiation (the 'us and them' method). Fourth, John uses 'flesh,' 'blood,' 'eating,' and 'drinking' in ways that are alien to us. It was already alien in the West by the ninth century when Eriugena wrote, commenting on this passage, *mente non dente comedimus* (we eat with mind not teeth); and it is further alien to us given the way we refer to blood in modern medicine.

So what key points can we extract from it? Sharing in the church's bread is the promise of the end times; the gathering now is an anticipation of the final existence of us as a people. In this symbol-system, 'eating' is appropriation of a common identity and 'flesh' is the reality of Jesus the Son of God. The identity of the church is this real existence in Christ now which is the promise of the fullness of life (cf Jn 10:10). 'Blood' is the actual life-force that keeps each body animated, it is life conceived of as a distinct reality from the individual bodies that have it now. It is not that 'I am alive' (as we say) but 'My body now has life' because it is participating in the created life force (think of the implications of the question: 'Is there any life in it?' or the statement 'There's life in the old dog yet!' – both assume that life is a distinct reality from the living body). This life that is in the blood of Christ is the divine life-force itself, the very life of God we are called to share in. 'Drinking' the life-force is asserting and establishing a common destiny (see Jn 18:11), which is the eschatological life of union with God. Life and life-force are about the future times, not about consuming the bread and cup now. The bread and cup now are the pointers (the *musteria*, the *sacramenta*) to that future time. The confusion that this passage has caused over the centuries (e.g. confusing real sacramental participation with hyper-realism, 'real presence' as if what is in the cup is equivalent to what one sees from a cut finger, or cannibalism) collapsing this eschatological time into everyday time. Sacraments exist in this time (what is measured with a clock) to point beyond it to another time that is beyond time.

HOMILY NOTES

1. Words should help us to draw out the significant in our lives. Words should be the seeds of meaning within us and between us. Words should be precious in letting us see the wonder and goodness of the Father.
2. Unfortunately, words also can obscure reality for us. They can bury us under so many layers of accumulated confusions that we struggle to see what is really important. In a communications age, words can be the vehicles of disinformation like never before and can confuse the chasm that should exist between the genuine, the true, the important, and the illusions of salesmen, marketers, and spin-doctors. Words also

can so fascinate us with their own magic that we fail to move beyond them to the realities they exist to highlight for us. Words should be illuminating, but they are often like a fog, and indeed sometimes a smokescreen separating us from reality.

3. What has this to do with the Eucharist? Well, the Eucharist is a sacrament, a sign, a mystery; and as such it should convey meaning and truth and authenticity and life. And so it always involves words: words, firstly, in the actual celebration, the words of thanksgiving and prayer to the Father that justify the name of 'The Eucharist'; and, words too that talk about what we are doing, explaining our actions to ourselves and to others. These words of explanation and exploration of meaning are what we call 'theology'. We see the process right from the start of the Christian journey: each week the community gathered and in its eating and drinking offered its prayer of thanksgiving. Then we see theologians explaining why this is significant: firstly, Paul writing to the Corinthians explaining it in terms of becoming one with the Christ, then the Didache in terms of the final banquet of the re-gathered Israel, then Mark explaining it in terms of a pre-existing understanding of the Passover (and in explaining a weekly meal in terms of an annual meal leaving a theological time-bomb that went off in Calvin's hands 1400 years later!), then John in terms of the manna in the desert, and on and on and on until we reach some of the books on the Eucharist that are on your shelves or the pamphlets in the church's bookrack.

4. But today we face a problem with all these words. For many the words about the Eucharist make no sense. The gathering makes no sense; its does not enhance their grasp of life or of the goodness of God. Just think of these two facts. First, English and Welsh hierarchy figures for Mass attendance showed a fall of 130,000 between 2002 and 2005. People are expressing their 'theology' (i.e. their understanding of what we are doing, whether it is an adequate theology or not) with their feet. Second, the fastest growing Christian groups are

the evangelical churches where the Eucharist is not considered central or significant (and which in some groups is even
considered superstitious). Yet the statisticians point out that
between 25% (Catholics bishops' figures) and 33% (the evangelical missionaries' figures) of South Americans now formally call themselves 'Evangelicals' as distinct from 'Catholics'.
And, this is a pattern of movement that is not confined to
Latin America. When we consider the centrality of this meal,
since the very first days of the church, that was the bonding
force of the little groups with their Lord whose resurrection
they proclaimed, then the poverty of such a jejune (literally)
non-Eucharist centred theology cannot but be a cause of sad-
ness.

5. That the Eucharist and its language are seen as meaningless,
   boring, or irrelevant either to life in general or the life of discipleship is, of its nature, a complex problem with many
   causes; and it is possible that it is beyond our ability to do
   anything about most of these causes. However, some parts of
   the problem are of our making and can be addressed. One of
   these is that many celebrations obscure the basic and original
   structure of this gift that Jesus gave us. This obscuring takes
   place in that we concentrate on all the various levels of meaning that have accumulated over the centuries such that participants cannot experience the answer to that constant
   human question: 'What's this about?' – nor can teachers give
   a concise explanation that might answer that question. Such
   accumulations of secondary issues are a normal part of
   human life and the constant bane of every group activity,
   and so common is it that we have the classic image of 'the tail
   wagging the dog' to describe the problem. In the case of the
   Eucharist this can take many forms: the celebration becomes
   primarily linked to the availability of a priest rather than the
   needs of a community; it becomes a teaching session and
   prayer service plus getting Holy Communion rather than the
   Lord's Banquet; the questions of who can or cannot receive
   become the central issue – and for a great many people this is

the sole question that concerns them about the whole affair –
rather than encountering the risen Christ; the Eucharist (the
name for an action) becomes subsumed under the notion of
Holy Communion (a commodity) or the Blessed Sacrament
(an object); and for many, priests included, it is hard to think
of 'sacrament' as the name of an activity of a group rather
than of a 'something' usually had by an individual.

6. So what can one do to address the problem? The starting
point is to remember that the Eucharist is the collective meal
of the community of the baptised. So why not meet for the
Eucharist on this day in the community hall rather than the
church building? Then stand around for the whole event
rather than be formally lined up in the way one might for a
class or a meeting where discussion is dominant. This is a
gathering, an assembly, a celebration of who we are in Christ,
not a meeting to transact business. Recall the gathering at
some 'reception', people stand and mingle, they get to know
each other, they recognise they have a common reason for
being there: they are not seated in rows. Then they can gather
around a single table that is the Lord's. Words like 'altar' are
secondary: they derive from a second century attempt to explain what we are doing as we gather at the one table. It was
basic to the message of Jesus that there was a welcome at his
table, there was room there for the poor, the outcasts, the
strangers, the sinners, and unloved. This gathering of those
who are reconciled and given new life (i.e. the baptised) is
the pattern for the whole life of the church, both now and eschatologically. So everyone should be able to gather around
that table, and know they have as much right to stand there
at the Lord's invitation as the mob of concelebrating priests
one sometimes sees huddling round it. A decent-sized dining
table, that is still clearly recognisable as such (i.e. not covered
to make it look like 'an altar'), is ideal. It is also worth recalling those lines from Eucharistic Prayer I (which date from the
time before we had formal churches) that say: 'Remember
your male servants (*famulorum*) and your female servants

(*famularum*), indeed, the needs of all who are standing around.'

Then we come to the basic activity of thanking the Father in Jesus. We often recite this as if its purpose was to ask God to consecrate elements on the table (and as such it becomes the skilled work of the priest alone). Presented in that light there is little adequate answer to the question someone asked me after the Eucharist recently: why does the priest not get all this done before-hand so that it is ready to give to us after the readings? It is strange how the culture of fast-food outlets matches the old practice of 'Mass and Communion (from the tabernacle, of course)'. So there has to be attention to the tone of the Eucharistic Prayer that it is recited as prayer directed to the Father thanking him for all he has given us in his Son. Use Eucharistic Prayer II as it is crisp and its theology elegant, and note that in the Missal of Vatican II there are no 'words of consecration', but an 'institution narrative' – there lies the core of the renewed theology of the council and it has major implications for how the Eucharistic Prayer is voiced at every celebration. We are recalling the Last Supper as part of our prayer and so justifying why we are now praying in this way (this recollection format is part of every collect: we praise the Father because of something that has occurred) not pronouncing a sacral formula. After all, in the final analysis, it is the gathered people that must be consecrated to become the body and blood of Christ.

Then we come to the basic form of the meal: Jesus used a single loaf from which each received a share, and passed around a single cup from which each drank. This is the basic symbolism of this particular meal: a common life as one body which is Christ (the one loaf), and a common destiny (see Mk 10:38-9; Jn 18:11) which is in Christ (the one cup). This eating and drinking by the gathering is, of its nature, a confusing and lengthy business, but that is fine. After all we are there to engage in just that activity.

7. This is a radical way to celebrate this feast and the homily

would be to point out that we are doing it this way to remind ourselves on this day of our eucharistic basics. There will be those who object, threaten to go the the next parish where the priest is sound, and indeed some who write to the bishop (or further afield) to 'just let him know what's happening'. This is, in every community, a well identified and easily quantified group and so they receive a lot of attention lest they be upset; however, that other group who are just drifting away without a word are not easily identifiable and are only quantifiable through statistics. In addressing those who day by day are being lost to the Eucharist, I suspect there is some guidance in Mt 18:12-3.

Sacred Vessels: What they say to us

1. Presuppositions

Imagination makes us human. We understand far more than we see, we know more than we encounter, we learn much besides what we are taught, we communicate far more than we say or write, and what we hear is different to that recorded by tape or transcript. This fact of our nature is both good and bad news for those responsible for liturgy. It is good in so far as it reassures us that human beings cannot be reduced to either isolated Cartesian centres of rational consciousness or biological processors of sensory stimuli: the world of a human being will always be more than the sum of its parts. It is also good news in that it reminds us that we are ritual animals and liturgy of some sort is 'hard wired' into our existence: we both establish our world and make sense of our living within it through complex social rituals, through community-validated narratives, and through symbols that reach us synaesthetically – speaking at once to senses, mind, and emotions. We in the contemporary western world may have a strong sense that we can distinguish 'symbols' and 'reality' – or even have a notion that 'symbols' are opposed to 'reality' – but that belief is most probably just one of the Baconian idols of our particular cultural market place. Being human is being able to read the 'vibes' of a situation or event along with the rationally intended communications of one person to another. Indeed, many would argue that there are basic human signals that operate within societies at so basic a level of interpersonal communication that we are unconscious of them, or even that such signals are to a large extent beyond our rational control. Thus a gesture that is a fixed part of a formal ritual may equally be a basic gesture that only takes on its most formal aspect when used within that specific ritual. A good example would be the formal Kiss of Peace within the eucharistic liturgy which has evolved various technical forms within the Latin rites over the centuries but which build on a basic linking symbol as studied by anthropologists. Eating together is a most basic human ritual creating and bonding societies, and it is that basic human reality that is given a specific formalised ritual role in such situations as Jewish *Shabbat* meals or Christian Eucharists.

However, this may also be bad news for theologians/liturgists/those concerned with religious communication. If humans must use symbols, and many basic symbols are not simply formless empty vehicles that can carry any consciously chosen meaning which we might want to impose on them, then they may be carrying a meaning/creating a world which is, at the very least, out of harmony with the rationally intended meaning network in which that symbol is used. That is, there may be cases where what the symbols communicate is the exact opposite of what is rationally intended by those anxious to use the symbol in communication. So, for example, someone who speaks about the equality of everyone in a situation but then behaves deferentially to some and patronisingly to others is rapidly identified as a 'hypocrite' and her/his discourse is considered a sham or pretence. There is a cognitive dissonance between the tacit/implicit signals and the explicit/formally espoused position: and, significantly, it is the unvoiced world of ritual and symbol that is taken as expressing the 'real' situation. It is this dissonance between symbols and intention that the gospel narrator expects will cause shock in his audience at the event of the arrest of Jesus when a kiss is used by the traitor as his identifying sign (Mk 14:44). In every ritual event there is a meaning conveyed in the very use of the symbols, *ex opere operato*, which is distinct from, and independent of, that which is conveyed in the accompanying words, the formal explanation of that ritual (e.g. its theology), or the intentions of those employing the symbols. The latent meanings (those tacitly conveyed in gestures or objects) may be in complete agreement (e.g. hugging a friend after a long absence while saying 'It's so good to see you'), complete dissonance (e.g. Judas's kiss), or somewhere in between these poles with the meanings contained in the voiced words at the event or, in the case of formal religious symbols, explanations usually offered. So in any ritual situation – from a simple shake hands at a meeting to the celebration of the Eucharist – we have to recall that words say one thing, gestures another, while the props and setting may perhaps convey something different again.

If this is accepted, then it has a curious implication for sacramental theology, and for the theology of the Eucharist in particular given the Eucharist's centrality in the religious life of Catholics. There may be three different eucharistic theologies – quite apart from the varying perceptions of what it is about which maybe as various as the number of participants – in circulation within a particular church:

Firstly, the formal theology of the Eucharist as this is found in textbooks, catechisms, and preaching, this is that community's 'theology': its conscious explanation of what it is doing. This can be referred to as its 'published theology' or the *lex credendi*.

Secondly, there is the understanding of the ritual that is conveyed within the language of the ritual, and which can be seen as embodying the belief of the community in a very openly communicative way in that it uses words. This is less than a published theology, but it is very easily recognised as being a theology, the *'lex orandi'* when thought of as the verbal element of liturgy. And, for the most part, when theologians use 'the liturgy' as a source of theology or seek to express the liturgy's inherent theology, it is to this part of the liturgy, its words, that they turn. A good example of the concern with this precise liturgical theology is the care that is manifested by reformers of liturgy that the verbal formulae (e.g. in an *anaphora*) should accord with that church's published theology, or the contemporary concern expressed by many today within Catholicism with 'the orthodoxy' of vernacular translations. This concern with the verbal orthodoxy of the liturgy (with little concern with the orthodoxy of other signifiers in the liturgy) can be seen in the document *Liturgiam authenticam* of the Vatican's Congregation for Divine Worship and the Discipline of the Sacraments (28 March 2001) which assumed in its opening sentence that not only is it the verbal element that is theologically paramount but that there can be no dissonance between that verbal element and the Roman church's published theology. Since there is no corresponding concern with the Christian appropriateness of the non-verbal elements of the liturgy, it appears that for many it is only this verbal element (i.e. the texts that can be printed in black in a liturgical book) that are seen as important bearers of a theology – or perhaps even of meaning – within the liturgy.

Thirdly, there is the communication of the actions, gestures, objects, buildings, decor, furniture, community atmosphere, and indeed the non-verbal aspects of public worship. Here we glimpse the 'operative theology' of those involved in how they behave towards one another and towards the ritual, in the style they adopt in celebration, be that as president or someone standing at the edge of the group, and in the nature of the objects that they use. This third theology may seem a *jejune* affair when compared with sonorous formulae or shelves of formal reflection, but it probably touches more people today, and over the centuries has informed the understanding of more people, than either of the other two theologies. Ritual/liturgy speaks to us more completely and more profoundly than any set of verbal propositions, as is evidenced by the number of times groups, be they big or small, use events rather than simple lectures to establish their agenda.

It is this third theology that is my concern here and the aspect that directly concerns me is the theology inherent in the vessels (e.g. chalices, patens, ciboria) used at the Eucharist in the Latin church today. This might appear a peripheral subject for theological concern since they are but 'vessels' (this would not deny they are inherently interesting to artists as they have a long tradition of being the *ornamenta ecclesiae*; nor that they are a concern for rubricians and canonists) and it is their contents that are of religious interest, but such an approach would ignore many important aspects of Catholic eucharistic culture in favour of an abstract theological analysis. Most obviously, since the Eucharist takes its fundamental ritual form from the experience of a meal, we are faced with the fact that the vessels used at any meal are seen as part of the significance of the meal. Whether this is 'the good half-set' of china that was kept for visitors in many Irish houses until just a generation ago, or some great dinner service: the utensils and table ornaments matter. The twentieth-century cult of informality might appear to be a counter-indicator to this, but this ignores the fact that this functionalism and informality is not itself informal but a carefully contrived part of the whole message of such meals, as is seen in the well-known regularity of everything connected with drive-through fast food chains: indeed, one of the reasons frequently adduced for the preference by customers for the very well known chains is that 'they know exactly what to expect' and how to order in that chain: there is minimal uncertainty about the demands the encounter will make on them! Moreover, whenever eating together is significant, the imagery of the vessels reasserts itself in, for example, decorated tables at wedding receptions or the fact that despite the ubiquity of the hot-dog sellers in our cities, they have not driven chic restaurants from the market. How we eat, and what we eat off, says much about us as groups and individuals. That the eucharistic vessels are not peripheral to our understanding of the Eucharist can also be observed in the fact that they are known as 'the sacred vessels', deemed worthy of special respect and care. They are specially set aside through consecration in a formal ritual regulated by law, their form and use is regulated by the highest authority, and they have a special place as deliberate vehicles of meaning within the church, both as part of its memory – the interest in the original chalice of the Last Supper – and today: a chalice with a paten are themselves, i.e. apart from what they can contain, seen as the *instrumenta propria* of the presbyterate in the rite of ordination. Lastly, the eucharistic vessels have become conceptual shorthands, icons, for the symbols that make use of them. Hence a picture of a chalice and a 'Host' become 'symbols' of the Eucharist, conveniently ignoring that the Eucharist is itself a symbol. In effect, these images have become the standard eucharistic decorations in missals, altar frontals, or on liturgical vestments. They have become symbols of symbols in the dense imaginative world where we seek to encounter the divine.

So given the importance of these vessels in our imagination, it, seems relevant to ask what theology is inherent in their form and use today. This examination may, in turn, illuminate the embedded understanding of the Eucharist of those who produce and use them, and throw up some interesting dissonances between what we claim today in our theology, what we proclaim in our liturgical formulae, and what we 'say' in our actions with concrete objects.

2. The Chalice

Of all the sacred vessels, none is more readily recognisable both in use and as an image than the cup used at the Eucharist. That this vessel carries with it a latent theology can be seen most simply in the names given to it. The standard Greek word for a drinking vessel is to *potérion*: used on 17 occasions in the canonical gospels, and on the 8 occasions in the New Testament where there is reference to the cup of the Eucharist. This was rendered consistently in Latin by *calix*. Already the combination of Mk 14:23 (and parallels) with Lk 22:20 which forms the background to the institution narrative in the Roman *anaphora* (i.e. the text which evolved to become what we refer to today as Eucharistic Prayer 1) had introduced this word *calix* to the liturgy: *hunc praeclarum calicem ... hic est enim calix sanguinis mei* (and this usage now extends to all the Latin texts of the Eucharistic Prayers of the Roman Rite). In Latin, *calix* has no specifically religious semantic field, although both *cuppa* and *poculus* are more widely attested in ancient non-Christian sources. However, by the time that Latin became the linguistic expression of western Christianity, the word had become wholly restricted to the eucharistic cup. Hence when a vernacular name was needed in Anglo-Saxon for this vessel, *calix* was not translated (e.g. by 'cup'), but simply transliterated to give us the word 'chalice' – a word denoting a specific sacred vessel that can be thought of without reference to the larger class of objects: drinking vessels.

Here we encounter a very basic dissonance: the cup of the Eucharist, no matter how sacred we might judge its contents, can only be understood sacramentally in terms of all the other cups we encounter in our everyday life, just as the entire Eucharist, whose fundamental form is sacred meal, can only be understood in terms of its uniqueness among our other meals. Yet the word 'chalice' does not immediately link this vessel with all our other vessels. A 'chalice' does not relate to other, merely, ordinary everyday vessels, but recalls a cult object *sui generis*. However, as a sacramental reality, we can only appreciate 'the cup of the Lord' (1 Cor 10:21) by what makes it distinct from other cups. A sacral name which does not call to mind everyday comparitors implies a cult object with an absolute, rather than a sacramental, sacrality: so our formal theology of the sacraments is not well served by the tightly defined semantic range of this name.

The continued use of the word 'chalice' – the usage is universal among Catholics not only in the common speech of those involved with the practicalities of the liturgy but in the rubrics of the current English-language missal – also creates another dissonance. When we read the New Testament today – in any translation – we do not encounter 'chalice' but 'cup', and even in the liturgy we now say 'he took the cup ... this is the cup.' However, this creates a curious situation in practice where we refer to 'the cup' when we are remembering the Last Supper or the practice of Jesus and his followers, while using 'chalice' in our descriptions of our own liturgical activity. Which of these announcements is more likely to be heard in a church on Sunday: 'When you come up to drink from the cup, please wipe it before giving it back to the minister', or 'When you have received from the chalice, please wipe it before giving it back to the minister'? The first is clearly linked to the language of the basic liturgical activity, the second usage is derived from the period when the notion of 'receiving communion' was conceptually distinct from that of 'hearing Mass'. Yet the first statement is unlikely to be heard in a Catholic context: it seems to lack rev-

erence, while mention of 'communion cups' belongs to the language of non-Catholic groups who are known not to share a
Catholic 'theology' of the Eucharist. Having two usages currently
in use potentially creates barriers in linking the activity at a
Eucharist with the proclaimed memory, and may indicate a
wider persistence of the distinctions between sacrifice/sacra-
ment and Mass/Communion than is generally acknowledged in
preaching. We conceptually speak of cups or 'the cup', we functionally refer to chalices and think of chalices as the actual props
of worship.

When we look at the form of most existing chalices – or the
majority of those advertised by suppliers of liturgical requisites
today – we encounter these older theologies in another way.
That form is an ornate variant in metal of an individual's stem-
glass for wine at a meal. The average chalice cup is similar in size
(dimensions and capacity) to a wine glass; the stem is usually
longer due to the need to have a node to give the priest a good
grip at the elevation – a legal requirement in Tridentine rubrics;
and the base is usually broader than a wine glass to give it
added stability lest the vessel be overturned accidentally by the
priest while making blessings over it or with his maniple swing-
ing in a destructive arc as he turned toward or away from the
altar during Mass. Our 'standard' chalices were designed, as a
glimpse at older rubrical books shows, for a rite we no longer
celebrate. This 'classic' chalice shape, about 25cm high with a
cup about 8cm in diameter and about 8cm deep, can be traced to
the high middle ages and evolved as a vessel perfectly suited to
the needs of the rite of the time and the standard explanations of
that rite. First, only the priest would be drinking from this vessel, and then only a token amount of liquid – the actual quantity
was not specified by law but the maximum was the contents of a
small glass cruet, while most rubricians stated that it should not
be more than what could be consumed in one act of swallowing.
Second, the chalice had to be of such a shape that it could be held
up higher than the head of the priest so that the cup of the chalice could be seen at the elevation. Third, the action of drinking

the contents was of secondary importance to their actual confec-
tion: the focus of the liturgy was on the consecration. The actual
drinking was entailed by this action, but it was not perceived as
the direct purpose of the action. Hence, the rationale of the vessel's decoration was that it should be a worthy container of most
sacred contents, rather than a sacred drinking vessel. Thus in
use their cups' lips are often not shaped with drinking in mind,
they are awkwardly long, hard to hand from one to another, and
often with a base that seems incongruous on a drinking vessel
but would make a worthy pedestal for a liquid container.
Ornamentation tends to make them something beautiful to look
upon rather than something comfortable to use in the basic
human act of drinking.

Now that today we have embraced a model of liturgy where
we speak of drinking from the cup ('Take this all of you and
drink from it'), where the practice of sharing the cup is increasingly common (even if this is still seen legally as exceptional in
the Roman Rite), and where there is an increased awareness
among theologians of the significance of the one cup, these older
chalices are both inconvenient and recollections of earlier theologies. If it is a vessel designed for the use of just one person,
then it is really the priest's cup primarily from which others are
simply given a sip – this is hard to align with it being the one,
common, cup of the whole assembly. If sharing the one cup is
what is distinctive of the Christian celebration, then a cup that is
really fitted to just one person is not semantically appropriate. If
its decoration says 'look at me as a container' rather than 'is this
not a beautiful drinking vessel – as this is our community's most
precious common cup' then there is an emphasis on it as a container of the Blessed Sacrament rather than on the basic eucharistic action of drinking. Such an emphasis accords well with
a theology of adoration, but not where part-taking of a single
cup is the unique dominical regulation regarding this aspect of
the sacred banquet. Lastly, if there are more than possibly a
dozen people at the celebration, then there is not enough liquid
in the container for drinking rather than sipping. The older

rubricians were insistent on the quantity being such that there was enough to satisfy the command *bibite* (but also that it should be no more than one mouthful) and there is wisdom in this: the cup should be able to allow each participant to drink a normal mouthful. By contrast, taking a sip is simply tokenism; and when symbols are reduced to tokens then usually their primary meaning has already been lost.

So what would a cup look like that had the present liturgy in mind? It would need these characteristics:

First, its size and shape assume the sharing of the cup by all who are celebrating – i.e. each of the baptised taking part in the meal – at the Eucharist is the norm; it is not the priest's cup nor is it something for special occasions.

Second, it must be handled, located on the table of the Eucharist, and referred to as the community's cup, not as a personal item over which a priest says the requisite prayers and performs the required actions. Locating it just a few inches in front of the priest when he stands at the table and all the other participants stand far away send the signal that this is my activity, this cup is my concern, and the rest of you (except possibly deacons or presbyteral concelebrants) are just looking in on my performance of my work. So the vessel must be big enough to convey to all: 'This is our community's cup.'

Third, it must assume that drinking rather than looking is the primary mode of eucharistic worship; it is not a monstrance for liquid. This raises a very practical issue about the rim of the cup. Older chalices often have a lip that curves slightly outwards and this makes drinking more difficult without slips. More recent chalices have simply the thickness of the metal at their rim, yet a glance at any glass will reveal that there is a little rounded rim on every vessel whose wall thickness is not sufficient to provide a comfortable edge to place against the lips – such a rounded edge is essential for a eucharistic cup.

Fourth, since using one cup for this meal (rather than individual cups as in every other meal we share) is what is distinctive of Christian practice since the beginning, and indeed the practice of Jesus himself, then it must be large enough for a sizable congregation. And, if they are one congregation, then they should have just one cup – since the basic sacramental forms of the Eucharist are one table, one loaf, one cup. Many will object that this is impractical, but we are not here dealing with the practicalities of fast food, but the distinctiveness of being gathered into one body in Christ. Moreover, for all of the first millennium Christians were able to do this without murmur and produced some magnificent poetry to engage the congregation during the process. The very time needed for all to share one cup brings home the basic symbolism of our sacred meal. By the same logic the practice of using a flagon – on the assumption that it does not clutter the table as do multiple chalices – which can then be used to fill cups, misses the basic symbolism: it is not simply about consuming a sacred substance, it is about a Christ-imitating participation in a sacred meal.

Fifth, just as it has to be large enough for all and convenient for drinking from, so it must be easy to handle at the table and to pass from minister to communicant. This means it must have handles and its shape must take account of the difficulties of one sort or another of people with disabilities. The simplest solution is to have horizontal handles near the rim for ministers and occasional use by communicants, while communicants cup the cup with their hands to drink from it.

Sixth, it is a symbol in itself as the one cup of the meal. Its 'cupness' is what it must communicate, not some additional 'message' in its decoration. So decoration must be to make it a beautiful cup, not a vehicle of 'symbolic images'. If, for instance, it is a chalice-shaped jewelled container, rather than a cup, then it once again re-enforces the notion that it is as a container of sacred material rather than as the one cup of our Eucharistic banquet in which finds its perfection. This cup is about drinking from during the rite of communion, it is not for looking upon at the elevation or for the edification of the priest as he gazes upon it on the altar at his Mass. This was a common reason given for the decoration of the bases of chalices until 1960 – while such

reasoning is no longer publicly expressed, the practice of decoration which went with the attitude has very often remained. A
very plain cup would also have the advantage of making it less
prone to damage in handling.

3. The Paten

It is not an exaggeration to state that the entire history of Latin
theology of the Eucharist, and indeed piety towards the
Eucharist, can be observed in the size and shape of patens.
Moreover, the nuances of those attitudes can be seen in the two
other vessels that were spin-offs from the paten's changing
shape: the ciborium and the monstrance. Hence, to treat the
paten's significance without reference to that of the ciborium is
to make a false distinction (the monstrance we can ignore, for
now, as it is not used in the celebration of the Eucharist). While
the word 'paten' derives from the Greek name for a dish-like
bowl, for more than a millennium the actual liturgical artefact in
the West was a very shallow round platter of a diameter between 8 and 14 cm. While there are other forms of paten in use
today, the almost-flat saucer form is still our standard image of a
paten; and, because it is convenient to lift at the doxology of the
Eucharistic Prayer and use at the Invitation to Communion (*Ecce
agnus Dei*), these are still being manufactured and are almost
universally used. So we have two questions: why did it cease to
be a dish-like bowl; and why did it grow smaller to the size of a
saucer? When the West used 'bread' for the Eucharist (the usage
of Latin liturgists today of 'unleavened bread' contrasted with
'leavened bread' is a later linguistic invention to attempt to find
an historical justification in the face of Greek opposition to the
introduction of azymes to the western liturgy) it was a single
large loaf of real living bread that was used. Such a loaf had to be
large enough to be broken into many pieces so that each communicant could have a particle, and this was a task which needed
a large container over which to do the breaking and in which to
hold the broken pieces of the sacred loaf while they were being
distributed. When azymes replaced bread the 'dishness' was no

longer needed; when receiving communion by most, or at least a significant proportion of the assembly, was no longer seen as a regular feature of Mass, then anything larger than a saucer was a waste of precious metal and priestly energy. So the paten as we have it is intended for a loaf designed to be only large enough for one person (i.e. the 2mm thick round wafer averaging 7cm in diameter). If there are more than half-a-dozen people in the assembly they, usually, have their pre-cut round wafers in a separate receptacle placed on the table but distinct from the paten. This practice (which is still the most widespread usage) is derived from the normative ritual of the 1570 Missal which assumed that usually at Mass there would only be one bread for consecration (i.e. the priest's wafer on the paten) and one person for communion (i.e. the priest himself) for its rubric at the consecration read: *Tenens ... Hostiam ... profert verba consecrationis ... super Hostiam, et simul super omnes, si plures sint consecrandae.* That is the priest is to speak the words over a single waver (note the accusative singular), unless there are many wafers to be consecrated when he should say them once over all of them. Moreover, that rite assumed that the giving of 'communion' to the congregation was an act distinct from the Mass being celebrated: hence there is no reference within the rubrics for the Ordinary of the Mass – prior to the Missal of 1962 – to anyone other than the priest receiving communion. When anyone was to receive, for example the server, then communion was given to him using an additional rite.

The standard shallow, small paten arose within that world of dysfunctional eucharistic theology to which, it was hoped following on the instructions contained in Vatican II's Constitution *Sacrosanctum concilium*, the rite of 1970 would act as a corrective. However, even if those older theological and ritual worlds, which generated those patens, are no longer with us, the continuing use of the artefacts convey a remarkably similar message to participants in a contemporary Eucharist. If such a vessel is held up at the Preparation of the Gifts during the prayer 'Blessed are you Lord God of all creation...', then the focus of the banquet is

on food that can only be eaten by just one person. The symbolism of blessing God for his gift is restricted just to a token of
food, and not the food the assembly will eat. That food may be
there, in another container, and many would argue is 'virtually'
held up when the paten is held up, but this is to forget that the
whole meal is the sacred symbol and we should not be using
symbols of symbols. If it is the church's food for which we are
blessing God, then it is its food and not that of one member of
the community that should be held aloft for this act of praise.
Equally, while it is only this portion of the church's food that is
held up or placed before the president on the table, it suggests
that all the other particles are somehow supplementary whether
they be on the table at that celebration or taken from the tabernacle. All in all, such patens are really only suitable for celebrations
with tiny communities – certainly less than a dozen – and at any
larger celebration they cry out that there is a distinction between
the communion of the president of the assembly and that of his
brothers and sisters who make up the assembly. But before anything else can be said about patens, we must look at the vessel
that came into existence correlatively with the shallow, small
paten: the ciborium.

4. The Ciborium

The key features of the ciborium are that it is, firstly, supplementary to the paten and, secondly but not necessarily, that it has a
lid. Each feature expresses in metal an approach towards the eucharistic mystery.

The ciborium came into use when any particles that were
going to be distributed to the faithful were additional to the one
particle that the celebrant would consume: these small 'breads'
were now pre-cut, round wafers. This sends out five messages:
First, the reception of the food of the meal they are attending is
somehow distinct from their actual presence at the meal: there is
the essential communion of the celebrant, and the additional, accidental communion of everyone else. So there is 'the Mass' and
there is an additional reality called 'receiving Holy Communion'.

Anyone familiar with Catholic liturgical culture prior to 1970 will know that a familiar liturgical cliché was 'Mass and Holy Communion' – two events that were notionally and practically quite distinct. Using a ciborium in addition to a paten corresponds to that distinction.

Second, using two vessels suggests that there are two levels of participant in the meal: the priest has his specific food in one container, that for the rest is in another. This division of classes might be naïvely justified by some misguided appeal to the 'essential' distinction between a priest and non-priests in a hierarchical assembly, but even if such an 'ontological' approach is used regarding the theology of ministry it is inappropriate in this case as such a distinction in this situation would sunder the 'one body' of Christ which is both indicated and established in the one cup and the one loaf. It was such distinctions of classes of food at the Eucharist that prompted Paul's criticisms of the Corinthian church.

Third, the notion that there is a supply of particles – such language is never used in liturgical textbooks but is part of our practice: how often has a sacristan told me that 'there is no need to consecrate any small hosts at your Mass, Father, as there's plenty in the tabernacle' – is a variant on the notion that the purpose of the Eucharist is to consecrate a sacred commodity. And, the reason someone turns up is to get that precious commodity. The emphasis is upon receiving 'Holy Communion' – thought of as an object, a sacramental thing, a sacred stuff. Thus, the reality of the Eucharist as the action of thanksgiving of the whole Christ (*Christus totus*) to the Father through the action of table sharing recedes into an academic background of abstract orthodoxy which little informs the actual imaginations of Christians. The movement from conceiving the Eucharist as an action to a thing – which occurred sometime in the early seventh century – has, arguably, been the single most significant shift in western eucharistic theology. However, at a time when the poverty of such a theology is being increasingly recognised both in terms of preaching and for ecumenical reasons, the use of ciboria that parallel that defective theology must be seen as a serious cause of confusion.

Fourth, ciboria encourage the use of pre-cut wafers and so eliminate any serious reflection of the significance of the fraction. It is sharing one loaf, not each getting their own sustenance as an individual, which is at the heart of the symbolism of the communal meal. Small pre-cut round 'breads' – ideally suited for groups of individuals – are symbolically the very opposite to all that is imagined in the notion of the broken loaf. At the Eucharist we gather as one people – the *populus Dei*, one body – the *corpus Christi*, and not as a collection of individuals who are only together in one place as each one of the collection wants the same object. If one goes to the world's best-known hamburger restaurant, one can see people all gathered and well-packed into one place with one object, and all knowing the ritual to order, collect, and find a place to eat their food – and even knowing the right verbal formulae for ordering their 'food'; yet this gathering is the exact opposite of sharing the banquet of the Lord. But if an anthropologist from a culture that had never seen a Eucharist or heard some of our explanations saw both gatherings, which would they consider the most expressive of human solidarity? The answer is, I suspect, one that most theologians or bishops would not like to hear!

While many in the body may have little appreciation of their corporate nature as Christians, this false understanding is not something that is to be condoned but challenged, yet our tableware – and our little pre-cut 'breads' – may be silently colluding with this 'cheaper-by-the dozen' ecclesiology.

The four false signals that have just been outlined apply both to traditional lid-covered ciboria and to the small soup-bowl shaped dishes that have been popular more recently. The fifth false signal only related to the covered ciborium. When the ciborium emerged, its distinctive physical feature was the lid, for it appeared at the same time that the notion that one could use particles consecrated at one Eucharist to give communion at a later Eucharist became acceptable. Thus the ciborium could be used to store enough particles that the need to share the actual loaf of the meal with those gathered at the table could be obviated for days. This utilitarian practice – once described by an Irish liturgist as 'giving communion from intervention' – destroys the central symbolism and skews the understanding of the Eucharist. It is practice that has been challenged repeatedly in the Roman documents on liturgical renewal and was even identified in *Sacrosanctum concilium* for special mention:

> The more perfect form of participation in the Mass whereby the faithful, after the priest's communion, receive the Lord's Body from the same sacrifice is warmly recommended.

While the continued toleration of the contrary practice is a fact, and indeed few priests seem concerned that their practice is out of harmony with the spirit of the revised rite, this does not diminish the fact that it fosters an understanding of the Eucharist which is not that which is found in our formal documents or indeed in most modern theological writing. The ciborium, in so far as it allows people to separate the eating from the meal at which they eat, introduces a note of semiotic absurdity unworthy of the mystery of Christ.

The most important problem of the continued use of ciboria is that it perpetuates the notion that using pre-cut breads and having a minimal fraction are matters of little consequence. These misconceptions are furthered by other practices such as that of asking people as they enter the building to place a small bread in a ciborium – ironically this is often done so that there would not be a large number of particles to carry over to the next celebration in the tabernacle – which re-enforces the message that the celebration is one of individuals getting 'what they come for'. However, this does not mean that the larger, chalice-shaped ciboria are no longer useful. The larger ones, i.e. those designed to hold several hundred particles, can be very easily modified by an adjustment to their rim to become ideal cups for an assembly of a hundred or more. Designed to be held by their stem, they are easy to hand to a communicant who holds the quondam-ciborium by cupping the bowl with both hands, and then to take back.

So what would a paten look like that did not send out these signals? Given that the use of azymes seems not to be negotiable (the canonists now seem to have convinced themselves that the practice is 'ancient' even if it only goes back to the ninth century and only in the west: see Code of Canon Law, 926) then it would be a dinner-plate sized dish that could take one very large bread that was then broken up. Failing this, for whatever reason, then such a dinner plate could still have a heap of 'small breads' upon it and these could be divided onto several plates at the fraction.

5. The Pyx

The pyx – literally a box – was originally that which held a fragment of the eucharistic loaf after the celebration for the purpose of bringing it to the sick, both immediately and as viaticum. With the rise of the practice of reservation – and the ciborium – and then the appearance of the 'tabernacle' in the later sixteenth century, the pyx became either the container of the lunette in the tabernacle or the portable container for bringing communion to the sick – in this latter function it became the size of a pocket watch capable of holding about half a dozen wafers. It is only of concern here in that the laudable practice of bringing communion from the celebration to sick and housebound within the community has often resulted in several pyxes being placed on the table: in effect, this conveys the same sub-liminal messages as ciboria. The inspiration for this revived practice – attested as early as the mid-second century – is that a part of the loaf is brought to someone elsewhere and they are thus linked into the celebrating eucharistic body. This is best done taking a particle from the paten and deliberately wrapping it up to be taken away from the table: and the ancient practice of wrapping the fragment of the loaf in linen, i.e. a corporal then put in a burse, is appropriate.

6. The Monstrance

This is not a vessel that belongs to the celebration of the Eucharist but to one of the consequences of that celebration. However, it too presents a theology in metal and it is worth noting that it only rose to its prominence as the most decorated of the vessels linked to the Eucharist with the demise of the paten as a large and elegant vessel. Until the tenth century anyone wishing to make an impression by presenting vessels to a church did so by presenting a big paten weighty with precious metals, stones, and decoration. Later when receiving communion was less frequent, azymes were the norm, and the cult of the Blessed Sacrament emerged as a significant factor in Latin piety, this vessel emerged as the sacred vessel of greatest size – there were even wheeled versions – and artistic virtuosity. However, with the monstrance's focus on an unbroken particle detached from the meal, the common table, and the single cup, we know that it represents a very limited eucharistic theology. But, its sheer size and magnificence can lead to people assuming that this is the perfection of the church's eucharistic activity.

7. Resolving ambiguities

It is a commonplace to observe that 'the people in the pews are not concerned about theology'; whether or not this is true, it is certain that they – as sentient symbol-using beings – pick up 'cues' in their ritual activity as in all their other human interactions and these cues form their imaginations and understanding of what surrounds them. Rituals create our worlds. Bad practices, therefore, are not simply breaches of some code of rubrics, but failures to bear witness adequately to that which we have received from the Lord (1 Cor 11:23).

At present, most of our vessels, and the ways we use them, emerged within an understanding of the Eucharist which a century of research and an ecumenical council have found to be severely 'limited'. There is now a dissonance between what we state in the formulae of the liturgy and in preaching, on the one hand, and what we convey in our actions and tableware. Yet such integrity is not some delicacy of semiotics: it is the integrity that befits the Lord's meal and us as his sisters and brothers. If this is not the meal of honesty, then what is? If we are to proclaim the Lord in this meal until he comes, dissonance in that communication marks out an inauthenticity that brings our larger message into disrepute.

The sacred meal is always eaten from within the context of all the other meals that we eat: it cannot be otherwise, and those meals mark out the imaginative space within which we encounter the mystery. In a world of hunger, this banquet must generate a challenge of justice and plenty; in a world of fast-food, this table fellowship must mark out a place of genuine human encounter; and in a world of deceptive appearance where the 'virtual' and the 'real' are presented as inter-changeable, everything connected with this meal must have a rugged authenticity. Alas, our common tableware promotes a standardised attitude of speedy convenience, betrays a tokenism, and suggests that much of what we say is simply sounds.

Eighth Sunday of Ordinary Time

CELEBRANT'S GUIDE

Introduction to the Celebration

Our first, absolutely fundamental, most important belief is that God has shown his love in creating the universe, the world we live in, and us. If we did not believe this, then everything else we say or do or think would be meaningless. We gather here to be united with Jesus our Saviour, but if we did not believe that God created us and loves us, we would be foolish to talk about him sending his Son to bring us the fullness of life! Yet everyday we forget that we are made by God, that our lives and our world are his gifts. We behave as if we were the lords of life and the lords of creation, and all around us we see the misery, suffering and destruction that this greed and these mistaken notions about our status in creation cause us. Today we remind ourselves of another way of living with one another and with the creation: the way of trustfulness, appreciation, and caring.

Rite of Penance

 For those times when we have acted without care for the environment, Lord have mercy.

 For those times when have been exploiters of human beings or of the planet you have given us as our home, Christ have mercy.

 For those times when have failed to appreciate that the world is your creation entrusted to us, Lord have mercy.

Headings for Readings

First Reading

God does not forget the creation but cares for it like a mother cares for her child

Second Reading

We must act humbly as Christians and not be quick to pass

judgement on one another: we can leave that to the Lord. We should spend our time in the service of God seeking that we may be found worthy of the trust he has placed in us.

Gospel
The gospel tells us how the Father cares for even the smallest animals and flowers in the creation; how much more does he love us?

Prayer of the Faithful
President
We gather for the Eucharist to express our thanks to the Father for all his goodness; but as creatures who depend on him for existence we also express our needs to him. So, in union with Christ our High Priest, let us pray:
Reader(s)
1. For the universal church, that we will become aware of our responsibilities towards the creation that has been entrusted to us. Lord hear us.
2. For all humanity, that we will learn to work in harmony with nature and not act mindlessly in exploiting the planet. Lord hear us.
3. For this community, that we will grow in our sense of acting as the stewards of creation. Lord hear us.
4. For all those who are working to preserve and enhance our environment, that they may act with wisdom. Lord hear us.
5. Specific local needs and topics of the day.
President
Father, all that we have and are is your gift; hear us now as we ask for our needs through Christ our Lord. Amen.

Eucharistic Prayer
Preface of Sundays in Ordinary Time V (P33) makes our position within the creation the basis of our song of thanksgiving. This preface does, however, contain two phrases that will annoy many in the assembly and, by so doing, are a distraction. These

phrases are (1) 'you chose to create man in your own image'; and
(2) 'you made man the steward of creation' (this latter phrase is
also problematic in that it uses the rhetorical figure of synec-
doche – the singular nouns 'man' and 'steward' standing for a
group – which is rare in normal English today). So change these
phrases to 'you chose to create us in your own image' and 'you
make us the stewards of creation'.

Invitation to the Our Father
Gathered here, conscious of all the gifts that the Father has lav-
ished on us in the creation, let us pray to him:

Sign of Peace
We are called to live in peace and harmony with each other, with
every human being, and with the whole creation. If we are ready
to accept this call, we should offer those around us the sign of
peace.

Invitation to Communion
All that we have is from the Father's bounty, but his greatest gift
is the presence of his Son among us. Behold the Lamb of God ...

Communion Reflection
Use of the credal statement from Bishop Tírechán provided for
the reflection in the resources for Trinity Sunday. Its basic
inspiration is that God is the Lord of creation in its many-splen-
dored details.

Conclusion
May God bless you with every good gift from on high. Amen.
May God keep you in harmony with one another and with all
humanity. Amen.
May God empower you to acts as stewards of his creation.
Amen.

Notes

Today's gospel is usually read as expanding on the choice that faces the individual between service of God and selfishness. I have chosen in these notes to read it in a completely different way: to begin by looking at how God cares for the animals/ inanimate things of the creation (e.g. the lilies) and then use this as a springboard to ask how we as humans relate to the creation so loved by God. This approach is not good exegesis, nor does it conform to the way the Second Vatican Council (and the missal and lectionary which expressed the council's mind for a less corrupted liturgy) envisaged the relationship of preaching with the gospel text. So why have I departed so consciously from the expected pattern?

One of the most important tasks facing humanity is the crisis that has come about from exploiting the planet without any sense of natural limits or of limits to our greed. One of the tasks that face Christians is to move from seeing morality almost solely in terms of individuals and to become aware of the moral demands of a theology of creation. Yet, faced with this situation, many see Christianity as having little to say that is positive; others see it as a negative force either in promoting the notion that we have preached (which we have) that nature is there to be subdued and used or else that the material creation is of no ultimate worth and so spiritually irrelevant; while others see the churches as saying little, even if they think individual Christians are interested.

Here we must face the simple fact that when Christianity was first preached, this was simply not an issue: a pre-industrial agricultural society makes very little demands on the planet and its carbon imprint is minimal. So we can look back over most of our tradition and there is little on the topic. So too with the liturgy, where there is no consistent theme of the need for humans to act with respect towards the inanimate creation. Even if the structures of liturgy are only decades old, they were composed before this awareness arose and, in any case, the structures were formed in continuity with the past. This means that even as the churches begin to develop theologies of the creation in the face of the global crisis, there will be few opportunities for the average Christian to hear these ideas if their only contact with reflection on the content of the Christian life is the liturgy and what is preached on Sunday. Therefore, if this is an urgent challenge to Christians, then we must drag it into the liturgy 'by the backdoor' if people are to hear it. These resources are written in a conscious attempt to do this. This gospel was not preached by Matthew to heighten awareness of responsibility for the creation. It was not selected for this Sunday with any thought that it would provide a springboard for such concerns to form a theme running through today's liturgy. But given the need to have these concerns placed before people when they come to be fed at the Table of the Word, then this day is an occasion on which it can plausibly be done. The notes that are given below may seem a very simplistic theology of creation, and so indeed it is. However, for many Christians this concern is so far beneath their horizon of consciousness (or if they are concerned about the environment that concern is so distant from their religious consciousness) that all we can hope to do in an occasional homily is let them know that this is a Christian concern.

COMMENTARY

First Reading: Isa 49:14-15

This is part of a section of Deutero-Isaiah where the salvation that God will give to Zion is announced. As excerpted here it is an analogy for the care of God for his creatures. There are two small points worth noting: first, this is one of the very few places in the scriptures where a female simile is related to God: God here is to be understood by analogy with a mother (the male similies of Ps 61 are far more common and 'normal'); and second, even a mother is expected to be more protective of a son than a daughter, and in the society that produced this text a son was a far greater gift than a daughter. We may wish to have continuity of teaching with Isaiah in stating that God is loving, but not with his notions about the respective worth of the sexes (even though he used his views on this matter to speak of God).

Psalm: 61 (62)
This was chosen to take up the image of the shelter and care
found in the first reading; here again, but with a very different
range of imagery, the Lord is shelter, and the source of strength
and protection.

Second Reading: 1 Cor 4:1-5
This reading can only be understood within the larger context of
Paul's concerns about division in the community and that they
should have the right attitude to the leaders in the community
(the stewards). In this snippet it can have little meaning except
as a source of a few maxims. It is the frequency of such out-of-
context passages from the epistles as second readings that has
made the whole notion of the second reading look like a simple
disruption in the Liturgy of the Word.

First Reading > Gospel Links
Continuity of teaching: God cares for the creation down to the
last detail.

Gospel: Mt 6:24-34
This passage is made up of two separate items: the first verse
which deals with the issue of serving two masters; and the remaining ten verses which deal with anxiety and failure to place
trust in the Lord's care. That the lection is, in reality, two separate items cannot, however, be blamed on the creators of the lectionary. These two items were already combined by Matthew
using the 'therefore' (*dia touto*) in verse 25 as the connection. This
'therefore' was already present in Matthew's source (we know
this because it is also in Luke) and it is possible that he, or perhaps the person who put together his source, went looking for
some statement for which verses 25-34 could be the explication.
Luke has both statements but they are not linked in any way in
his gospel (16:13 and 12:22-31). The effect of Matthew's presenting verses 25-34 as the consequence of verse 24 has created a
mighty muddle in the exegesis of this passage down the cent-

uries as more and more imaginative solutions have been invented
to show how the teaching of 25-34 could be the logical outcome
of v 24!

In effect, we make better sense of the whole by breaking it
into its parts and regretting the presence of 'therefore'. Viewed
in this way, v 24 is a challenge to discipleship that there is a basic
option to be made in our following of the way. It is a stark choice
and one which does not admit of mitigating circumstances. The
second section, vv 25-34, is sapiential, proverbial advice directed
against those who keep labouring to be certain of tomorrow
without realising that one cannot have such total security.
However, as with all such proverbial advice, it cannot be read in
an absolute fashion or we could just let rip and trust in God
would be just a pious name for fecklessness. To the anxious who
are always seeking a hedge for tomorrow there is this advice; to
the feckless who are not preparing for tomorrow nor acting with
prudence, there is the counter-balancing wisdom of the parable
of the unjust steward (Lk 16:1-9) which Luke uses as the preface
to his use of 'you cannot serve God and mammon'.

HOMILY NOTES

1. We sometimes think of the creation as 'just there'; it is the
   background of our activities, it is the stage and scene where
   we get on with what is important in our lives. Such an attitude is at the heart of most industry and commerce, but it is
   also present when we do not care how much of the earth's resources we use up selfishly. When we do value the creation,
   perhaps by admiring a sunset or a landscape, it is no more
   than a moment's respite from the serious business of life:
   such admiration belongs to the holidays, not to work.
2. We Christians can slip so easily into this attitude that if one
   were to look at Christians across the globe today they would
   not stand out from the madding crowd in terms of their distinctive attitudes to the earth and its resources, or in their
   concern over the size of their Carbon Footprint, or in terms of
   their opposition to the destruction of fragile ecosystems on

which many indigenous peoples depend. That we Christians do not stand out in this way should be a source of shame, for we profess that we believe that God is the creator of all that is, whether it is visible or invisible.

3. We need to have a simple way of remembering the basics about how we as Christians should interact with the material creation about us.

First, if everything that exists has come into existence because of the will of God, we should respect it as his gift. It is not just a heap of riches to be plundered.

Second, when we think about the creation we perceive order and harmony and we see that as evidence of the Wisdom of God 'through whom all thing were made'. This Wisdom has become a man like us in all but sin in Jesus. So we as his people must seek to act in an orderly and harmonious way towards all that exists, as creatures in the creation. Creation is to be a place where we discover wisdom.

Third, we need to recall our prayer of blessing over the bread: 'Blessed are you Lord, God of all creation, through your goodness we have this bread ... which earth has given and human hands have made ...' Everything we have and do is a work of co-operation with God. God works with us and through us, we share in his creation and work with him. This vision of collaboration must be deeply implanted in our lives.

4. We can express these as:
   • Respecting creation as a gift;
   • Becoming aware of the Wisdom of God in the creation;
   • Collaborating with the Creator.

   If we can grow in these things we will be on our way to being stewards of creation.

Ninth Sunday of Ordinary Time

Introduction to the Celebration

One of the most chilling passages in the whole gospel is the statement 'Not every one who says to me, "Lord, Lord," shall enter the kingdom of heaven, but he who does the will of my Father.' We can do everything that is demanded by the outward show of religion, may even be thought to be 'good Christians', but if we do not love God and love others like we love ourselves, if we do not work for this new set of relationships in the world, then we may have missed the point!

Rite of Penance

Option c vii (Missal, p 394-5) is appropriate.

Headings for Readings

First Reading

The path of following the commandments, doing the will of God, is the path to life.

Second Reading

Paul is reminding people that God has promised to give life to all who were part of the community of the Law and the Prophets, those who were born Jews; now Jesus has come to bring that promise to fulfillment by extending it to every nation.

Gospel

The challenge of discipleship is to live our lives doing the will of the Father.

Prayer of the Faithful

The sample formulas for this Prayer remind us of its well-defined structure as a prayer of the priestly people (hence its title 'of the Faithful') in union with our High Priest to the Father. General Formula I (Missal, p 995) is ideal for this day.

Eucharistic Prayer

Eucharistic Prayer IV has the notion of the series of covenants that picks up a theme from the second reading (Eucharistic Prayer IV can now be used on the Sundays of Ordinary Time, cf *General Instruction on the Roman Missal*, n 365d).

Invitation to the Our Father

Let us ask the Father for the strength to do his will:

Sign of Peace

The will of the Father is that we should love one another. Let us express our willingness to act in this way through exchanging the Sign of Peace.

Invitation to Communion

The Lord bids us to join him at this banquet, and by doing the Father's will to prepare ourselves to sit at the Father's banquet in heaven.

Communion Reflection

Lord Jesus Christ,
By your birth, we are reborn;
By your sufferings, we are freed from sin;
By your rising from the dead, we rise to everlasting life;
By your returning to the Father in glory, we enter into the Father's heavenly kingdom.
Amen.
Preface 32, adapted

Conclusion
Solemn Blessing 14: Ordinary Time V (Missal, p 373) is appropriate.

Notes
People often complain that they do not 'get anything out of the readings' or that they do not appear to make sense. Most priests' first reaction is to try to defend the lectionary while also claiming that it is 'all very complex'. However, given that every lectionary is a compromise between differing demands, this is one Sunday when choices have not gone too well. So there is a case for concentrating on the gospel – which today is a well-formed unit – and gently ignoring the rest.

COMMENTARY

First Reading: Deut 11:18, 26-28, 32
Deut 11 is a call to Israel to remember its past, recognise that it must choose the Lord, and that it must hand on that relationship to its children. As such, it is an ideal place to study the nature of commitment with a religious tradition. However, that is completely lost in this lection which is really just a selection of snippets to form a preamble to v 32: 'You shall be careful to do all the statutes and the ordinances which I set before you this day.' This is read as simple command, which is then seen as setting the scene for the gospel.

Therefore, it is little use studying the context and background to today's reading, as it is a scissors-and-paste job that is intended to be its own explanation.

Psalm: 30 (31)
This psalm looks as if it is a preparation for the gospel with its reference to God being a rock of refuge and the gospel's reference of building on rock. However, this is no more than a chance similarity of words in English. The 'rock of refuge' is what we would call a 'strong point' or a 'redoubt' – a term derived from military engineering. The 'rock' of the gospel is what we would

call 'bed-rock' or 'firm foundations' and is derived from house construction. They are two very different image-ranges and should not be confused.

Second Reading: Rom 3:21-25, 28

This is just one link in Paul's very long argument to show that in Jesus Christ the possibility of righteousness is now available to every human being without distinction. The key to this correct relationship with God is faith in Jesus.

There are two problems with this reading as it is found in the lectionary. First, one cannot make any sense of the Letter to the Romans when read in such little bits once a week. The lectionary compilers seem to have been aware of this themselves because that is why they omitted vv 26-27 today as they pick up other themes found elsewhere in the letter for the reader, and so are meaningless if one just reads these few verses. Romans is neither episodic nor a chain of small pieces: it can only be read in much larger chunks than what is laid out for these Sundays. Second, the Jerusalem Bible version is more an interpretation than a translation of this passage, and its specification of 'Jew and pagan alike' does damage to the very point Paul wants to make here.

The second reading can always be dropped for a good reason, and the likelihood that it will not be understood as presented in the lectionary looks to me like a good reason. If you do read it, then this is one day when it is better to opt for the RSV or NRSV.

First Reading > Gospel Links

Continuity of teaching in both covenants: the worship of God must be internalised and express itself in the way life is lived.

Gospel: Mt 7:21-27

As Matthew works with this material the basic teaching is a warning against self-deception (vv 21-23), followed by teaching on what is the opposite of self-deception: being genuine hearers and doers of the will of God (vv 24-27). By putting these two elements together in this way (in contrast to Luke's use of the same material), Matthew produces a very well rounded piece of instruction where the second element comments upon and complements the first. However, if it has integrity as a piece of teaching, it is also the conclusion to the whole of the Sermon on the Mount (Mt 5:1–7:27) and gives the whole sermon a sharp and precise ending.

In the sermon, Matthew has been presenting Jesus as the New Moses setting out the New Law and, as is common in other pieces of formal legal teaching, he concludes with a parable: the house on rock versus the house on sand. The parable is the dramatic end of the whole sermon as much as of this concluding part: the person who takes heed of all the words of Jesus is the one who has built on rock. As parables go, its meaning is straight-forward – the simile 'foundations of sand' has entered our speech so thoroughly that we forget its origins lie in the gospels – but given the way we read the text today, it has to be related to just the passage rather than three whole chapters and this does place a strain upon the preacher.

HOMILY NOTES

1. We humans are prone to two constant faults.
2. The first of these is that we get so absorbed with the immediate and the instantaneous, that we loose sight of long term goals. We confuse the imminent with the important. That this is a major problem for people can easily be seen: just look at the number of management consultants that are out there helping companies find their 'long-term strategic aims' or look at the number of 'life-style consultants' who offer to train people (for a price) 'to prioritise'. Not confusing the issues of today with our overall goals is one of the aspects of wisdom (or as the Jerusalem Bible translates it: 'sensible').
3. The second fault is that we tend to become so infatuated with outward appearances that we ignore the reality of situations. The proof of this is the amount of energy and money that it spent on promoting a good 'image'; and there is no shortage

of 'image consultants' as a subsection of marketing consultants. How many people in the assembly have felt cheated by the reality of a product because they were attracted by a slick website? When we know that we can be so easily distracted by appearances, it is important that we have regular 'reality checks' just so that we are not falling into the trap of believing our own propaganda. This link between the inner person and the other person is at the heart of integrity. We have captured that nugget of wisdom in the saying: 'The habit does not make the monk.'

4. The gospel today is a call to have a reality check. To look at what is really important in our lives: this is building on rock.

5. It is easy to have the appearances of religion and all the professional panoply of religion: speaking in the Lord's name; prophesying in the Lord's name; casting out demons. It is much harder to contribute to building the civilisation of justice, peace, and love.

6. One of the problems of preaching is that there is no one in the assembly today who is not aware of more than a decade of clerical scandals, possible cover-ups, and attempts at protecting the institutions of religion given priority over helping victims. That such problems have undermined the integrity of preaching the gospel is undeniable. Therefore, the preacher must make himself the first recipient of the call of today's gospel and make that explicit. As the examples chosen by Jesus make clear: no group is more prone to deceive themselves about their integrity before God than religious professionals.

7. Reality checks are never easy. Making the changes that take place after such a check is also hard. But we do not engage in this process alone: the Spirit of God moves within us to lead us into the truth, strengthening us, and purifying us.

Lectionary Unit III

This unit comprises Sundays 10-13, and its focus is on the spread of God's kingdom.

There is one Sunday devoted to narrative: Sunday 10 which highlights the call of Levi.

The remaining Sundays' gospels are seen as discourse: the Mission Sermon.

Tenth Sunday of Ordinary Time

CELEBRANT'S GUIDE

Introduction to the Celebration

We have gathered here around the table of the Lord; he has invited us to share in his meal; and by becoming one with him at this table, we are enabled to offer thanks to our heavenly Father. We come here as his guests and he makes us welcome: saints and sinners; some of us here are very fervent disciples, some of us are struggling to keep going along. But he wants all of us to share with him in his meal; to encounter his forgiving love; for he came 'not to call the righteous, but sinners'. Let us reflect that we are here around his table, sharers in the mystery of his forgiving love.

Rite of Penance

    Lord Jesus, you sit at table with sinners. Lord have mercy.
    Lord Jesus, you sit at table with outcasts. Christ have mercy.
    Lord Jesus, you sit at table with us. Lord have mercy.

Headings for Readings

First Reading

The prophet reminds us that love of one another and knowledge of God are truly precious, and we must not think that these can be replaced by religious show.

Second Reading

We refer to Abraham as 'our father in faith' because he is a model for us of believing in God's promises.

Gospel

This gospel reminds us that to answer the call to follow Jesus is to be willing to sit with him, and with sinners and tax collectors, at his table.

Prayer of the Faithful
President
Jesus addresses us as 'Friends' when he gathers us for the Eucharist and enables us to place our needs before the Father. Let us do so now, confident that he will hear us.
Reader(s)
1. For the whole church of God, that we will grow in the healing and forgiveness offered to us in Christ. Lord hear us.
2. For this community, that we will become aware of our common identity as the People of God gathered at the Lord's table. Lord hear us.
3. For all those who belong to this community but cannot be with us today, that they know the Lord's loving care. Lord hear us.
4. For all those who find difficulty in joining us in this holy mystery, that their hearts and minds may be transformed. Lord hear us.
5. Specific local needs and topics of the day.
6. For all those who have gathered for this meal and who have now died, that they may come to its fulfilment in the heavenly banquet. Lord hear us.
President
Father, you hear our prayers, you give us healing and welcome, you call us to yourself. Hear us now for we make our prayers as the People of your Son, Jesus Christ, our Lord.

Eucharistic Prayer
Preface of the Eucharist II (P 48) with Eucharistic Prayer I which refers to those gathered around the table (it also, incidentally today, picks up the line from the second reading of 'Abraham, our father in faith').

Invitation to the Our Father
Through Christ's love we have been called to be at this table offering thanksgiving to the Father. So, in union with Jesus, let us pray:

Sign of Peace

The Lord desires mercy before sacrifice, so let us show our desire to extend mercy, forgiveness, and peace to those around us and to the world.

Invitation to Communion

The Lord Jesus once used to gather tax collectors and sinners to his table. Today he gathers us as well, because we are all in need of his healing. Happy are we to be called to this supper.

Communion Reflection

The Prayer of St Thomas Aquinas for the 'Preparation for Mass' (Missal, p 1018) is appropriate as a reflection today as it picks up the gospel's theme.

Conclusion

Solemn Blessing 13 (Ordinary Time IV) (Missal, p 373) is appropriate.

Notes

When pre-1970 church buildings were changed to suit the new liturgy, the process was often described in terms of 'the priest no longer having his back to the people' and 'people being able to see the altar'. These were simple explanations that made little demand for liturgical catechesis of the communities, seemed 'sensible,' and often allayed the fears of conservative-minded members of the community – and we should remember that ritual is intrinsically conservative – about 'tearing down the lovely High Altar'. The problem with such explanations was that they were rooted in a notion that one participated in the Eucharist by observation: the more one could see, the closer one was to seeing the event at the altar, the more that one was involved. Again, there is a note of truth in this: if one is engaged in any activity one likes to be able to see what is going on. Indeed, even at a committee meeting, people who cannot be seen by the rest of the group feel left out. So a person should be able to see all that is

happening at an event at which s/he is present. However, a
main driver of all liturgical renewal was that there should be a
richer notion of participation than participation by observation.

The Eucharist was not to be the action of a priest at which
people were present 'hearing Mass', but 'the action of the whole
people of God hierarchically assembled'. The community is now
the celebrant with an ordained president. The activity of the
community is that of offering the thanksgiving sacrifice to the
Father (Eucharist) which established the new covenant, and the
form of that sacrifice is the meal of the Lord. To bring out this aspect of the work of the whole community (which is practically
the reality of being gathered at the Lord's table) the table (which
we can interpret as an altar, i.e. a place where a sacrifice is offered) had to be positioned so that we could actually gather
around it just as was taken for granted when the First
Eucharistic Prayer was being formed in the third century:
'Remember O Lord, us, your men-servants and your women-
servants, gathered around.' So the aim of the changes was to
allow people to gather around the table (impossible when it was
shoved against a wall like a sideboard), but, in effect, what happened was that it became the teacher's bench in a laboratory:
everyone could see what he was doing, rather than feel that this
is what *we* are doing. So how do we convey that we are called to
the Lord's table, we sinners along with all those other sinners
and tax-collectors? We must actually find ways to break the notion of participation by looking, and have the actual gathering
around. It will require planning; it will encounter opposition;
but to refuse to attempt it or refuse to challenge those who oppose it, is to tacitly accept an inferior theology born not from an
examination of the Eucharist but out of the need to make sense
for people of being present at a ritual they could not see properly,
nor for the most part hear, and what they did hear was in a language that most could not understand. So, keep words to a minimum today; instead, do as Jesus did.

COMMENTARY

First Reading: Hos 6:3-6

This is part of Hosea's call to Israel to return to the way of true faithfulness: God is greater than the rituals which we need in order for us to relate to him. The truly valuable realities transcend the forms and words (sacrifices, offerings, prayers) which are a necessary part of the order of the people. Here Hosea makes this basic truth of faith in a creator serve the topic of false repentance: if Israel is to return to the Lord, it will have to use the rituals of repentance but, these without the love and awareness of the divine presence, are not sufficient.

Psalm: 49 (50)

This continues theme of Hosea: the reality of God is greater than the image contained in the liturgy; the service is more demanding 'services' (in the sense of liturgies). Every believer and every community walks this tight-rope: without words and rituals we would be condemned to a silence that would be untruthful to what we do know of the mystery of God, while at the same time, when we think we know that mystery through knowing its necessary expression in our world of images, then we have lost the plot. Or, as Aquinas put it more elegantly: *Hoc est ultimum cognitionis humanae de Deo: quod sciat se Deum nescire!* (A person has reached the summit of human knowledge about God when he knows he cannot know God).

Second Reading: Rom 4:18-25

Part of the whole argument of Romans is the place of believing in God's promises and, in particular, his promise of the resurrection of Christians in the resurrection of Jesus. So Paul wants a model of such believing in the face of so much evidence: what better example than that of the father of the people who believed in the promise of becoming the father of a multitude despite every appearance to the contrary.

The preaching/apologetic strategy which Paul employs in this argument (you can believe how God will act now, on the basis of how he acted in the past) is typical of much of the theology of the first churches: you can explain 'now,' by appeals to examples of what happened 'then'. Here Abraham becomes the model of what faithful hope is; in other places the temple service of the priesthood becomes a way of understanding Jesus's death; while the Passover Meal becomes a way of understanding the Christian meal. The strength of the approach is that it explains the new through the old, a variant of the unknown through the known strategy used by every teacher. Its weakness is that the new easily became identified with the old, and with it, the explicatory analogy becomes a definition which limits the new to the older paradigms. Illumination parallels easily became defining theological straightjackets.

First Reading > Gospel Links
The relationship is not at all obvious but seems to be this: Hosea shows that love is greater than the bounds of ritual purity; Jesus too sees love and mercy being greater than the bounds of ritual purity. If this is the link (and it is a valid connection between the readings, even if we cannot be certain it was the link intended by the lectionary's compilers), then the link is that of the continuity of teaching, and perceptions of God, between the two covenants.

Gospel: Mt 9:9-13
This gospel reflects the evangelists' memory of a defining moment in the ministry of Jesus linked with the calling of a man named Levi (Mk and Lk) or Matthew (Mt), who was a tax collector, to follow him. This event seems to have prompted the questioning of just what sort of people were linked with Jesus. And the acid-text of that link, crucial for our understanding of the centrality of the eucharistic meal in the practice of Jesus, was not just why he would talk with them, but that he would eat with them. Others preachers took differing approaches, but all avoided sinners: John the Baptist announced the coming kingdom and warned sinners to repent; the people in Qumran practiced separation from the sinful world; while the Pharisees preached

renewal through adherence to the law's demands. Now we are presented with the practice of Jesus: the kingdom is a new set of relationships, founded on healing and God's generosity in forgiveness. And this new presentation of the relationship of God to sinful humanity is modeled for all in their equality and welcome around the table. Here in the intimacy of a meal is the expression of the quality of the kingdom. This is to be contrasted with what is presented as archetypal of the kingdom for the others: penitential frugality in a desert (John), a life of strict ritual separation from the world (Qumran), a life of precise interpretation of divinely sanctioned texts (Pharisees).

HOMILY NOTES

1. Meals are, by nature, selective: family, then friends, then those who are invited. There is a difference between being invited to a meal, and lots of people sitting at different tables in a cafeteria.
2. If you want to know about someone, watch the company he keeps. This is ancient wisdom, but we all use it as a rule of thumb.
3. Jesus called to his table not just the disciples, but the outcasts: he was forming a new kind of community. A community offered healing by Jesus, which had heard the prompting of the Spirit, and which was loved by the Father. This new community had both the intimacy of a group invited to a meal, combined with an openness that broke down barriers.
4. We too are invited to gather at that table. When we gather here, we share in his healing and his forgiveness. Indeed, we share in his very life: our lives become one with him; his blood flows through us giving us his life-energy.

Eleventh Sunday of Ordinary Time

CELEBRANT'S GUIDE

Introduction to the Celebration

Today we recall how God has called us to be his people, his chosen ones. We retell the story of the first calling of a people to be a priestly people, and we remember how Jesus gathered around him the apostles and sent them to make disciples of all nations.

Rite of Penance

Option c ii (Missal, p 392) is appropriate.

Headings for Readings
First Reading

The people chosen by the Lord become a 'nation of priests': they can gather and stand in God's presence and ask him for his help and care.

Second Reading

In this reading we hear one of Paul's great messages to us: Christ died on the cross so that we who have sinned can be reconciled with God.

Gospel

We are not simply a collection of people with a common religious philosophy: we are called to become members of a community, the body of Christ, which has the apostles as its foundation members.

Prayer of the Faithful
President

Gathered as a priestly people as the first reading reminds us, we can now stand before the Father and make our needs, and the needs of all humanity, known to him and ask his help.

Reader(s)

1. For the whole church of God, that we will have a greater sense of being the community founded on the apostles.

2. For all who are leaders of communities and nations, that they will seek peace and justice in our world.

3. For all who are in need of reconciliation with other human beings or with God, that they will be given the strength to seek reconciliation.

4. For ourselves, that we will grow as a Christian community and may minister Christ's reconciliation to our neighbours during the coming week.

5. For all who are sick, suffering from disease, and in need of healing, that they may know the healing that comes from God, and our care as a community.

6. Local needs.

7. For our sisters and brothers who have died, that they may be reconciled to the Father in the new life of the kingdom.

President

Father, we are your chosen people and we rejoice in having been given a share in your Son's reconciliation. Hear us now and grant our petitions in Christ Jesus, our Lord, Amen.

Eucharistic Prayer

Use Eucharistic Prayer I and include all the names of the apostles, thus emphasising the gospel's theme that we are an apostolic community.

Invitation to the Our Father

We seek forgiveness and we must seek to forgive, so let us pray:

Sign of Peace

As disciples we are called to love one another and remove bitterness from between us; let us express this in a sign of peace.

Invitation to Communion
This is the Lamb who called the apostles to follow him, and who calls us now to share in this banquet.

Communion Reflection
The gospel presents the notion of the apostles being sent out to heal and 'cure all kinds of diseases and sickness' – it is a basic part of the ministry of the Lord. The community that rejoices in the Lord must always be conscious of the suffering around it. This is a day when that gets some conscious expression. It could be that there is a formal sending off of Ministers of the Eucharist to bring particles from the Lord's Table to sick members of the community. It could be when a representative of a health charity tells of their work. Or it could be something else ... what would fit in your community? Contemporary society likes to hide sickness and live in an illusion that it is not part of life; such delusions must be challenged in the more real grasp of our human condition that should characterise us as Christians.

Conclusion
Blessing n 17 [Apostles] (Missal, p 375) picks up the theme of the gospel.

COMMENTARY

First Reading: Ex 19:2-9
Within the wilderness narratives there are frequent reminders that the identity of Israel depends on the covenant between the people and God. Obeying the Lord's voice makes them the Lord's people and so they can stand before him and pray ('kingdom of priests') and receive his blessings ('consecrated nation'). This piece of text plays an important part in how Christians view their identity as the new People of God – the nation formed not by passing through the waters of the Red Sea but through the waters of baptism – as it is quoted (in its Septuagint form) in 1 Pet 2:9: 'But you are "a chosen race, a royal priesthood, a holy nation," the people God has taken to himself.'

Psalm: 99 (100)

The people of the Lord form a single entity, 'the flock,' and the Lord cares for them. The assembled community today are to read this psalm as applying directly to themselves. We, gathered for the Eucharist, are his people, and therefore we thank him, i.e. offer the Eucharist, and praise him, join together in hymns and prayers, because the Father is good to us, 'faithful from age to age.' Such direct appropriations of the voice of the psalmist by the Eucharistic community are rare in the Sunday cycles of readings.

Second Reading: Rom 5:6-11

Between the Ninth and Twenty-fourth Sundays of Year A the second lection is a series of successive snippets from the Letter to the Romans. Given that the letter has an internal logic as Paul sets out his mature theology in a more coherent manner than in any other of his letters, what we have on any one Sunday is no more than a step in his argument. Today his emphasis is on the importance of the death of Jesus in our reconciliation with the Father.

First Reading > Gospel Links

The link is continuity in pattern in the divine action towards the holy people in the two relationships (i.e. the Old Testament and the New Testament). In each the Father provides care for the people's needs: first through Moses, then through Jesus (and this introduces a sub-theme of Moses being an anticipation of the Christ).

Gospel: Mt 9:36-10:8

In this passage Matthew brings together (within a structure that shows some influence from Mark) four distinct items of his tradition, all connected by the theme of the preaching ministry of the church: first, the need for labourers in the harvest and that each church should pray for the advancement of the kerygma; second, a tradition regarding the appointment of exorcists – a min-

istry in each community – by Jesus; third, a list giving the names
of 'the twelve'; and lastly, teaching on the lifestyle of the ministers of the gospel. Matthew gathers these pieces of tradition by
seeing them as each having their origin in the immediate group
around Jesus whom he calls 'the twelve apostles' (10:2). Within
this short text we see the complexity of how the gathering of
people around Jesus mutated over the course of the first generations of Christians to become a conflated memory within the
church – much as it has continued down to this day – whereby
the initial group is identified as 'the twelve disciples/apostles'
and these form the basic pattern for all later ministers. When we
try to get behind the Synoptic Tradition (see J. P. Meier, *A
Marginal Jew III: Companions and Competitors,* New York 2001, pp
125-97 for a very clear recent study) we find that among the followers of Jesus we have a large outer circle of 'the crowds' that
followed him, then a smaller group of men and women who either followed him or provided him with support: 'the disciples',
and then an inner group of men who symbolised the new in-
gathered Israel: 'the twelve.' Then there are those disciples who
were sent out to the house of Israel to proclaim the kingdom:
'the apostles'. However, as time passes these distinctions became blurred and the terms 'apostles,' 'the twelve' and 'disciples' became almost identical. Moreover, the special role that
'the twelve' had during the lifetime of Jesus seems to have been
forgotten quite early by the church for they became the paradigm 'apostles' (as here) and indeed they become the only group
of disciples who were imagined to be following Jesus. Thus in
this passage we have a reference to 'the disciples' at 9:37, to 'the
twelve disciples' at 10:1, and to 'the twelve apostles' at 10:2 –
and we are invited to imagine that it is the same group being referred to on each occasion; moreover, at no point is there a reference to 'the twelve' as such. The best indicator that the special
function of 'the twelve' within Jesus' ministry was soon forgotten within the church is that not only do they become simply the
paradigm group of 'apostles' (i.e. those sent on a mission), but
that the exact composition of 'the twelve' was forgotten: see the

variation in the names between Mk 3:16-9; Mt 10:2-4; Lk 6:14-6; and Acts 1:13.

Matthew's task in this collection of four items of tradition was (1) to retain the traditions, and then (2) give a clear focus to his communities on the importance of sending apostles now to all the nations. He does this by presenting apostleship as a basic function of the followers of Jesus, initially to Israel (10:6), but now in the evangelist's time, after the resurrection, to all the nations (28:19).

HOMILY NOTES

1. Why do we bother recalling all these early disciples? We list them off in this gospel, we recall them in the first Eucharistic Prayer, we name children after them, we dedicate church buildings to their memory, and until recently any group of twelve (be they a collection of spoons or Michael Collins's hit-men in 1921) would be labelled 'the twelve apostles'. We refer to the church as 'apostolic' in creeds because 'it' comes from them and was 'founded' upon them – but this seems like the point of a dilettante, surely it is 'the message' that is important rather than these people long ago? This attitude that the early members of the church – or the lists of saints in between them and now – are 'simply history' (= irrelevant to our belief) is part of the atmosphere we breath. You can check this attitude out quite simply: when was the last time you heard all the early saints' names read out when Eucharistic Prayer 1 was used? There is a real danger today that we reduce the good news to being the 'teaching of Jesus' and so see the Christians as simply those who follow a partic-ular set of religious/moral beliefs and who have rituals and structures simply to promote this philosophy.

2. Today's gospel reminds us that Jesus did not come to impart a teaching or a philosophy of life, but to establish a community bounded in prayer together (all our rituals and practices) and which shared a vision of God and his love for us (all his teaching). Put simply, if you are not living as part of the com-

munity of the Good News, then the teaching of Jesus will make little sense or else seem commonplace.

3. Celebrating 'the twelve' reminds us that Jesus came to establish a group of people who would share their lives, and love, and work, and vision. A group that would try to reflect in the way they lived the coming kingdom. That group grew and spread and established other groups – for most of Christian history the groups have been quite small, usually no more than a hundred or so people in one building: hence the density of medieval church buildings seen in old cities or in the countryside – and those groups remained in contact and shared a larger world-sized vision of their identity. So the Christian-event is that there are groups who are each the Body of Christ at their Eucharist there and then, and all the groups are one group – the 'one church' of the creeds – that is the Body of Christ. That we are in such a gathering today is not because we have simply selected a particular religious teaching, but because there is a bodily link between this group and all the groups going right back to the group around Jesus.

4. Recalling the earliest group, the twelve, shows us who we are when we gather. It reminds us that one cannot be a follower without playing one's part in the community (one's ministry) or sharing in its common life in Christ (its regular eucharistic meals, its prayers, its fasts, its works of charity). It challenges us to have the Christian lifestyle. It challenges us to live as a community who are reflecting to the world new Life and the coming kingdom.

Twelfth Sunday of Ordinary Time

CELEBRANT'S GUIDE

Introduction to the Celebration

We are here because we believe that God the Father loves us, and loves us with such care that we can say, in the words of today's gospel, that he even knows the number of hairs on our head. Let us reflect on that love for a moment.

Rite of Penance

Option c vii (Missal, p 394-5) is appropriate.

Headings for Readings

First Reading

The prophet describes terror all around him, but trusts that God will be with him and deliver him.

Second Reading

God's goodness to us always outweighs human wickedness and sin.

Gospel

The Lord knows us through and through, and we must bear witness to the Lord, and his law, and his love.

Note: the phrase 'in the presence of men' (v 32 and v 33) is both awkward and not gender inclusive. The text reads equally accurately if this is rendered: 'before others'.

Prayer of the Faithful

President

Friends, in the gospel today we heard Jesus instructing the Twelve on how they were to act in bearing witness to him. Let us now ask the Father for the gift of these qualities in the way we live our lives.

Reader(s)

1. That we Christians will not be afraid to proclaim the message of Jesus from the housetops. Lord in your mercy hear our prayer.

2. That our sisters and brothers who are suffering for their faith will be given the strength not to fear those who can kill the body but not the soul. Lord in your mercy hear our prayer.

3. That human beings everywhere may come to know that God knows them and cares for them. Lord in your mercy hear our prayer.

4. That each of us may have the courage to declare himself or herself for Jesus in the society in which we live. Lord in your mercy hear our prayer.

5. Specific local needs and topics of the day.

President

Father, we acknowledge and thank you for your care of us, indeed you know the number of the hairs on our heads. So hear our petitions and grant our needs for we pray to you in Jesus Christ, your Son, our Lord, Amen.

Eucharistic Prayer

No preface or Eucharistic Prayer is particularly appropriate.

Invitation to the Our Father

Jesus has revealed to us the depth of the Father's love for each of us, so let us say:

Sign of Peace

The Lord has reconciled us to the Father, let us offer reconciliation now to one another.

Invitation to Communion

This is the Lamb of God who has revealed the Father's love to us; happy are we who are called to his supper.

Communion Reflection
Read Mt 25:34-45 which can act as a focus to today's gospel: in both the case of the righteous and the unrighteous it is communities not individuals that are addressed (not clear in modern English as we lack a distinctive second person plural, so change the text to the old-fashioned 'ye'), and the witness of the communities (or lack of it) is in service to their suffering fellow humans.

Conclusion
Solemn Blessing 14, Ordinary Time V (Missal, p 373) is suitable.

COMMENTARY

First Reading: Jer 20:10-13
This lection is taken from a section of the book where the prophet gives vent to his despair (20:7-18). Here we have two seemingly incompatible statements: first, a desperate statement of how he is being persecuted with terrors all around, and then a confident statement of his trust in the Lord of Hosts to deliver 'his poor one' (i.e. someone who has only the Lord to depend upon). It would be a mistake to seek a logical connection between these two statements: together they simply reflect the psychological situation so many, including the prophet, have found themselves in. People may be simultaneously despairing and overwhelmed by those seeking to destroy them, yet also trusting in God as their caring deliverer.

Psalm: 68 (69)
This is interpreted within today's liturgy as the prayer of the prophet in his conflict, and so it is also the prayer of every believer in a similar paradoxical situation of despair yet trust.

Second Reading: Rom 5:12-15
Between the Ninth and Twenty-fourth Sundays of Year A the second lection is a series of successive snippets from the Letter to the Romans. Given that the letter has an internal logic as Paul

sets out his mature theology in a more coherent manner than in any other of his letters, what we have on any one Sunday is no more than a step in his argument. Today his aim is to identify the origin of sin in the world that makes necessary Jesus' work of reconciliation.

First Reading > Gospel Links
Similarity of situation between a message found in the prophets and in the teaching of Jesus: the caring presence of God is all embracing.

Gospel: Mt 10:26-33
This section of Matthew is derived from Q (see Lk 12:2-9), but is made up of several sayings and we have evidence that these were also circulating as individual sayings in the churches (see Mk 4:22; Mk 8:38; Gospel of Thomas 5 and 6). As they are found here the focus of the sayings is to highlight the difference between a fear of ordinary human consequences and genuine ultimate fear. It employs a Hellenistic dualist notion of the human being as a body and a soul which are separable. The normal fear is that which concerns the body (which this passage assumes the hearers will think of as transient) but genuine fear should be that the soul (which this passage assumes its hearers will imagine as immortal and incorruptible) be annihilated. This notion that ultimate divine punishment is equivalent to annihilation is uncommon in early Christian writings, and soon disappeared completely from the kerygma in favour of the notion of a continuing subject undergoing punishment. Even when later writers, e.g. Irenaeus, struggled with the problems inherent in the notion of 'eternal punishment,' they did not return to this concept of annihilation of the soul.

HOMILY NOTES

1. There are several notes of fear in today's gospel. There is the fear that what they – the matthaean churches represented by 'The Twelve' – are involved in as Christians is unclear and

hidden from the eyes of the ordinary people around them, yet they are expected to proclaim it from the housetops. There is the fear of those who are persecuting the group – they must rather fear God who can destroy them utterly than the earthly persecutor who can only destroy their bodies. This seems cold comfort. You may be worth 'hundreds of sparrows,' but there is still the threat of one's body being killed. Then there is the fear that if the community do not witness to Jesus before others, then he will disown them before the Father. This seems to offer support to the old conundrum: 'The Christian way is a free and joyful choice; but if you do not choose it, you will be condemned to hell for your refusal.'

2. This passage also brings before us the fact that it was part of the primitive kerygma that there is a genuine ultimate fear of God's justice and, so, of his punishment. Yet 'preaching hell fire and damnation' is not a strategy that is in line with the overall thrust of the good news. The problem arises from the fact that we want a consistent 'message', yet there is no such consistency to be derived from the surviving early Christian texts. Many people from many different branches of Judaism became followers of Jesus, and so there were many flavours of Christian belief, emphasis, and lifestyle. Here we see traditions preserved that probably reflect the sort of preaching we see with John the Baptist: there is a crunch coming and God will mete out his punishments, while the more characteristic message of Jesus is that there is a crunch coming so form a community of love and God will mete out his mercies. These various strands came together in the traditions of the churches and left a mosaic of positions that has defied nearly two thousand years of attempts at systematisation in catechisms and doctrinal systems.

3. So can these statements be presented today in such a way that they do not become the basis for a gospel of fear? That is the task we face as preachers: accommodating these particular perceptions within a larger picture of what we say about the Father on the basis of what Jesus taught and did.

4. Jesus formed a people and presented God relating to us as members of that new people, not as isolated individuals. This is seen in this text in that it is addressed to The Twelve – a unified highly identifiable group – not to twelve individuals who just happened to be together. This warning of fear must be to us as a community, not to each individually. So the question is: are we as a community sufficiently serious about the message of God in Christ; do we realise the importance of the message entrusted to us; do we realise its urgency? On the whole as a community we fail in this and the evidence is all around us: we live in fractured communities, we often condone injustice, we know that there is poverty and suffering in the world – and yet we do nothing. We may 'fear for our souls,' but a glance at a news bulletin shows that most Christian communities are not too fearful for other people's bodies.

5. So the task of the community is to act together to bear witness to the love and care of God before our fellow human beings. If we seek forgiveness from God, we must forgive fellow humans (the Our Father); if we seek love and care from God, we must offer love and care to others. So can this community organise itself to that it can witness before men and women as caring for those suffering from injustice, hatred, sickness, the exploitation of the environment? If the community can be so seen as the body of Christ, then it can stand as the body of Christ in the presence of the Father.

Thirteenth Sunday of Ordinary Time

CELEBRANT'S GUIDE

Introduction to the Celebration

Welcome! Welcome to this assembly of the baptised who have gathered to give thanks to our Father in heaven. 'Welcome': it is such a simple word, and one we use freely and often with little thought. We welcome friends and guests to our homes; from time to time we welcome visitors; we talk about giving and receiving warm welcomes; and we sometimes have little plaques near our front door with 'Welcome' written on them or even have it bound into the weave of the front door mat.

Because we have been baptised into Jesus the Christ, we have been welcomed by the Father as his daughters and sons. Because we are disciples we are welcomed now to the Lord's table. Because we are followers of the Way we look forward to being welcomed to the banquet of heaven. We can thank the Father that we are a welcomed people.

But do we always welcome the Christ in his teachings in our lives? Do we always welcome the Christ in the stranger? Do we always welcome the Christ in the poor? Do we always welcome the Christ in those in need in our society?

Rite of Penance

For those times when we have not welcomed Christ in the poor. Lord have mercy.

For those times when we have not welcomed Christ in those who are strangers to us. Christ have mercy.

For those times when we have not welcomed Christ in those in any kind of need. Lord have mercy.

Headings for Readings
First Reading
We recall the welcome given to Elisha when he was on his trav-
els in the land of Shunem: Elisha was stranger to the people who
welcomed him and who repeatedly gave him food and shelter,
and who recognised that in him God was visiting their household.

Second Reading
We are here in this church as the community of the baptised; in
this reading Paul reminds the church in Rome about what that
means.

Gospel
Jesus reminds us of the demands of discipleship; and one of
those demands is that we must be a welcoming and openhearted
community.

Prayer of the Faithful
President
'Whoever gives to one of these little ones even a cup of cold
water because he is a disciple, truly, I say to you, he shall not
lose his reward.' With these words ringing in our ears, let us
pray for ourselves, the other members of this community, and
the whole People of God.
Reader(s)
1. That the church throughout the world will heed the call to
serve the poor. Lord hear us.
2. The women and men of all nations and religions will seek the
ways of peace. Lord hear us.
3. That this community will hear the challenge of the Lord to
lead lives of discipleship. Lord hear us.
4. That anyone in pain or distress or need in our society may receive mercy, help and comfort. Lord hear us.
5. That anyone who encounters this community may find us
welcoming. Lord hear us.

6. Specific local needs and topics of the day.

7. That the dead who have trodden the ways of discipleship shall not lose their reward. Lord hear us.

President

Father, your Son taught us that anyone who welcomes him welcomes you who sent him. Hear us now for we seek to welcome the Christ, to take up his cross and to follow his footsteps; and we make this prayer in Christ Jesus, our Lord. Amen.

Eucharistic Prayer

Eucharistic Prayer IV which presents Jesus as our model for caring for the poor, for prisoners, and for those in sorrow.

Invitation to the Our Father

The Father has made us welcome as his family. Let us praise him and ask him to forgive us those times when we have not welcomed others as he has welcomed us:

Sign of Peace

We are all poor and needy of the Lord's mercy and glad to be welcomed to the Lord's table. Let us express this welcome and love to those around us.

Invitation to Communion

We are all poor and needy of the Lord's mercy and glad to be welcomed to the Lord's table; happy are we to be sharers in this banquet of the Lord.

Communion Reflection

The response to the litany: Blessed be the Lord who has welcomed us.

For making us his sisters and brothers. *Response.*
For gathering us to be his holy people. *Response.*
For showing us the way to life. *Response.*
For giving us light for our life. *Response.*

For sharing with the consolation of the truth. *Response.*
For gathering us as this assembly. *Response.*
For establishing peace among us. *Response.*
For offering us reconciliation. *Response.*
For calling us his friends. *Response.*
For making us his table companions. *Response.*
For our sharing in the one loaf. *Response.*
For our sharing in the one cup. *Response.*
For giving us a participation in the body of Christ. *Response.*
For giving us a participation in the blood of Christ. *Response.*
For the promise of being welcomed into the kingdom at the end.
Response.
Amen.

Conclusion
Solemn Blessing for Ordinary Time I (Missal, p 372).

Notes
The notion of welcome presented in the gospel could be developed in terms of the welcome that is to be the attitude of the church to visiting prophets. However, that approach could be seen as very narrow and only of historical interest. So the notion of welcome has been broadened to take account of the style of disciples: they cannot be an exclusivist group.

COMMENTARY

First Reading: 2 Kings 4:8-11, 14-16
This is the scene-setting preamble to one of the great miracle stories of the Elisha-cycle: the Shunammite Woman (4:8-37). She gives hospitality to the man of God; he rewards her with the miraculous birth of a son; the son dies; she begs Elisha's help; and eventually, through his intercession, the child is restored to life. This miracle has now receded into the 'non-active' memory of the tradition; but its significance as a pointer to one of the essential qualities of holiness can be gauged by its influence in the gospels where it is echoed in at least three miracles of Jesus:

Jairus's daughter (Mk 5); the centurion's servant (Mt 8); and the widow's son at Nain (Lk 7); not to mention umpteen miracles in the tradition of hagiography.

One can extract an example of welcome and hospitality from the beginning of the story – as is done here – but that is not to suggest that that is part of the structure of the narrative.

Psalm: 88 (89)

This is a psalm of praise of the steadfastness of God's love. It does not, however, relate in any particular way to the common theme of welcome that links the first reading and gospel.

Second Reading: Rom 6:3-4, 8-11

This is part of Paul's exposition of what it means to be the new creation, free people in the kingdom, through union with Christ; and this union is achieved through baptism. Quite what purpose it served by cutting three verses out of the middle of this reading is unclear: not even time is saved as they take less than a minute to read aloud; but these seconds are saved, if that is why they are omitted, at the expense of noting a key part of Paul's argument (the link of baptism with death), and also by furthering the notion that the scriptures are a treasury from which a few nice verses can be selected from time to time.

First Reading > Gospel Links

The first reading provides a concrete example of what is given as teaching in the gospel.

Gospel: Mt 10:37-42

This is the conclusion of the Mission Discourse (10:1-42), and collects together a number of sayings, all concerned with discipleship in some way, that must have seemed to Matthew to need a home somewhere in his gospels. The first three verses are also found in Luke, and while the second three verses are unique to this passage, they have echoes elsewhere. They cluster around two distinct themes: first, the nature of the claim which discipleship of Jesus makes on each person – the bonds of discipleship are to be stronger than even the bonds of flesh and blood; and second, the welcoming of the disciple is the welcoming of the one who has commissioned the disciple.

It is the latter theme that is highlighted in the liturgy by its choice of first reading and it provides a suitable point for the nature of the welcome that Matthew envisaged as existing in the churches for brothers and sisters from other communities.

HOMILY NOTES

1. It is always worth giving time to a few unpalatable facts! Here is one: religions are forces for conservatism in societies – in effect, changes (such as the arrival of new people) tend to be seen as frightening and sources of danger. Here is another: religions tend to build cohesion between groups that engage in ritual together – in effect, they establish a *status quo* that becomes increasingly rigid and adverse to change (so adding hymns that make the assembly more friendly to parents with young children will be a war of attrition ['attrition' in its military rather than its theological sense!]). Here is a third: most religious groups tend to have high perceptions of their own identity and so, in effect, become either excluding of members drifting in from outside or positively exclusive. In effect, you might come to the group as a visitor, but either you would always feel on the periphery as a 'blow in' or you would get a set of signals that this was not really your kind of place.

2. This might appear to be an interesting piece of religious anthropology, but it certainly would not apply to our community: surely it was only last week that we all shook hands at coffee with the two foreigners that bought the house round the corner that old Mrs Smith lived in! Alas, there is a fourth fact: we all drift down this route of being unwelcoming and must positively choose to act differently if we are to answer the Lord's call to be welcoming. We want to be like this precisely because we have been so warmly welcomed by the

Christ into the family of the Father. This is not some other morally good attitude, but is at the heart of the Christian vision of the universe. We who have become estranged from God through sin are welcomed back; so too we must act in welcoming those who are strangers to us.

3. This problem with unwelcoming communities is not a new problem. Paul criticises the church in Corinth for its social stratification: the 'nice people' do not like having to eat with the have-nots. There were disputes in several churches between those who were slaves thinking that at the Lord's table they could be equal to non-slaves. There were those of Jewish background who did not like eating with Christians who were uncircumcised. And even Jesus' own welcoming of prostitutes, sinners, 'enemies of the people' and foreigners to his table caused many to decide that they simply wanted nothing to do with him or to see him as clearly a false prophet.

4. The need to be welcoming stands behind many incidents in the gospels, for example the Zacchaeus story (Lk 19), and many of the concerns of Paul about the internal arrangements of the churches reflect his concern that the communities would not be exclusive to one social level but would recognise in practice that they were models for a new God-like vision of the world.

5. So the question is not whether the odd visitor is welcomed by the community, but whether people would find this a community where there is a sense of acceptance and recognition that we are all children of God. This means that every community must positively pursue the question of whether it is welcoming, and can be perceived as such by a stranger, as part of its own following.

6. The questions to ask are whether or not the liturgy, or the groups that take part in the liturgy, reflect just one social group within the area. Does the liturgy reflect the concerns of one strand of participants? Does the liturgy reflect one racial group among the locality? For example, in the locality there

may be two housing estates: one detached properties with gardens, the other high-density local authority housing. Are they represented *pro rata* in the groups in the church? Does the community only reflect the liturgical needs of the middle-aged or the young families? Does the community show its acceptance of immigrants from other cultures in those who read or assist with the sharing of the Eucharist? These are hard questions for any community because it tests 'welcoming' by practice. And, once someone says in reply: 'But they don't want to be involved anyway!' you can be certain the community has a problem because they are already thinking of brothers and sisters in Christ in terms of 'them' and 'us'.

7. Every congregation, and every group within it, must audit its practice: is this group inclusive and including; is this group exclusive or excluding; are there subtle signals being sent out that there are 'insiders' and 'outsiders'; are there ways of sending out subtle signals that we are all poor and needy of the Lord's mercy and glad to be welcomed to the Lord's table?

8. If the perfect expression of our existence as the church – our gathering for the Eucharist – is an event of true welcome, then those attitudes of welcome and social concern will begin to embed themselves in the community's discipleship as a whole. And the converse also hold true: if a community cannot be genuinely welcoming in its liturgy, then it is most unlikely that it will be concerned with the poor, the needy, or the stranger.

Lectionary Unit IV

This unit comprises Sundays 14-17, and its focus is on the mystery of God's Kingdom.

There is one Sunday devoted to narrative: Sunday 13, whose theme is the revelation to the simple.

The remaining Sundays' gospels are seen as discourse, which together make up the Parable Sermon.

Fourteenth Sunday of Ordinary Time

CELEBRANT'S GUIDE

Introduction to the Celebration
Every Sunday we gather here because we have heard the Lord's invitation: 'Come to me, all you who labour and are overburdened, and I will give you rest.' We rejoice that God in his generosity has given us this day of rest, this day of rejoicing, this day when we can just be happy and reflect on the wonder of the creation.

Rite of Penance
Option c iv (Missal, p 393) is appropriate.

Headings for Readings
First Reading
The prophet calls on the people to rejoice that the Lord is goodness and love, the Lord is king yet he is humble, and the Lord cares for all people

Second Reading
St Paul asks us to reflect on our identity as the church: we are the community in whom the Spirit has made his home.

Gospel
Part of the mystery of the kingdom of God is the mystery of the gentleness of God's love where we can find rest.

Prayer of the Faithful
Sample Formula 9 (Ordinary Time I), (Missal, p 1002) is appropriate for today.

Eucharistic Prayer
No Preface or Eucharistic Prayer is particularly appropriate to carry on the theme of the readings.

Invitation to the Our Father
The Father, the Lord of heaven and earth, has hidden his mysteries from the learned and the clever and revealed them to us who are his children; and, as such, we pray:

Sign of Peace
The Lord takes away our burdens. Let us pledge ourselves to remove burdens of bitterness and disquiet from one another by giving each other the sign of peace.

Invitation to Communion
In this celebration the Lord reveals the mystery of God to us, and with him we bless the Father. Happy are we to be called to share his supper.

Communion Reflection
Bestow on us, O Lord,
minds that know you;
Give us, O Lord,
wisdom in finding you;
Help us, O Lord,
to live in ways that please you;
Grant us, O Lord,
perseverance that waits for you;
Inspire us, O Lord,
with confidence that we shall embrace you at the end. Amen.
(Adapted from St Thomas Aquinas)

Conclusion
Solemn Blessing 12 (Ordinary Time III), Missal p 372, is appropriate.

COMMENTARY

First Reading: Zech 9:9-10
This reading, because of the role it plays as the backdrop to the triumphant entry of Jesus into Jerusalem and the events of Palm Sunday in the gospels (it is quoted in Mt 21:5 and Jn 12:15), is rarely read in its wider context, despite being the best-known verse from the whole book.

It is a prophecy written at a time when there is no king in Jerusalem and it looks forward to a coming king. This king will preside over peace and that dominion of peace will be world-wide. This appeal 'to the ends of the earth' is one of the earliest explicit statements about the universal importance of the Lord's dealings with Israel. While the first verse of this reading stands behind the liturgy of Palm Sunday, the latter verse stands behind the whole mission of the first Christians, after Easter, to the gentiles.

Psalm: 144 (145)
This is a celebration of the kingship of the Lord, which expands the themes of the first reading.

Second Reading: Rom 8:9, 11-13
The whole of Rom 8 forms a unity within the epistle and is concerned with the nature of the Christian life. The first characteristic of that is that it is life lived in the Spirit. And it is for this life in the Spirit that Jesus has freed us. In this reading v 10 has been omitted, but while such excisions usually make little sense, that is not the case today. The verse is a parenthetic comment, and when the passage is heard, as in the liturgy, it just makes following the reading more difficult, while its omission takes nothing away from Paul's pneumatology.

First Reading > Gospel Links
This is the classic link of the Lord being spoken of by the prophets, and then that prophecy being fulfilled in Jesus. The coming king will inaugurate the universal reign of peace. This

was brought about when Jesus announced that the kingdom is revealed.

Gospel: Mt 11:25-30
Matthew combines two items of tradition as a single event: first, Jesus' act of thanksgiving to the Father (found also in Lk 10:21-22); and, second, a saying on the comfort for the heavy-laden and the rest that the Christ will give. This latter point is only found here in the canonical gospels, but this notion that rest is a gift of the Christ was certainly a more widespread part of the initial kerygma than this one citation would suggest, for echoes of it are present in the Gospel of Thomas and the Gospel according the Hebrews. Matthew's cutting-and-pasting of the elements is not well done, for even a casual listener wonders how the invitation 'Come to me ...' follows on from the statement that the only ones who know the Father are those to whom the Son chooses to reveal him. Therefore, for the purposes of exegesis, the two passages (vv 25-7 and vv 28-30) have to be read separately.

The passage about 'blessing the Father' frequently gives rise to misunderstanding: 'How can you bless God? Is not God already holy?' and it is worth noting this confusion in the context of the Eucharist. We use 'bless' as a transitive verb: one blesses an object and then that object is blessed (e.g. water, salt, houses, or whatever). However, in the early church, carrying on from Jewish usage, 'bless' was also used intransitively in that one 'blessed God' and this is a basic form of Jewish prayer (often referred to by liturgists as 'the *beraka* form'). Here 'to bless' is equivalent to offering praise, a sacrifice of praise, giving thanks, and worship and God alone is the recipient. In Christian usage, the Father alone is the recipient as we see in the Our Father: 'hallowed be your name' could be rendered 'may your name be blessed' or in prayers over the gifts at the Eucharist in the rite of 1970: 'Blessed are you Lord God of all creation ...' When early communities heard the words of today's gospel they would have immediately linked it with the Eucharist for they would have recalled that practice of Jesus at table when he blessed God when he had taken the loaf. Despite the fact that the word *benedixit* has been rendered 'gave you thanks and praise' or 'said the blessing' in our Eucharistic Prayers we still are inclined to think – as was the common error in the previous rite – that Jesus took bread and blessed *it*. To bless the Father is to offer prayerful thanks for his goodness; this is the sacrifice of praise; and for Christians this is the Eucharist around the Lord's table sharing the one loaf and cup.

HOMILY NOTES

1. The challenge with a text such as today's gospel is to find something particular that can give expression to the aspect of the kergyma which it represents. I am picking up the notion of the rest that God gives us, and particularising it in terms of the notion of Sunday as the divine gift of a day of rest.

2. This is, of course, an ancient theme. And, deviant notions of Sabbatarianism apart, there has been a standard way to present both the Sabbath (in Jewish sources) and Sunday (among Christians) down the ages. These presentations have a common theme: 'This is the day.' Whether it is the day of creating or resting from creating, or the day of resurrection or some other day. Then this actual day, Sunday now, is a means of participating in that original 'day'. This notion that time forms mystical unity with the fundamental moments in the history of salvation is deeply embedded in both Jewish and Christian notions of ritual and celebration. However, possibly Christmas and Easter apart, they seem not to excite people today in the way they did until quite recently. Whatever has caused this change is one matter, the fact is that in a 'leisure society' the notion of a Day of Rest, or a Day belonging to the Lord, just does not move people – even if they are Christians. This can be seen in that many people are willing to opt for alternative 'worship services' that would take place on weekday evenings because they do not want to have 'to go on Sunday' as it 'messes up their weekend'. The

time of leisure, the weekend, is so sacrosanct that it cannot even be interrupted for prayer. Older books spoke of the dichotomy of people who gave 'Sunday to God; the rest to mammon'; now it is more complex. Monday to Friday is for work and duties; weekends are pure leisure time; God does not belong to my leisure time, so he can be squeezed in during the week.

3. So how do you speak about Sunday and 'a day of rest' to people when many of those listening will be viewing their presence there as an interruption in their leisure time? Indeed, there will be individuals in every assembly who will be suffering from stress because of the tension that her/his decision to go the Eucharist has caused their families who see it as an unwarranted interruption the family's leisure. Today, in every society where there is a five-day week and work is limited by a maximum number of hours, Sunday is a problem for Christians!

4. The first step is to acknowledge the problem. Ask rhetorically how many know this dialogue: the family want to go somewhere on Sunday and to leave to get there for lunchtime. Only one parent is a church-goer. That person's desire to attend the Eucharist is throwing the plans out. So someone asks: 'Why can't you just skip church this week – you can worship God anywhere – you don't need to go into a special building!' Reply: 'It's not as simple as that!' Another voice: 'Well, OK, but can you not make an exception for today, it's such a nice day!' Reply: 'But I made an exception last week and this week I'm down on the list to do the reading!' Another: 'Oh Yes! Someone else's list. Strange religion this: someone else is more important than your family's happiness. Strange religion this! Loving God means you don't love your family.' Another voice: 'You better go on to your Mass. We're too late to get there now anyway. You might as well go off and look after your religion!'

5. This acknowledgment of the stress that many are under can be a way of ventilating a problem that people have never

named and itself lessens the stress and the consequent feelings of guilt.

6. So the first step in preaching Sunday is to say to people that
resting is having burdens removed: so, just for now, relax.
God loves us and knows the strains and stresses we live with.

7. Then, step two, just point out the irony: in a 'leisure society'
the pressures to use 'leisure time' often become so great, that
the time is as stressed as for work-time. We have industri-
alised leisure time! How much leisure is left? Yet God wants
us to have leisure and rest from work.

8. Life is greater than our pressures and concerns and work:
that is the insight of the Day of Rest being the Lord's Day.
Our life is greater than the sum of its parts. Yet, if we do not
reflect regularly on this, and be thankful to God for all his
gifts – of which life is basic – we lose the plot and lose the
leisure. That is why we Christians call on ourselves to stop
regularly, relax and reflect on life and work and leisure, and
to bless the Father for his goodness. And our word for 'blessing the Father' is Eucharist.

Fifteenth Sunday of the Year

CELEBRANT'S GUIDE

Introduction to the Celebration

Today our thoughts during this celebration are guided by the Parable of the Sower: seeds fell along the path, on rocks, among thorns, and into rich soil. Only the seeds which fell into the rich soil bore fruit. Christ is the sower, and while we desire to be good soil, we know there are times when we are pretty shallow like the depth of soil along the path. There are areas of rock in our lives where God's word has not taken root, and there are areas where God's word finds difficulty in taking root. So as we prepare to celebrate the mystery of Christ's love, let us acknowledge our failures and ask the Lord for pardon and strength.

Rite of Penance

Lord Jesus, for those times when our hearts have grown dull in our desire to follow you; help us to turn to you to heal us. Lord have mercy.

Lord Jesus, for those times when our ears are heavy of hearing your words; help us to turn to you to heal us. Christ have mercy.

Lord Jesus, for those times when our eyes have been closed to the path you show us, help us to turn to you to heal us. Lord have mercy.

Headings for Readings

First Reading

The prophet Isaiah likens God's word to a seed that is planted and then bears fruit.

Second Reading

The full glory of how the universe is transformed by the Christ will only become visible at the end of time, for now we must live by hope; but we do have a foretaste of that glory in that the Spirit of God dwells within us.

Gospel

Jesus likens God's word to seeds sown under different conditions, but which when it takes proper root can yield a great harvest.

Prayer of the Faithful

President

Let us pray now, as members of the kingdom, that we will be those who hear the word and understand it, and bear fruit, and yield, in one case a hundredfold, in another sixty, and in another thirty.

Reader(s)

1. For the people of God, that we may grow in our knowledge of the secrets of the kingdom of heaven. Lord hear us.

2. For ourselves, that we may not be a community whose heart has grown dull, whose ears are heavy of hearing, and who have closed their eyes. Lord hear us.

3. For those who have heard the word and who therefore face tribulation or persecution, that they may be given the gift of perseverance so as not to fall away. Lord hear us.

4. For all those whose cares of the world and delight in riches make them unable to follow the Lord, that their hearts may be converted so as to yield much fruit. Lord hear us.

5. For our sisters and brothers who have died in Christ, that they may present at the harvest the fruit of the word of God within them and yield, in one case a hundredfold, in another sixty, and in another thirty. Lord hear us.

President

Father, you have revealed the mystery of the kingdom to us through your Son, hear us as your children through that same Son, Jesus our Lord. Amen.

Eucharistic Prayer
The eschatological dimension of the gospel, the mystery finally come to its fullness in the presence of God, is well expressed in Preface of Christian Death IV (P80); none of the Eucharistic Prayers picks up the theme is a special way.

Invitation to the Our Father
By letting the word of God take root in our lives we have been made sisters and brothers of the Christ, and so in union with him we can pray:

Sign of Peace
If the word of God has taken root in our hearts, then it will blossom when we seek for peace. Let us express our willing to offer and receive peace from one another.

Invitation to Communion
Behold the Sower, who has planted his seed within our hearts and who bids us to be a people of rich harvests, and who calls us now to share in his banquet.

Communion Reflection
George Herbert's poem 'The Call' (Breviary, III, 786*).

Conclusion
That the Lord may grant us eyes that see his wonder and love in all creation. Amen.
That the Lord may grant us ears that hear his voice calling on us to act as disciples. Amen.
That the Lord may grant us wisdom to understand his ways and yield a rich harvest with our lives. Amen.

COMMENTARY

First Reading: Isa 55:10-11
This comes from the finale to Deutero-Isaiah (40:1-55:13). It is a re-iteration of the message with which this book began: Israel,

you can take comfort! Why? Because God's word moves in world history and effects his purposes.

Psalm: 64 (65)
This is only linked to the first reading and gospel in that it uses agricultural imagery.

Second Reading: Rom 8:18-23
Paul continues his treatment of the life in the Spirit that is the life of Christians. In this section of chapter 8 he seems to have in mind those who want the glory of God to be visible now, so he replies that the Christians, just like the whole creation, must wait for the End in hope. For the time being, Christians have the consolation of having the first fruits of the final harvest: the Spirit dwelling within them.

First Reading > Gospel Links
The same image for God's word is used in both passages. However, there the similarity ends for in the first reading the purpose is to show that God's word is indefectible, while in the gospel the variety of seedbeds is to show how God's word often fails to take root. Since Isa 6:9-10 is quoted by name in the gospel, it might have formed the kernel of a first reading that would have shifted the emphasis of today from the parable and its interpretation to the teaching between those sections.

Gospel: Mt 13:1-23
The third of the sermons that form the teaching structure of Matthew's gospel is usually called 'The Parables Sermon' or 'The Parable of the Kingdom' and it comprises Mt 13:1-52. How many parables it contains depends on how one counts, but the number usually given is eight. The whole of this Parables Sermon is read over three Sundays (today and the next two weeks), and it makes up the discourse element of this unit of the Year of Matthew.

In today's gospel we read almost half of the whole sermon

which comprises the Parable of the Sower (at the beginning and end of the passage) along with the 'explanation' of why Jesus spoke in parables. While most of today's reading is also found in Mark and Luke, Matthew is a fuller text and makes it clear that the focus is on how many heard Jesus but were un-affected by him. For Matthew the reason that many did not (or do not) hear Jesus, and why Jesus will only speak in parables is inter-connected: the kingdom is a mystery which is both seen and hidden. At one extreme there are those for whom it is a silly irrelevance, while to others it is the gateway to a great harvest.

HOMILY NOTES

1. There is always a danger that the Eucharist is transformed from a celebration into an affair of words, words, and yet more words. Picture this situation: people have just sat down after listening to the (long) parable of the sower when they have heard the story (13:3-8), then teaching, then the explanation of the story (13:18-23); then they listen to the preacher explaining the story yet again, and possibly telling yet more stories 'to bring the story home' or else an explanation of 'the mystery of the kingdom' (alas, if it is that simple we should not refer to it as a mystery!). The result is information overload: so many words that people become tired and hearing yet more words, they hear nothing.

2. An alternative would be something like this. Once people have settled in their seats, introduce a few moments reflection with an introduction like this:

    We have heard the words of Jesus about the mystery of the kingdom and his words on how the word of God must bear rich fruit in our lives. Let us reflect in silence about what it means to us to have been called by Jesus to become members of the Father's kingdom.

3. Conclude the period of reflections (you need only wait a minute or so after the coughing and clearing the throat phase has passed) with the invitation to stand for the profession of faith.

Sixteenth Sunday of Ordinary Time

Introduction to the Celebration

Use the Asperges option, with this introduction:

Sisters and brothers, today's gospel reminds us that we, because we are Christians, have to be like a leaven in our society and our world. So let us begin our assembly as the Body of Christ by re-affirming our identity as those who have died in Christ in baptism, and have risen with him to new life and so stand here today.

(If your use a Rite of Penance, then Option c vii (Missal, p 394-5) is appropriate.)

Headings for Readings

First Reading

This reading is a hymn of praise to God as almighty; yet such is the nature of God that we see his might not in terrifying displays of power but in his mercy, his leniency, and his willingness to grant us the possibility of repentance. Moreover, in showing us this love, he is showing us how we should live virtuous lives: we must forgive those who trespass against us because God forgives us our trespasses.

Second Reading

St Paul reminds the church in Rome how the Spirit acts in our lives.

Gospel

Use the shorter version.

This is a parable that shows God's care: even the wicked are not punished in this world lest such punishment would damage the righteous.

Prayer of the Faithful
Use Sample Formula 1 (Missal, p 995).

Eucharistic Prayer
No preface or Eucharistic Prayer is particularly appropriate.

Invitation to the Our Father
The Lord Jesus has told us that 'the righteous will shine like the sun in the kingdom of their Father'. Let us pray for that kingdom's coming:

Sign of Peace
The Lord Jesus has told us that 'the righteous will shine like the sun in the kingdom of their Father'. May we learn to be righteous through being builders of peace.

Invitation to Communion
The Lord Jesus has told us that 'the righteous will shine like the sun in the kingdom of their Father', and as we journey towards the Father he feeds us now at this table.

Communion Reflection
Have a structured silence.

Conclusion
Solemn Blessing 12, Ordinary Time III (Missal, p 372) is appropriate.

COMMENTARY

First Reading: Wis 12:13, 16-19
This book, often referred to as 'the Wisdom of Solomon,' only exists in Greek and has the distinction of being the most recent book included in the Catholic and Orthodox canons of the Old Testament. The book is usually dated to the last decades before the birth of Jesus (on the basis that its theology is so close to that of Philo (20BC-54AD)), but it could just as easily have been writ-

ten during the lifetime of Jesus. Because it came from one of the branches of Judaism that was very similar in theological stance to that of Jesus, it comes as no surprise that the first Christians took it into their canon of readings (its life within Judaism rapidly faded away after the First Revolt (70AD)), and theologians down the centuries (with the exception of Jerome, and the sixteenth century Reformers who followed him) have found its teaching remarkably close to that of the gospels.

However, by the careful use of the scissors, today's lection is even closer to the gospels than if one read the text outside the liturgy: vv 14-15 dwell on God's just punishments – and the omission of these verses, while it produces a lovely reading, prevents us appreciating the author's position. The lection is taken from a hymn, i.e. poetry addressed to God, on God's mercy and power that runs from 11:17 to 12:22. It is worth looking up this reading in a copy of the scriptures to see how the overall message is changed by including vv 14-15.

Psalm: 85 (86)
The psalm continues the theme of the first reading: the characteristic of God is his mercy and forgiveness.

Second Reading: Rom 8:26-27
In this snippet, which is at least a natural unit of text within the letter as a whole, Paul explores yet another aspect of the new life and destiny of those reborn as Christians. In these people, the Holy Spirit has come to dwell in such a way that he transforms their individual spirits; and if they desire it, the Spirit can act for them in place of their own spirits.

First Reading > Gospel Links
The first reading sets forth something that is basic to our theology. It seems to be used here as a counter-point to the prediction of eschatological trauma that is placed in the mouth of Jesus in the longer form of the gospel. Such a link is the exact reverse of how most people view the relationship between the documents of the two covenants.

Gospel: Mt 13:24-43 (shorter version: 13:24-30)

This gospel text is made up of a series of parables which are laid one on top of another. There is (i) the Parable of the Weeds (vv 24-30) found only in Matthew; then (ii) a version of the Parable of the Mustard Seed (vv 31-32) found in all the synoptics; then (iii) that of the Leaven (v 33) found also in Luke; then (iv) a statement on the use of parables (vv 34-5) which is Matthew's variant on one of the texts regarding the Messianic Secret in Mark; and lastly, (v) an interpretation of the Parable of the Weeds (vv 36-43). Since the Parable of the Weeds forms a boundary around the other three elements, the whole passage (vv 24-43) is seen as a unity and the work of Matthew the editor. For this reason it is given as a single reading today. However, the whole package is so complex just as the sum of its parts (not to mention its place in Matthew's preaching) that if used at a Eucharist, it just creates communication overload. Any one piece (with the exception of item v) is more than enough to work on in a homily. So this is a day when the shorter version is much to be preferred.

If one reads the parable alone (i.e. ignore vv 36-43) one finds we have a typical parable that should be addressed as such: a story that dramatically makes just one point. In this case it seems that the story is designed to answer the question as to why God does not visit wrong-doers with the immediate and visible punishments that their actions are perceived to deserve. In Jesus's presentation of the action of his Father, there are no lightning bolts, no displays of divine anger, and no exemplary punishments. Sin may indeed punish itself (cf Mt 26:52), but the Lord's justice will only take place at the End. Equally, there are no immediate 'rewards' for acting justly – simply doing 'the right thing' does not ensure that we will have a happy life or that things 'will go well' for us or that we will succeed in our aims however noble. These are hard lessons for all of us; but there is a contemporary tendency among Christian fundamentalists to see 'disasters as punishments' for this or that, and to a tendency to preach 'a gospel of profit' (if you become a 'believer' then life will go well), and all such notions have their rebuttal in this parable.

HOMILY NOTES

1. During the Year of Matthew we encounter, Sunday by Sunday, a very large range of parables – as commonly defined – as the gospel readings. The repetition of themes can, therefore, be a problem. One solution would be to select topics from the second readings, but this cannot be done on every occasion without provoking the question: 'How does the gospel fit with this?' Sadly, most people cannot appreciate that there is no planned link between the two New Testament readings, no matter how often they are told this. Another solution would be to pick significant topics for preaching, irrespective of the gospel readings. However, apart from this being out of harmony with the logic of the liturgy, and the *General Instruction*, it also destroys the greatest gift any lectionary confers: it sets a limit to preachers going off on their hobby horses. So preaching, if it is part of the Eucharist and so part of the supreme ecclesial expression of a community of the baptised, must be linked to the readings and, normally, the gospel.

   So we need a more sophisticated strategy to provide homilies for the Sundays on which there are parables, which acknowledges the content of the reading, but does not reduce the homily to exegetical notes on particular snippets of text which would be found only of antiquarian value by those members of the community who are not interested in the study of the gospels as such. What follows in these notes, and those of other Sundays (i.e. on Sundays 17, 19, 27, 28, 29, 30, 32), is an attempt to have a preaching strategy that can overarch a wide selection of parable, and parable-like, material.

2. There is a fundamental question that we have to ask ourselves: How do we learn to be Christians?

3. Is that a silly question? Note two specific elements of the form of the question. First, it is not a question about Christianity, but about people. Second, it is not a question about an individual engaged in learning, but about a community engaged in learning.

4. It is very easy to learning about 'what we believe' or about 'what the church believes' or 'what the church teaches.' There are umpteen books, catechisms, and classes on this topic. You will find little booklets on it at the back of the church and posters in the porch advertising courses. It is also easy to find out about 'The Church'. Again, there books on its history, structures, its position as a social force in various societies, it art, customs, architecture, and what not. But all this is learning *about* something. But Jesus calls us to a new life-style, a new way of acting, a new way of life. And one learns how to be and how to live through doing it. Its more like an apprenticeship than a course of studies.

5. The question is how do we learn to be Christians. Most learning is an individual activity, we just happen to do it in a group because there are not enough teachers to go round. So we go to a group evening class to learn French after we have been on a holiday in France. But we worry that our children's class-sizes are too large. We think of learning as *my* learning. But how could you learn to play football on your own? To learn to play football requires slowly building up skills through practice and more practice. But while one can practice one or two little moves on one's own, real practice needs to take place with the team: because it is learning to play together as the team that is the key to success. One cannot say, except as a joke, that 'I won the game; pity that my team lost!'

6. We hear about 'the kingdom' in almost every reading from the gospels. We hear about 'the disciples,' 'the apostles,' and about 'the followers', and in almost every reading from St Paul we hear about 'the church in this or that place' or 'the body of Christ'. In every case we are talking about the groups: the kingdom is the group who have united themselves with Jesus Christ, are given life by the Holy Spirit, and have come into the Father's presence. This is the group we pray for when we say 'thy kingdom come'. The kingdom that is just one individual is a joke!

7. So we have to learn how to be members of this group, the

Christians; and we have to learn how to be this new people, how to live this new lifestyle of Jesus. We have to see ourselves as learning by practice, and working with sisters and brothers (that is why we use these terms about one another) to be 'the kingdom,' 'the church,' 'the People of God.'

8. Today's gospel gives some insights into the tasks facing the group learning to be Christians. First, they have to cope with the fact that the group will not be perfect at this stage of its pilgrimage. It would be nice to be part of a perfect group, but it is the actual community that we must work with, learn to act as a group, learn to act with harmony keeping our minds fixed on the lifestyle of generous, peace-making love. Second, we have to learn to act as a group so that we are like a tiny seed that grows to be a great tree. We must be willing to collaborate to take on the great tasks needed so that the Father's kingdom grows. Third, we have to work as a community to transform situations of injustice and suffering. As yeast turns an unappetising mass of starch into joy-giving, living bread, so must our community act within the society. The world must be a better place because of our community.

9. Learning *about* is easy; Jesus calls his people to learn *to be* his people.

Some 'Defects' in Eucharistic Celebrations

The 1570 Missal contained a list of the 'defects' that could occur during a Mass, assessing each problem, judging whether con-secration had occurred, and giving remedies so that the Mass could be completed successfully. It makes curious reading today partly because some of the defects seem so unlikely (e.g. forget-ting to say the Canon – though I once saw it happen), and partly because its underlying theology takes the notion of 'a work fully done' (*opus operatum*) to extremes. Collectively, its main concern was to ensure the completion of the operation of lawfully chang-ing the bread and wine into the Body and Blood of Christ. If that happened, then Mass had taken place; if not, then nothing had happened, the operation was a failure with collateral legal con-sequence: people deceived by assuming spiritual benefits when there were none, possible materially committed idolatries by worshipping what was still bread, and a stipend taken unjustly. This work could go wrong at several points, and the list of de-fects was to pick out the most serious, and show a way out. A modern analogue to that notion of an *opus operatum* is that of in-stalling a computer programme where, if you have the right ma-chine (the matter) and follow the instructions correctly (the form), on completing your task a message appears such as 'suc-cessful installation', or if something has gone wrong: 'invalid ac-tion.' The 1570 Missal's list of defects was equivalent to the 'trouble shooting' section of a computer manual, and its reme-dies equivalent to 'work arounds'.

However, if that famous list was dropped without comment from the 1970 Missal, that does not mean that defects do not still occur which detract from our Eucharistic celebrations and cause them to give many a false understanding of what we believe. In contrast to the old list which focused on validity, the defects here are small matters in themselves, and all are common to greater or lesser extents. However, taken together they present or perpetuate a view of the Eucharist at odds with the under-standing inherent in the present rite. Equally, they are easily put right.

1. Hiding behind a lectern or the altar

The rite assumes there are three distinct locations: the chair from where the priest presides – it is not a *sedilia* where you just sit down when not doing something; the ambo where the Word is proclaimed during the Liturgy of the Word – it is not a ros-trum/lectern intended for a speaker's notes; and the table for the Liturgy of the Eucharist which is not the focus of attention throughout the celebration. The practice of beginning the cele-bration from the altar harks back to the dynamics of the old rite, and make the Lord's Table into a teacher's desk. Likewise, a lectern balancing the ambo, or using the ambo itself to begin and conclude the Eucharist destroys the unique dignity that is to be given to the place of the Word's proclamation. However, always having a structure (be it table, ambo, or lectern) is bad body language in that it sends out a signal of 'me and them' – it is like the counter in a bank which is designed to separate, it is a barrier between 'first' and 'second class,' the 'ins' and the 'outs'. Opening the celebration, there should be no barriers between president and those celebrating with him. If you do need notes then put them on a card, and use a small missal or leaflet – that you cannot extend your hands for the Opening Prayer without a book-bearer is less of a loss in communication terms than that of having a barrier, however flimsy, between you and the others taking part.

2. Using the Confiteor option

If a Penitential Rite is used – and this is the Missal's second choice for Sundays, then saying the Confiteor is the option remi-niscent of the pre-1970 rite. Because of this, it is for many the de-fault setting. However, using option 'B c' with focused lines in-troducing each 'Lord have mercy' allows the introductory words of welcome and the Penitential Rite to be seamlessly joined together. It allows for the desire for mercy to be linked to the aspect of the mystery of salvation being celebrated or referred to in the readings on that day; and it leads from the welcome to the joy of the Gloria without a jarring note. By contrast, the emphasis on sinfulness contained in the Confiteor, while it fitted well with the old Fore-Mass, does not sit well with the tone of the Introductory Rite. It splits what is said about the mystery being celebrated in the priest's opening remarks from actual prayer, and it often creates a sequence of joy, sin, joy which is not conducive to a reflective mood in preparation for the readings. When you are about the use the Confiteor, ask yourself if the tone of the celebration could not be better expressed using one of the eight forms of option 'B c' in the Missal (pp 391-5), or in one specially composed for the occasion. Three tailored calls for mercy voiced reflectively, with slight pauses between them, are more likely to strike a cord than beating out a formula on the cue of the words 'I confess ...'. Note, also, that this is a place where a member of the assembly, other than the president, can take the lead.

3. Hearing only clerical voices
Many celebrations still silently continue the notion that it is the 'priest's Mass': something done by the priest, who has a server and the congregation in attendance. Such a signal is sent out whenever the only single voice heard is that of the priest. That the Eucharist is a celebration by all present is seen when there are a variety of voices and they are not all clergy or people in robes. A variation on this is when at concelebrations to involve the extra clergy, all other participation disappears. This signals that it is a clerical affair, non-clerics are but substitutes.

4. Hearing and seeing only males
A criticism of Catholicism today is that it does not give women a sufficient role. The parish Eucharist must include women prominently so that they can bring their voices, experience, and presence into the community's celebration. If the procession has

no woman taking part, it signals that all the significant people in this assembly are male. The perception is reinforced if there are no women readers or ministers of the Eucharist. Avoiding such signals must be a conscious element in planning each Sunday Eucharist

5. The Homily: 7-minute maximum

Many of us labour to produce content-rich, 'catchy' homilies; but few are good at pruning to size. A three-minute radio reflection requires more careful crafting that a full lecture. Every idea has to be carefully thought out, the structure that will deliver your point has to be clear in your mind, and many ideas and beautiful images have to die in the waste basket. Yet, such is the average attention span that many people find following words for even three minutes difficult. Short verbal attention spans is just the way it is; we as people of the Word may find that distressing, but we must live with it. Many still have an idea that 10 minutes is a suitable length for a homily, yet when was the last time you listened to a politician's speech for that long? In any case, if you preach for more than 7 minutes at a parish Eucharist the length of the homily unbalances the length of the Liturgy of the Word, turning it into a short lecture preceded by some bits of reading: unless the Psalm is sung, the readings rarely take more than five minutes. Certainly, if you preach more that 10 minutes you unbalance the rhythm of the whole celebration so that it is a Liturgy of the Word with the Liturgy of the Eucharist tacked on.

Some believe their congregations would not accept such short homilies! Two points: first, such anecdotes are meaningless if they come from a handful of people at the door after Mass; to have any worth they must be based on a some numerically tested research covering the sweep of the parish or a particular Mass-time's congregation. Second, if you have a congregation that is steadily asking for more of your insights: rejoice, for truly you are a blessed man.

6. The Prayer of the Faithful

This Prayer is not just a time for shared prayers or the equivalent of the old practice of reading out some of the petitions of those taking part in a novena. When the people of God come together for the Eucharist they become a priestly people who in virtue of that priesthood make intercession for themselves, the wider church, the entire human family, and the whole of creation. See Missal, p xxix, n 45. It is not a Sunday addition, but something that should be in all parish celebrations. Omitting it regularly in parish weekday celebrations is certainly a defect in our Eucharistic understanding. Omitting it on Sunday is something for an emergency. Recently, when I asked a friend why he omitted it in a parish on Sunday he replied that he had not had time to make one up! In such situations, just use one of the exemplars in the Missal (pp 995-1004). Occasional use of these shows the correct form this priestly act should take. The quaint term 'Bidding Prayers' should be allowed to disappear. It does not bring out the specific corporate nature of this prayer, and in using 'prayers' it emphasises the idea of a list of requests rather than a single formal act of intercession.

7. Notices in the Middle of the Celebration

The collection is a necessary part of the celebration, but it is best carried out between the Liturgy of the Word and that of the Eucharist. At that point it can provide a hiatus between the parts and emphasise the move from word to sacrament, from ambo to altar, from one table to another. But if the time is then filled with an assortment of notices it becomes a jagged period, non-time, and something that introduces a note of unquiet into the celebration when we would actually want a new note of focus and concentration. That this is so can be observed in the amount of shuffling and 'noise' in the church. After the Prayer of the Faithful, the collection can take place with the minimum of disturbance if it is seen as a time to just sit for moment 'between things', the ear can be pleased by instrumental music or a choir piece, but not with a hymn (such as those which accompany processions of gifts) indicating that the Liturgy of the Eucharist has already begun. If action is needed, then this could be a time for the preparation of the altar by putting the cloth, candles, and a book upon it.

The Missal assumes that notices will be read just before the final blessing along with the priest's final words. Since these are about things other than the Eucharist itself, they are wholly disruptive if read earlier in the celebration. It is worth noting that the bad habit of reading them soon after the homily is another legacy from pre-1970 where the preacher in the pulpit was not the celebrant, and since the former did all the bits and pieces other than say the Mass, it fell to him to read the notices and the banns while there.

8. Keeping your prayers to yourself

The present liturgy runs the risk of becoming too wordy: words, words, and more words. Changes in rhythm, pace, sound and silence are becoming rarer. That being so, the practice of reciting the private prayers of the priest for himself (1) before the gospel, (2) after the blessings over the bread and wine, and (3) before receiving communion just destroys the last moments of silence that can help pace the liturgy.

9. Bells

In the old rite the server watched out for the priest extending his hands over the offerings (when reciting in silence the text *Hanc igitur* [= Father accept]) and its purpose was not to give a heightened sense of importance to that text, but practical. At a *missa cantata* once the preface was finished the choir began the *Sanctus*. However, the priest did not wait for them but recited the whole *Sanctus* himself and proceeded with the Canon. The first bell was to tell the choir to stop, there and then, or they would hold the priest up since they could not sing during the consecration. Then after the second elevation the choir proceeded to sing the *Benedictus*. Hence, in older musical settings there is a distinction made between the *Sanctus* and the *Benedictus* which seems strange to modern ears as we always recite or sing a single text.

This bell is now meaningless, and a simple interruption in the Eucharistic Prayer for several reasons. First, choirs no long need this information; second, the extension of the hands has now been moved in Eucharistic Prayer I from the *Hang igitur* to the *Quam oblationem* [= Bless and approve]; third, in the other Eucharistic Prayers it is noise at the moment when we call by name for the gentle descent of the Spirit.

The communion bell was there to indicate that this was a Mass with a 'lay communion' (an extra rite after the priest's communion pre-1962) and since only the server could hear what point the priest had reached, it was necessary to signal the congregation when to approach the rails. Since a communion rite for all present is integral to the 1970 rite, and it assumes people can hear, see and understand the priest, the need for this bell is removed.

As to the 'elevation' bells, while they do not fit with the modern liturgy, their removal can provoke more trouble than their abolition is worth. However, neither should anything be done against helping these bells moving towards oblivion.

10. The 'elevation'
The old rite demanded that the priest raise both Bread and Cup high over the head so that they became visible. Now that we face the congregation this is no longer necessary. By continuing the older practice we ignore that 'the elevation' is not a feature of the rite any longer. The consecrated elements are to be shown to the people, and this is followed by the moment of adoration. That is far better achieved by holding the elements outwards at shoulder level in a gesture of showing, rather than a gesture of stretching upwards as if mimicking some act of 'sacrifice' to on high.

In some places, although on steadily fewer occasions, the older military salutes – drawn swords, flags dipped, bugles – are still found, even if only sloppily by a few boy scouts. Are these really appropriate to the intimate meal of those whom Christ calls his friends? It certainly represents a view of the Eucharistic Prayer's structure that is without any foundation in the Missal.

The common feature running through most of these defects is that they represent a failure to think through the differences demanded by the 1970 Missal in the way we act. As such they are old bad habits re-establishing themselves and preventing the adequate celebration of what we formally declare we want to do when we assemble for the Eucharist.

Seventeenth Sunday of Ordinary Time

CELEBRANT'S GUIDE

Introduction to the Celebration
When we gather here each Sunday we are not simple a scattering of individuals, but a family who are brothers and sisters in Christ Jesus. He has called each of us, and transformed us from being isolated individuals into being a community: his body. Now as that community he wants us to gather about his table and share in his one loaf and one cup. By doing this he is sharing his life with us, and we are showing our willingness to share our lives with one another.

Rite of Penance
Option c ii (Missal, p 392) is appropriate.

Headings for Readings
First Reading
Solomon is held out to us as an ideal: he was dedicated to the wisdom and law of the Lord above all things.

Second Reading
We are gathered here as sisters and brothers. In this reading we hear Paul telling us that Jesus is the Son of God and our elder brother.

Gospel
We are called to be dedicated to living in the way of the Lord above all else.

Prayer of the Faithful
President
Gathered here in Christ, let us ask the Father to help us to learn how to be disciples.

Reader(s)
1. For all who describe themselves with the name 'Christian': that we will recognise our need to work with others if we are to discover God's love for each. Lord hear us.
2. For the whole church of God across the world: that we will grow in love of one another and work for that unity for which Jesus prayed. Lord hear us.
3. For all the communities of Christians: that the Spirit will remove internal factions, heal old wounds, and give us a new energy for collaboration. Lord hear us.
4. For this community gathered at this sacred banquet: that sharing here in the Lord's loaf and cup will strengthen us to work together as a community in the coming week. Lord hear us.
5. Specific local needs and topics of the day.
6. For all who have gone before us marked with the sign of faith: that we will all be, one day, reunited in the community of heaven.
President
Father, your Son came to form us into a new people united in him. Hear these prayers, for we make them not as a collection of individuals but as the holy body of Jesus Christ, your Son, our Lord. Amen.

Eucharistic Prayer
No preface or Eucharistic Prayer is particularly appropriate.

Invitation to the Our Father
The kingdom of heaven is like a treasure hidden in a field, like a pearl of great price. Let us pray now for its coming:

Sign of Peace
The kingdom of heaven is like a treasure hidden in a field, like a pearl of great price, and it is the kingdom of true peace. Let us declare our willingness to live by its standards.

Invitation to Communion
He calls us to this banquet; he invites us to share our lives with
one another; he offers to share his life with us; happy are we to
be his people.

Communion Reflection
The Lord Jesus has called us to this banquet;
The Lord Jesus has invited us to share our lives with one another;
The Lord Jesus has shared his life with us;
The Lord Jesus sends us from his table to be his presence.

Conclusion
May the Father who has created us as a human family empower
us to act with love towards all our sisters and brothers during
this week. Amen.
May the Son who has gathered us here and united us as his body
teach us to work together as his presence on earth during the
coming week. Amen.
May the Spirit who gives life and reconciliation energise us to
act together, bringing harmony and reconciliation during the
coming week. Amen.

Notes
Today's gospel is a collection of four images presented one after
the other. Any one of them is enough to 'give a headline' for a
congregation, many of whom are convinced that the readings
are a kind of 'thought for the day.' However, Matthew intended
them to be read as a sequence, and the simple fact is that one
cannot have a 'one image fits all' theology. So go for the longer
version, conscious that no matter how many ways we try to describe the mystery, there will still be one more image that may
add some wee bit more to our understanding: *Deus semper maior*.

COMMENTARY

First Reading: 1 Kings 3:5, 7-12
The ideal ruler in Egypt was the just king (in arbitrating disputes) who was also the perfect expression of the ideal civil servant/scribe/man of wisdom. Wisdom was not simply our philosophical notion, but the possession of proverbial lore of statecraft. In this part of 1 Kings we are reading the hagiography of Solomon as an ideal for any king of Israel; therefore he is a model of 'wisdom' but receives this as a direct gift from the Lord (not as an automatic consequence of his ritual possession of the kingship).

Psalm: 118 (119)
If one reads the first reading as an example of dedication to the Lord's Law above all else, then this psalm expresses that notion in prayer.

Second Reading: Rom 8:28-30
Paul's argument at this point in the letter is that those who belong to the church are in a completely new human society: not only are they human images of God (the gift of creation), but they are images of Christ (the gift of the new creation). And this new identity transforms their own relations within the community: they are now brothers – a radically new idea in any highly stratified ancient society based on privileges and the *cursus honorum* – and within this egalitarian society they even have a relationship with the Son of God.

We should note, however, that Paul only thinks of being 'brothers' within this new society, and so we should silently alter the text to 'brothers and sisters'. While undoubtedly some of the self-appointed guardians of antiquity in the congregation will see this as 'unwarranted meddling', we must recognise that these texts are read to help us celebrate now, not as an invocation of antiquity.

First Reading > Gospel Links
The link depends on reading the first reading as a moral tale about Solomon's dedication (a notion reinforced in the psalm): he is dedicated to the wisdom of the Lord above all else; likewise should the person who has discovered the kingdom be dedicated to it. So the first reading is a moral example of the activity demanded in the gospel.

Gospel: Mt 13:44-52 (shorter version 13:44-46)
These four parables are only found in Matthew, and make the same point using different ranges of imagery. Used together they make the point that no set of images can capture the unique relationship that draws each of us towards the k ingdom. They pose us the task of asking what ranges of images we, as different individuals and as communities, would chose to express the unique relationship that God establishes with us.

HOMILY NOTES

1. How do we learn to be Christians?
2. We learn to be Christians by long periods of apprenticeship: working in groups at being the presence of Jesus in our ways of thinking, playing, working, and living. Just as you can only learn to be a pilgrim by setting out with a group of pilgrims, so you can only learn how to move on the pilgrimage of life by travelling and acting with other Christians.
3. The kingdom is the group of people; and each of us has to see working with the group as a treasure we desire to own. Learning to be a Christian involves recognising that working as part of the group must have priority over our tendency to wander off to work as isolated individuals.
4. Take our gathering here today. We learn to pray together with one voice as a priestly people. We commit ourselves to working for peace. We learn to share our talents. We learn to share our joys and sorrows. Contrast that with spiritualistic individualism. This is the notion that I do not have to join with others to pray, I can pray on my own, I can be spiritual

on my own. Interesting sentiments that are true as far as they go – but they do not go very far.

Jesus did not come with to sell ideas to individuals, but to form a community. We can only learn to pray *as* that community by praying *with* that community. Jesus did not invent a set of rituals for several individuals, but wanted his people to have the ethos of sharing among themselves. Indeed, the very heart of his community is mirrored in the sharing of a family around the meal table.

5. If I want to learn to be a Christian, then I must commit myself to gathering with the group, to praying with the group, to sharing my talents and resources with the group, and collectively we must share them with the poor.

6. Even when I pray on my own, I must remember that I pray as part of the community. Even alone I pray 'Our Father' not 'my Father'; even alone I pray that the Father 'give us this day our daily bread' not that he give me my needs; I pray 'forgive us our trespasses' not just that he forgive me mine; I pray that 'as we forgive those who trespass against us,' so he should forgive us; and I pray that he does not 'lead us into temptation.'

7. Discovering that I can become truly the person God wishes me to be is a pearl of great price, but that in turn demands that we learn to live and work in loving communities. Such communities of love mirror within the creation the community of love that is the Father, the Son, and the Spirit.

Lectionary Unit V

This unit comprises Sundays 18-24, and its focus is on God's Kingdom on earth – the church of Christ.

There are five Sundays devoted to narrative:

Sunday 18: the feeding of the five thousand;

Sunday 19: Jesus walking on water;

Sunday 20: the healing/exorcism of the Canaanite woman's daughter;

Sunday 21: Peter's confession of Jesus's identity (and to which the lectionary adds the comment 'the primacy conferred'); and

Sunday 22: discipleship and the prophecy of the passion.

This set of five Sundays has less unity than the other units in this Year's lectionary, and the sequence of three Sundays each with a miracle story poses its own difficulties.

The remaining Sundays' gospels (Sundays 23 and 24) are seen as discourse: the Community Sermon.

Eighteenth Sunday of Ordinary Time

CELEBRANT'S GUIDE

Introduction to the Celebration

Today we recall one of the great miracles of Jesus: a large group came to hear him and he saw their need and fed them with five loaves and two fish. We might look back and think that that is just a story, yet here we are today being fed by him at his table. We might look back and think that things like that do not happen, yet here are we who still look to him for the bread of life to give us strength and hope in our lives. We might look back and think of the miracles as just fables, yet we too gather today to listen to his teaching as the word of life.

Rite of Penance

> Lord Jesus, you feed your people with the word of life. Lord have mercy.
> Lord Jesus, you feed your people with the bread of life. Christ have mercy.
> Lord Jesus, you feed your people with the food of eternal life. Lord have mercy.

Headings for Readings

First Reading

The prophet tells of the time when God will care abundantly for his people: then the poor will feast from the generosity of God.

Second Reading

God's love for us is greater and more constant than anything else in the universe.

Gospel

When Jesus saw the large crowd he took pity on them, he taught them, he healed their sick, and he fed them with the food of life.

Prayer of the Faithful

President

We have assembled here to eat and drink at the Lord's table and, gathered here in union with the Christ, we must now ask the Father to bless us, those around us, and the whole of humanity with his gifts.

Reader(s)

1. That the church throughout the world may rejoice in the food that comes from the Lord's table. Lord hear us.

2. That people everywhere may find in the gospel the words of truth and life. Lord hear us.

3. That those who have wealth and resources may know their obligations to share with all who are hungry. Lord hear us.

4. That all of us may learn to use our individual gifts to serve this community. Lord hear us.

5. Specific local needs and topics of the day.

6. That all who have shared in the Lord's table in this life may share in the banquet of heaven. Lord hear us.

President

Father, your Son raised his eyes to you in prayer and you answered him. We now raise our eyes and voices to you in our needs. Answer us for we pray in union with Jesus your Son, our Lord. Amen.

Eucharistic Prayer

There is no specific preface or Eucharistic Prayer that is particularly appropriate for today.

Invitation to the Our Father

Jesus raised his eyes to heaven and prayed to the Father. Now let us pray to the Father as we say:

Sign of Peace

Jesus made the multitude that listened to him into the new community of peace; he now makes us into that community. Let us reflect his gift by exchanging signs of peace with one another.

Invitation to Communion
The Lord fed the multitudes with the five loaves he broke for
them; he now feeds us with this loaf which he has broken for us.
Lord I am not worthy … .

Communion Reflection
If you have had a proper fraction, then offer this as a reflection:
The cup of blessing which we bless,
is it not a participation in the blood of Christ?
The loaf which we break,
is it not a participation in the body of Christ?
Because there is one loaf,
we who are many are one body,
for we all partake of the one loaf. *(1 Cor 10:16-17)*

Conclusion
Solemn Blessing 12 (Ordinary Time III) is appropriate.

Notes
This is one of the days when the gospel refers to one of the central eucharistic actions: 'blessing' the Father (i.e. what we refer to
as the Eucharistic Prayer) and 'breaking the loaves'. So this is a
day when that emphasis can be brought out clearly. If you cannot get an altar bread which is large enough to be broken for the
whole assembly to share in just one of them, then you may be
able to procure breads that are large enough that five of them
would supply the needs of the community. If so, then draw attention to this and have a proper fraction (which takes time),
making it obvious that all are sharers in the loaf/loaves.

COMMENTARY

First Reading: Isa 55:1-3
These are the opening verses of the final part of Second-Isaiah. It
looks forward to a time when Zion will be comforted, and cared
for directly by the Lord. All the good things will be in abund-
ance, and there will be the new covenant that replaces that based

on trading and selfishness: all will share in the gracious generosity of God, and this will be the pattern for the perfect society.

Psalm: 144 (145)

This psalm was chosen as it continues the theme of the generosity of God, which is beyond any notion of meriting by the creatures. It is God's love for his creatures that is the source of his generosity.

Second Reading: Rom 8:35, 37-39

The key to this passage is the verse that is, quite inexplicably, omitted! Paul reflects on his sufferings and those of the whole church – which might indeed have some notion that they should have the most pleasant of lives if they are the ones chosen by God – and tells the Christians that part of being in Christ is that they share in his paschal reality of dying and rising. But such is this relationship with Christ that nothing can break it.

First Reading > Gospel Links

The choice of the first reading and the psalm show that the lectionary planners read Mt 14 primarily as an example of the divine generosity – which of course it is – but without linking that generosity to its liturgical, and kergymatic, expression: the Eucharist. Read simply as the miraculous expression of God's loving care for his people, then the relation with the first reading is one of promise – fulfilment in terms of the coming of the Christ. But in so far as the gospel is a miracle story, the lectionary planners were thinking in terms of both readings having an eschatological link: the first reading looks forward to the time when God's care will be complete, so too does the gospel in that the miracle is but a foretaste of the Final Times, so both are one in continuity as God's enduring promise, brought 'closer' in the Christ. However, some of these more complex 'senses of scripture' (i.e. strategies for seeing links between Old and New Testaments) are very far from the understanding of most people today.

Gospel: Mt 14:13-21

The story of a miraculous feeding must have been part of the very earliest preaching of the gospel. We know this because by the time of the first gospel which has come down to us, Mark, the story has changed its details and been duplicated in the preaching memory of the church and so we find it in Mk 6 and again in Mk 9. Matthew then follows this as here and then again in Mt 15; while both Mk (8:19-20) and Mt (16:9-10) have echoes of the story drawing out its significance. The story also figures in Lk 9 and in Jn 6. In all these cases the story is inexplicable apart from the evangelists' theologies of the Eucharist. This is more obviously the case in Luke and John and, as such, is a demonstration that the story's original context in the kerygma was in terms of drawing out the meaning of the meal of the Christians. That the story has lodged itself so firmly in the preached gospels is, therefore, not in the least surprising in that all these gospels were first heard at the very assemblies for the churches' meals that were the subject of the story.

Therefore, here we have one of the strange moments in the liturgy when what we read refers to the very event at which we read it, and when we read it at a celebration of the Eucharist we read it in the context of its first preaching.

It is worth noting the very last line of the gospel today, to note just how different our culture is from that of the early church. The gospel counts men, males, five thousand of them; women and children, literally, didn't count! For most of our history, and indeed still for many cultures, that situation did not raise an eyebrow! However, can you imagine that today? Can you imagine saying that women (or indeed children) do not count simply because of what they are? It is worth drawing attention to this point as many in the gathering will pick it up; and failing to acknowledge the gap in attitudes on the public significance of women between the early church and our own is just to attract the accusation of being obscurantist.

HOMILY NOTES

1. Miracles cause embarrassment within our world. The miraculous is suspected as fraud or foolishness; those who accept them as the gullible. Indeed, the whole study of the scriptures has been linked with the case for or against miracles: can one accept the teaching of the scriptures, yet leave this whole miraculous dimension parked somewhere either out of sight or somewhere it will not provoke questions such as 'Do you think that actually happened?' The problem is that so long as we read the primary stories of the tradition, we will encounter miracle stories like this one. So how do we react?

2. First, we must be honest about our own discomfort with such questions. Many people who grow up within the faith, when they begin to question, hear us refer to these miracles (without noting our discomfort or even admitting how they are not harmonious with our sense of rationality) just abandon belief on the secularist assumption that miracles are the province of the simple-minded and such 'beliefs' are endemic to religion, so the whole should be abandoned as a fairytale. For anyone today, such stories as are found in today's gospel should raise eyebrows.

3. Why do we find miracle stories a problem anyway? Most people in our society use a very simple model of what constitutes 'truth.' Truth is no more and no less than what can be observed by the senses directly. This model of truth has replaced the classical, medieval, renaissance, and now even the Marxist ways of viewing reality. This is not expressed by the average person as they go about the shopping in terms of a theory of verification; it is expressed far more concretely with something like: 'Well if I were there on that lakeside with Jesus what would I have seen? Would I have been able to video it if there were videos?' If the answer is no, then it is 'just a story' (and we know that when something is just a story, then it is lies). If truth is just what you can video, then meaning, values, belonging (at the lower level), justice,

beauty and love (at a higher level), and the mystery of God interacting with us (at the highest level) are all just stories.

4. Whenever we encounter their more precious aspects of life we know that they are more than we can see or touch or taste, yet we only meet them amidst the fractured moments of daily existence. So to bring out the significant within the everyday our memory extracts, combines, and presents the meaning in restructured historical narrative. We all know this in our everyday lives when we try to make sense of experience by highlighting, dramatising, and exaggerating some aspects of the past so that the structure of meaning stands out. Here lies the role of the miracle story for it is the memory, here that of the community, restructuring events to bring out meaning. Nowhere is this gift more needed than in seeking to speak of the mysteries of God, and for us whose faith is founded in the Word made flesh this means that we express the totality of our beliefs about Jesus in stories anchored (on the one hand) in times and places, yet (on the other hand) greater in their dimensions than the scope of normal space and time. Such memories, elucidating the mystery of the Son of God who is the man Jesus, are our miracle stories. We need stories bigger than what our videos can record for mysteries bigger than our physical senses.

5. So what aspect of the mystery of the presence of the Word made flesh are Matthew, the churches who heard him, the later churches that read him down to this assembly today, remembering in the miracle of the feeding of the 5000 men? This is the genuine question we are called to reflect on and believe, not the question of the video camera.

6. Just look at what the scene involves. We have a people gathered. They are listening to Jesus and being taught by him. We have people wanting food. We have loaves. We have Jesus blessing the Father (i.e. he offers a prayer of thanksgiving to the Father for the gift of the food; and note that he blesses God, not the loaves). Then Jesus breaks the loaves. And from a few loaves a whole multitude was able to eat as much as they wanted.

7. Here we have the mystery of our own gathering: it is no ordinary feeding, no ordinary meal. It is with Jesus we have gathered, not just us but communities in literally thousands upon thousands of gatherings at the same time. Yet all are hearing the same Jesus, and being taught by him, and are with him as he offers the prayer of thanksgiving to the Father – just look at the words we will use with regard to our bread: 'Blessed are you Lord, God of all creation … ' – and all of us are going to eat the loaf broken by him.

8. If we realise we have to expand our minds to take in the meaning of the miracle in today's gospel, we will see that we have to expand our minds in just the same way to take in the mystery we are celebrating in our gathering today.

Nineteenth Sunday of Ordinary Time

Introduction to the Celebration

We live in a world that is shot-through with the glory of God. The Father has made us for himself that we might praise him; the Son has come among us to lead us towards the fullness of life; the Spirit dwells within us to enlighten our minds to the mystery that is greater than all we can see, touch, and taste. Part of living a Christian life is becoming attuned to this presence. This is the focus of our reflection today as we gather to en-counter Jesus in our common meal. But in this encounter we recognise that God is greater than all creation and is the very source of our being.

Rite of Penance

Lord Jesus, Son of God, we gather here in your name. Lord have mercy.

Lord Jesus, Son of God, we seek your company and your friendship. Christ have mercy.

Lord Jesus, Son of God, we ask for your help and salvation. Lord have mercy.

Headings for Readings

First Reading

In this reading and later in the gospel we hear of extraordinary encounters with God: Elijah knows of God's presence in the sound of a gentle breeze after an earthquake; and because he then is in the divine presence he covers his eyes.

Second Reading

Paul wants to remind his gentile Christians that they are not to think that because God now has made them his people, that he has abandoned the people he chose at the time of the patriarchs.

It is not a case of God swapping 'favourites', but extending the range of those who can call on him by name.

Gospel
Peter recognises Jesus coming towards the boat on the water, yet despite his lack of faith can call out for mercy, and in the process discover that Jesus is the Lord of creation.

Prayer of the Faithful
Use Sample Formula 1 (Missal, p 995).

Eucharistic Prayer
The notion of the sequence of covenants mentioned in the second reading means that this is a Sunday on which Eucharistic Prayer IV is suitable.

Invitation to the Our Father
As the daughters and sons of the Father by adoption, let us pray:

Sign of Peace
The Lord Jesus has brought us salvation and peace. Let us celebrate that peace with one another.

Invitation to Communion
The Lord calls us to come to him now at his table as he once called Peter to come to him over the water. Happy are we to be in the presence of the Son of God.

Communion Reflection
The Lord Jesus calls us into his presence.
The Lord Jesus shares his table with us.
The Lord Jesus gives us his life.

The Lord Jesus offers our thanks to the Father.
The Lord Jesus carries our praise to the Father.
The Lord Jesus presents us to the Father.

The Lord Jesus empowers us with his Spirit.
The Lord Jesus sends us out to be his disciples.
The Lord Jesus awaits us at the End.

Conclusion
Solemn Blessing 11, Ordinary Time II (Missal, p 372) is appropriate.

Notes
Liturgy Planning Groups, quite naturally, like to have clear and consistent themes running through the variable parts of each liturgy: this not only allows for some sensitive planning of hymns, decorations, activities, but it is very sound communications theory. Any event that tries to communicate too many ideas or a jumble of a few ideas, usually ends up communicating nothing in particular. However, on every Sunday in Ordinary Time the presence of the epistle reading – always Paul in Year A – frustrates cohesion (by coming between the first reading and the gospel) and consistency (by having no thematic connection with them). For such planning groups, today is going to be especially frustrating because the second reading is actually long enough to express a distinctive theological theme, whereas on many Sundays it is little more than a pious soundbite. Moreover, it breaks up the very clear theme of theophany linking the first reading and the gospel. This is a day to consider omitting the second reading.

COMMENTARY

First Reading: 1 Kings 19:9; 11-3
This is one of the 'classic' theophany texts in the scriptures, and indeed its memory was influential among the followers of Jesus in forming the theophany we read in the gospel today. The recipient is an individual, but as a prophet is intended within the story to be remembered as representing the whole community to whom he is sent. There is a display of nature's powers, but 'the Lord' – not just our name 'God', but God whose very own

name we know although we refer to him as 'the Lord', is not to be identified with any of these forces. Because the Lord is greater than all of them, indeed transcending all of them, his presence is, in comparison to them, a stillness. This stillness beyond the whole might of the universe must not be seen as just one further element within the universe (such a reading misses the dynamic of the theophany story), but that the Lord is beyond all the forces of the universe (and not just its loudest, biggest bit). This is negative theology in narrative.

Psalm: 84 (85)
Having accepted the theophany, we can now relate to 'the Lord' in prayer.

Second Reading: Rom 9:1-5
This is the opening section of the next step (which runs from 9:1 to 11:36) within Paul's much larger chain of reasoning in Romans. In these verses he is concentrating on showing that the new life offered in Jesus does not contradict the promises already made by God to Israel.

First Reading > Gospel Links
This is a perfect combination: the classic theophany from the Old Covenant is read with the classic theophany from the New Relationship. Together there is the continuity of the Lord revealing himself as beyond the universe (the continuity link); between them there is the contrast that in the first there is the voice of God, in the second there is the man Jesus who enters the boat (the anticipation-fulfilment link).

Gospel: Mt 14:22-33
This story, found in its longest form here, was an important item in the early kergyma for it is found in both Mark (6:45-52) and in John (6:15-21). In its basic form it is a theophany where Jesus is the one revealed and those in the boat, 'the disciples' (a word whose choice implies that we have to think of the whole group

of followers), are the recipients. The content of the theophany is the divine identity of Jesus as the one who is unaffected by the winds (within the mythic system of the time this is the hostile forces within the world) and the waves of death (an image found in the scriptures). The theophany centre lies in hearing the words 'It is I' and then accepting that Jesus enters the boat. By being a stillness greater than all the forces of nature, Jesus is identified with the Lord; but he identifies with the disciples (not simply by being heard by them for that would be just the voice of God) but by entering the boat with them.

In Matthew there is an intrusion of four verses into the story which give special prominence to Peter (vv 28-31). This fits with Matthew's tendency to highlight the special position of Peter with The Twelve. However, it is a secondary theme within the miracle story and distracts from its clarity as a theophany.

HOMILY NOTES

1. How do we learn to be Christians? The most common answer to that question is to say something like this: 'I will
   study the teachings of Jesus and see if I believe them. If I
   think they are true, I shall then be a believer' (while subcon-
   sciously adding: and if I call myself a believer in Jesus's message, then I will be called a Christian).
2. The problem with this is that Jesus is not just a religious wise
   man who offers us teachings. We do not simply believe his
   teaching, we believe in him. To believe in him is to believe
   that he is the Anointed, the Son of God. We do not simple believe that what he said is true, but we believe that he *is* the
   truth.
3. The church's message is not just a set of teachings that he has
   given us; the teaching of his followers is that Jesus *is* the message of the Father to all humanity. Our teaching is Jesus: that
   he is the Christ.
4. The task we face is to learn to live in Jesus, to live in a style
   that is consistent with affirming our basic teaching as
   Christians: that Jesus is the way to the Father.

5. This is the challenge that lies behind today's gospel. It is not
    just enough to listen to Jesus, we have to get out of our security
    zone and go to him, to commit ourselves to him, to trust him.
    To learn to be a Christian is to learn to behave with an obedi-
    ent trust that amidst life's difficulties and fears, he is the sav-
    iour.

6. The challenge of the gospel is not to ask whether you think it
    happened, or indeed whether or not you think it could hap-
    pen. Such questions are not questions about faith, but about
    history or physics. The challenge is that each of us, and all of
    us as a community, has to be prepared to leave our boat and
    venture toward Jesus. It is only in going toward him in trust
    that we discover who he truly is.

7. In a moment we will stand up and profess our faith. Note
    that we do not subscribe to a series of teachings or ideas
    which we might call 'the teachings of Jesus'. Rather, we pro-
    fess that we believe in Jesus, and we believe him to be the Son
    of God in union with the whole church. We believe him to be
    the Son who has shown us the Father, and who has sent us
    the Spirit who gives us life.

8. Now, let us assert together through the power of the Spirit,
    who transforms us from being a bunch of individuals in the
    church, that we are the people who believe that Jesus is the
    Christ, the Son of God, who comes from the Father.

Twentieth Sunday of Ordinary Time

CELEBRANT'S GUIDE

Introduction to the Celebration

When we gather each Sunday to celebrate being the People of God, we address Jesus as 'our Saviour'. But we often forget that the basic image of 'saviour' is that Jesus came to bring healing. We are addressing Jesus as the one we look to for healing, health, and wholeness. This aspect of the ministry of the Christ is brought out in today's gospel when a woman calls on him as 'Lord' and 'Son of David' asking him to heal her daughter.

So just like that woman long ago who asked Jesus for healing, during our gathering today we shall keep our need for healing in mind in our prayer.

We all need, in one way or another, healing for our bodies when afflicted with pain, we need healing for our minds when they are distressed or embittered, and we need healing for our spirits which become damaged by sin. To encounter Jesus is to encounter the Father's gift of wholeness. Let us pray now that we shall share in it through this Eucharist.

Rite of Penance

O Lord, Son of David, you come bringing us healing. Lord have mercy.

O Lord, Son of David, you come bringing us forgiveness. Christ have mercy.

O Lord, Son of David, you come bringing us peace. Lord have mercy.

Headings for Readings

First Reading

The whole of humanity can come before God and ask for his mercy.

Second Reading
The divine mercy reaches out to every human being.

Gospel
A woman professes her faith in Jesus as the one whom God promised to send to Israel to bring healing and reconciliation.

Prayer of the Faithful
President
All of us who call on the name of Jesus as our Saviour, our healer, know that in some way or other we are in need of the gifts of healing, wholeness, reconciliation, and renewal. So now standing before the Father, and in union with Jesus, let us intercede for ourselves, our absent sisters and brothers, and all humanity.
Reader(s)
1. For all who are sick in body, that the Lord may give them healing. Lord hear us.
2. For all who are sick in mind, that the Lord may restore them. Lord hear us.
3. For all who are sick in spirit, that Lord may grant them forgiveness and hope. Lord hear us.
4. For all who seek wholeness in their lives, that the Lord may grant them an awareness of his love. Lord hear us.
5. For those who are sick in this community, especially ... ... who have asked our prayers. Lord hear us.
6. For all who care for the sick, that the Lord will give them strength, patience, and joyfulness. Lord hear us.
President
Father, you sent your Son to bring healing to suffering humanity; hear the prayer we make to you in union with him, and grant us healing, pardon, and peace. Amen.

Eucharistic Prayer
Use the Preface from the Rite of Anointing within Mass (Pastoral Care of the Sick, p 114) and Eucharistic Prayer 2 with the special insert (Pastoral Care of the Sick, p 115).

Invitation to the Our Father
With God there is healing, mercy and the fullness of redemption. Let us pray as Jesus taught us:

Sign of Peace
If we are to be healed and become whole we must overcome bitterness, divisions, and seek out the way of peace. If you are ready to embark on this process, then offer your neighbours the sign of peace.

Invitation to Communion
Behold the Lamb of God who takes away the sins of the world, brings us healing, offers us the gift of wholeness, and grants us peace.

Communion Reflection
The Prayer of St Thomas Aquinas from the 'Preparation for Mass' prayers (Missal, p 1018) can also be use as a reflection. It is appropriate today as Thomas presents the Eucharist as medicine to heal our infirmities.

If there is not a formal sending out of eucharistic ministers with particles of the Eucharist to the sick and housebound at this point as a formal part of the Sunday liturgy, then this is a good occasion to introduce the practice in some way. This care of those sisters and brothers who cannot join the common meal by sending the Eucharist to them can be traced back to, at least, the mid-second century and is a precious part of our whole eucharistic practice, stressing the role of the Eucharist in bonding us together to become the community of loving care that should be the church.

Conclusion
Solemn Blessing A (Pastoral Care of the Sick, p 117).

Notes

Today's gospel has a remarkable ability to generate distracting questions. The first reaction of most people when they hear it is to question whether or not demons exist. Then if they do exist, to wonder about such matters as exorcism, possession, and a host of questions more closely related to the horror film business than the gospel. Then there are the attempts to rationalise the story and say that the demon is really a psychosis or some form of mental illness. If that is the case, then there are the questions about how sick people have been cruelly and, indeed horribly, treated down the centuries by people who were hunting demons or engaging in 'deliverance ministry'. Such behaviour (and it still occurs in some communities today) is the unaccept-able face of Christianity. Indeed, there are many social workers and mental health practitioners who would earnestly wish that Christians would drop all talk of possession by demons, espec-ially of children being possessed by demons, because of the damage it causes. So the very act of reading this gospel, when we do not know how those who hear it will react to it, must be seen as a rather risky affair. The good news of God's love is not proclaimed if some unbalanced person in the congregation starts to think of her/his child, who may be behaving in some unusual way, as possessed, and who then seeks to 'drive out the demon' from the child.

Even leaving aside the attraction of the bizarre and the para-normal, this pericope attracts other questions such as how did the woman know that she should go to Jesus, why was he so 'hard' as to liken helping her daughter to throwing bread needed for children to the dogs? Is the divine mercy so restricted? These questions cannot be answered in a couple of minutes as they touch upon the structure of the gospel's preaching in the first communities. But our inability to give simple and coherent an-swers brings the whole gospel into disrepute.

This presents the president of the assembly with a question: in this actual community (for this is a practical question that can-not be answered in the abstract) will reading a text about a little girl possessed by a demon be likely to upset people and, through distraction, lead them astray. This judgement must take account of the overall educational standards of the community, its economic status, the presence of immigrants from cultures where cults for 'deliverance from demons' are common-place. If it is likely to cause unhealthy interest in demonic possession or likely to be used as a 'proof' that such demonic possession occurs, then it is perhaps better not to use this gospel and to use the next three verses of Matthew (Mt 15:29-31) which have been omitted from the lectionary. These three verses form a well-defined unit in the gospel, are concerned with healing (and so fit the overall structure of the Year of Matthew), but have no reference to demonic possession.

If today's gospel is read, then (given that it is impossible to convey a nuanced theology of demons in the normal course of the Eucharistic liturgy) it is best to ignore the demon references altogether and make the theme of the whole liturgy the universal need for healing.

COMMENTARY

First Reading: Isa 56:1, 6-7
This section of Third-Isaiah imagines the time of the Anointed One as the time when the whole of humanity, 'the foreigners,' can have access to God through being able to take part in the Temple's liturgy. It bases itself on the notion that the God of Israel is not a sectional god, but the God of all creation, and that his mercy is unbounded. The whole of humanity can by faith enter into the promises of the Lord and become part of the holy people.

Psalm: 66 (67)
This psalm picks up the theme of the first reading and offers a link towards how that theme is developed in the gospel. All nations shall have access to 'the face of God' and the kerygma shall spread outwards to the ends of the earth.

Second Reading: Rom 11:13-15, 29-32

This lection is really two separate thoughts simply butted to-gether; as such one cannot really examine its meaning in terms of Paul's theology in the letter. However, if it is not a real 'read-ing from the letter,' its concluding remark gives it, accidentally, a link with the first reading and the gospel: God's mercy is not limited to some group or sect, but reaches to all.

First Reading > Gospel Links

The theme one is expected to draw from the gospel is that the gospel message, and the event of Jesus Christ, is not bounded to the people of Israel but reaches out to all. This is foretold in the prophecy of Isaiah. So the link is one of promise-fulfilment.

Gospel: Mt 15:21-28

Within both Matthew and Mark (who has the same story but with different scenery in 7:24-30) the focus of this story is not that Jesus brings healing or that even the demons are subject to him: that is a theme that is made in any number of incidents. Rather, the focus is that the message of Jesus is not confined to the community of Israel, but reaches out to all nations. This going beyond the boundary of the People of Israel was undoubt-edly a major issue in Jesus's life, but we know directly that it was the first major question that affected the churches. Were they to be another sect within the larger religious grouping known as Judaism, or were they to be a group who would set their own boundaries? We see the debate directly in Galatians and we have a later re-telling of the debate in Acts. Here in this story we see another way of looking at the issue: Jesus asserting that he was sent first to Israel, but that his work is not limited to Israel but extends to all who accept him as Lord. It is significant that the person who brings forth this move to cross the boundary is made deliberately as small and insignificant a person as possible (and a far more insignificant person than that in Mark's story). First, the person who needs mercy is a child (and this in a culture where children were not given the significance that children have had since the eighteenth century in the west); second, it is a girl (even less useful than a son); third, the petition is made by the mother, not the father; and, finally, both daughter and mother are Canaanite – the historical unbelieving enemy at the gate of the Chosen People. If mercy can extend to a Canaanite, female child, then it can extend to anyone.

However, if the focus of this story in the gospels is the universality of the gospel message, and this is the focus which interested the lectionary's creators as witness their choice of first reading, we have a problem. Given that (1) it is now 1900 years since the kergyma went beyond the bounds of Israel, and (2) that since the end of the first century Christianity and rabbinic Judaism had emerged as distinct, and all too often antagonistic, religions, this is not a message that the average reader takes out of this reading as its significant content. For us, and indeed for most Christians since the mid-first century, the question of whether the gospel is confined to Israel or not is simply not an issue. Therefore, when we hear the story – whatever the lectionary's creators might wish us to hear – we hear about a healing by Jesus. It is this fact that underlies the approach taken to this reading in these resources.

HOMILY NOTES

1. There are two basic facts that stare us in the face every day. First, we know that there are areas of our lives which are just a mess, they are not as they should be, they are awry, they are somehow a problem to us. It may be a physical affliction, it may be a cause of stress, it may be a memory that haunts us, it may be a relationship that has broken down. Whatever it is, we know that we would love to have it sorted out, mended, fixed, renewed.

    Second, we are all aware that our lives are fractured, broken up into little pieces that do not seem to mesh with one another. We want to live peaceful lives, yet we are caught up in various stressful pursuits. There are conflicts between what we would like to do and what we actually do. There are stresses between the demands of family and work. There are demands from various quarters that seem to contradict one another.

2. This need for healing and renewal takes on many expressions. Some people try to ignore it, others seek out various miracle cures, other seek out alternative medicine, lifestyles, or exotic New Age spiritual paths. We as Christians see it as a cry from within our deepest selves that we are incomplete without seeking God. 'You, O God, have made us for yourself, and our hearts are ever restless until they rest in you,' prayed St Augustine, while generations of believers have prayed that God would show them his face, turn his face toward them, and show them his mercy.

3. Every occasion of human sickness should somehow, in some way, and to some extent remind us that we are not self-sufficient, that we need others, need forgiveness and mercy, and need God's love and mercy.

4. The awareness of the fractured nature of our lives, of our brokenness, is what provides the basis for the 'wholeness' industry which promises a 'holistic approach' to this, that, and the other. But the fact that there are people cashing in on this human need should not cause us to forget that there is a really human desire for wholeness, to bring the various parts of our lives into connection, and to give our lives direction. This quest for wholeness has been an aspect of the Christian search for holiness down the centuries. Part of our wisdom is that this brokenness is somehow related to sin and so a first step towards a more integrated life is an acknowledgment of our sins and a willingness to accept forgiveness from God. Another part of our wisdom is that wholeness cannot be attained without prayer and care for others.

5. Lastly, while we seek healing and wholeness, we must be suspicious of 'instant solutions.' Healing comes in many forms, but it is usually slow, and always partial. Wholeness is never 'just there for the picking,' and its pursuit is the life-long quest. Again, as believers in the God of infinite mercy,

we know that complete healing and complete wholeness will only be ours when we enter into the fullness of life in the divine presence.

6. This last point seems rather dull given that we are bombarded with advertising promising us both healing and wholeness in a simple package: all that stands in our way is our willingness to pay for it! In the face of such illusions, bursting the bubble may seem churlish, but it is good news.

An Alternative to Preaching

The Sacrament of the Sick is in many ways the hidden sacrament, the one that is least understood, and the one that is wrapped up most in fears and myths. Just look at the way the media refer to 'last rites' or the fears that are often expressed that if a priest is allowed near a sick person's bed that it might be 'too traumatic' for him/her. The scene of a black clad functionary dabbing some mysterious substance, making religious looking gestures, while mumbling formulae in Latin is a cliché in films for finality and death. Such long-established cultural fears have been created over generations and they will not be easily changed. However, it is a good idea to try to make the church's care for the sick more visible. One way to do this would be to replace the homily today with a blessing of oil.

Introduce the Blessing with something like this:
Since the time of the apostles, we as a community have expressed our concern for our sick sisters and brothers by gathering specially to pray for them, and to anoint them to invoke the God's mercy and healing. During the coming weeks I will be called upon to anoint sick people in this community. Some will be anointed in their homes, some in hospitals. Some will be suffering from long-term illnesses, some will be distraught, some will be feeling the effects of old age, and some indeed will be at the moment of death. So let us now join together to pray for all the sick and infirm in our community.

Now have a procession with a glass jug of olive oil that can be seen by the community.

Then read the Instruction from the Rite of Anointing outside Mass on pp 84-5 of the Pastoral Care of the Sick, making the last sentence plural: 'Let us therefore commend our sick brothers and sisters to the grace and power of Christ, that he may save them and raise them up.'

Then use the Blessing of Oil B from the Rite of Anointing within

Mass on pp 109-110 of the Pastoral Care of the Sick.
   Conclude this with the collect, formula B, from p 111.
   Then continue with the Profession of Faith.

Twenty-first Sunday of Ordinary Time

CELEBRANT'S GUIDE

Introduction to the Celebration

We have gathered here as the disciples of Jesus, we declare that he is present among us, we are about to share his table. But who is the One we follow? That is the question that is posed in today's gospel, and we hear Peter's resounding answer: 'You are the Christ, the Son of the living God.' Let us spend a moment in prayer and reflection, asking the Father to reveal to us now a deeper awareness of who it is in whose name we have assembled and into whose presence we have come.

Rite of Penance

Lord Jesus, you are the Christ. Lord have mercy.

Lord Jesus, you are the Son of the Living God. Christ have mercy.

Lord Jesus, you are the Christ. Lord have mercy.

Headings for Readings

First Reading

This reading recalls that God chose many individuals to minister to his people during the time of the first covenant.

Second Reading

We all try to imagine God, we all have images of God in our heads; but Paul now reminds us of a basic truth: God is always greater; God is greater than everything we can imagine.

Gospel

This gospel poses a question to each church and each believer: Who do we, as disciples, believe Jesus to be?

Profession of Faith

Since the gospel is concerned with the church's profession of faith, it is appropriate that this be highlighted today in some way. One easy way to do this is to replace the declaratory form with the question-and-answer form we use on Easter Sunday (Missal, p 220). The whole text, including the introduction 'Dear friends … ', can be used as every Sunday is a celebration of Easter, and every celebration of the Eucharist is an activity of the church within the Paschal Mystery.

Prayer of the Faithful
President
We have gathered here because we are the people who declare with Peter that Jesus is the Christ. Now as the Christ's priestly people let us stand before God and make our needs known.
Reader(s)
1. For the whole church of God that we will always confess that Jesus is the Christ, the Son of the living God. Lord hear us.
2. For this church, gathered here today, that each day we will grow in our relationship and knowledge of Jesus the Christ, the Son of the living God. Lord hear us.
3. For the Bishop of Rome, Pope N, for all the patriarchs, and all church leaders that they may confess with Peter the identity of Jesus the Christ the Son of the living God. Lord hear us.
4. For our bishop, N, and everyone called to preside over local churches, that they may help us to know and confess that Jesus is the Christ, the Son of the living God. Lord hear us.
5. For all our sisters and brothers who are suffering on account of their profession that Jesus is the Christ, the Son of the living God. Lord hear us.
6. For all those who persecute the holy church of God, let us pray for them to the Father in Jesus the Christ, the Son of the living God. Lord hear us.
7. For those who have yet to come the knowledge of the identity of Jesus as the Christ, the Son of the living God. Lord hear us.

President

Father, we are assembled in the name of your Son as the church founded on the rock of the apostles. Therefore we ask you to hear our prayer and grant our petitions through Jesus, your Son our Lord. Amen.

Eucharistic Prayer

Given the gospel, the appropriate preface is Preface of the Apostles II (P65) that speaks of the foundation of the church upon the apostles (this is better than the Preface of SS Peter and Paul whose focus is on the complementarity and contrast of those two apostles). Eucharistic Prayer I, which always names Peter and which can include the names of the Twelve, is appropriate. Otherwise, use Eucharistic Prayer III and today include Peter's name in the gap for including particularly appropriate saints' names.

Invitation to the Our Father

As the church founded on the apostles, let us pray with one voice to the Father in heaven who has revealed himself to us in the Christ:

Sign of Peace

We are here in the presence of the Christ, the Lord's anointed, the Prince of Peace. Let us celebrate this gift of peace with one another.

Invitation to Communion

Behold the Anointed One, the Christ, the Son of the living God; happy are we to be called to his supper.

Communion Reflection

We give thanks to you, our Father,
For the life and knowledge
You have made known to us
Through Jesus your servant;

To you be glory forever.
Just as our broken loaf
Was scattered upon the mountains
And then was gathered together
And became one,
So may your church
Be gathered together
From the ends of the earth
Into your kingdom
For yours is
The glory and the power
Through Jesus Christ forever.
Amen.
(*The Didache* 9:3)

Conclusion
This combination of Solemn Blessings 16 with 17 would fit:

The Lord has founded his church on the apostles.
May he bless you through the prayers of St Peter. Amen.
The Lord has set us firm within his church built upon the rock of
Peter's faith.
May he bless you with a faith that never falters. Amen.
The teaching of the apostles has strengthened your faith.
May God inspire you to follow their example and give witness
to the truth before all. Amen.

Notes
See Homily, note 1, on the problem of the diversity of directions
the liturgy must take today.

COMMENTARY

First Reading: Isa 22:19-23
This is a prophetic justification for a transfer of power from one
high official (Shebna) in the palace, referred to as the House of
David, to another (Eliakim). It is therefore probably the most

pious description of a political downfall or palace coup ever
written! What is interesting is that we see the rituals that were
used at the time of Isaiah to invest high civil servants (Shebna is
referred to elsewhere as a 'scribe' which is the generic design-
ation for all those involved in the palace-based administrations
of the ancient near east) with their responsibilities. He becomes a
key-holder and is given authority to judge cases himself.

The text is used today because of its reference to keys in v 22:
'And I will place on his shoulder the key of the house of David;
he shall open, and none shall shut; and he shall shut, and none
shall open'; and this is intended to be linked with the keys referred to in Mt 16:19 ('I will give you the keys of the kingdom of
heaven, and whatever you bind on earth shall be bound in heaven,
and whatever you loose on earth shall be loosed in heaven')
which echoes its wording. But this text is usually read in the
liturgy with reference to Jesus himself (not Peter or the apostles)
for it forms the text of the Great 'O' Antiphon, *O Clavis*, of
December 20.

Second Reading: Rom 11:33-36
This is the conclusion of the doctrinal section of the letter (1:16-
11:36) and, as such, it is a doxology which is at once a prayer and
a summary of basic belief. It is sometimes referred to as a 'hymn
to the merciful wisdom of God' – and some have suggested that
it may be a liturgical item that Paul has incorporated into his letter – and so it has a unity that makes it ideal as a lection.

Much effort has been expended on what are its 'sources' and
whether or not it reflects Greek philosophical thought (both
sides seem more interested in either finding or disproving such
influence, following out a Reformation agenda, than asking
what such an overlap of ideas might mean for understanding
the text!). However, it makes two central points about our belief
in God: first, God is not another element in the universe but its
origin, its sustainer and its end; second, the divine infinity
means that our thoughts, ideals, and words are but shadows. In
every age we have had to create theological short-hands to ex-

press these ideas (e.g. *creatio ex nihilo* or 'the non-mutual real relation' for the first point; *aliquid quod maius cogitari non potest* or *Deus semper maior* for the second point); but these fundamentals have probably never been expressed with such elegance as here.

First Reading > Gospel Links

At an obvious level the link is one based in the theology of fore-type and perfect fulfilment such as is envisaged in the opening lines of the Letter to the Hebrews: 'In many and various ways God spoke of old to our fathers by the prophets; but in these last days he has spoken to us by a Son, whom he appointed the heir of all things, through whom also he created the world' (1:1-2). In this case that becomes: there were many and various anointed ones in the earlier days: now the last days have come, now there is a final and unique Christ – the Son of God.

However, there is a symbolic connection between the two readings if one focuses on the gospel as the text underlying the gift of the keys to Peter. Then as Peter is given keys that can bind and loose as Christ's deputy, we have a prefigurement in the transfer of the keys from one minister of state to another. This type of prefigurement has usually been interpreted to show continuity in the pattern of the divine activity.

Gospel: Mt 16:13-20

This text has such a history as a 'proof text' for (1) the apostolicity of the church; (2) the unique place of Peter in 'the apostolic college'; (3) the role of Peter as Christ's vicar; (4) the Power of Keys; (5) the Tridentine understanding of the Sacrament of Penance; and (6) the perception of the papacy, that trying to read it as part of Matthew's preaching is, for many, well-nigh impossible. However, we have to try to dig down through these later issues which used it as 'a proof from scripture' and attempt to see what was being preached by Matthew in the churches of the later first century.

The text forms a unified item of narrative within Matthew's gospel, but we can see it is made up two items: first, the confession of the identity of Jesus (vv 13-16) which is common to all three synoptic gospels; and second, the blessing of Peter as the new Eliakim within the House of David which is found only in Matthew (vv 17-19). These two themes cannot be separated, however, in Matthew's preaching for it is in the second section that we find the source of his ability to confess the identity of Jesus (v 17). The fundamental starting point for reading the 'confession' is to note the context in which Matthew locates the question 'Who do they say the Son of Man is?' In this formulation, it is not a question about people in general, or even the Jews in Palestine that is the concern, but who do those who follow Jesus say that he is. This, indeed, may also be the concern of Mark and Luke, but their question is less precise than Matthew's: Mark asks 'Who do men say that I am?' (8:27) which is followed by Lk 9:18 with just a slight change of wording. Matthew's text involves who do those who consider him to be 'the Son of Man' (which he presents as a generic title for the hoped-for leader of Israel in the final time) think he really is. The answers reflect the positions of various groups who became part of the church and whose varying interpretation of the nature of the Christ were to cause tensions well into the second century. Some, presumably those who had been followers of John and had moved over to Jesus had not really shaken off his apocalyptic vision in favour of the very different view of the final time presented by Jesus. Others wanted a christ who would engage in demonstrations of power, others again just wanted a reiteration of the Law in the prophetic tradition. Matthew was aware of these tensions and wished to present a formal moment where Jesus is distinguished from these notions and this is shown to be the express revelation of the Father. It is the churches who have this adequate view of Jesus, and the kind of kingdom that he announces (so different to that of John, Elijah, or other reformers) that are well-ordered households of God. And what is the sign of such a well-ordered household? That it has been given the traditional sign of God's care for the House of David: the keys mentioned in Isa 22:22.

HOMILY NOTES

1. There are, at least, three different directions that a homily based on today's gospel can go down: first, the confession of who Jesus is, and then the homily focuses on christology; second, who/what the church is that was founded on the apostles, and then the homily focuses on ecclesiology; or third, the focus is on Peter and/or the keys, and the memory of Rome and the papacy, and then the homily will have an apologetics or ecumenics focus because this Petrine ministry is an aspect of the church that is not just disputed with the churches of the Reformation, but with the ancient churches of the East (e.g. the Greeks and the Syrians) and of Africa (e.g. the Copts and the Ethiopians).

   The problem is that all three of these themes have to be given attention in today's liturgy; but if you try to give all equal prominence, then you overload the whole system. More pointedly, if in a homily of 7 minutes, or less, you try to cover all of them, then you will probably fail to communicate any one of them adequately. The nature of human communications decrees that you choose one of the three possible directions and focus on it in the homily, and then let the rest of the liturgy draw attention to the other themes (e.g. The Preface of the Apostles can draw attention to the apostolic nature of the church).

2. I am opting in the rest of these notes for the theme of christology. My reason for this choice is that there are likely to be many people in an average congregation with a defective understanding of who we believe Jesus to be, and sound doctrine on this core of Christian faith (as this gospel itself makes clear) is the presupposition of concerns with ecclesiology or ecumenics.

3. Let us begin, just as today's gospel does, with a question. Who is Jesus? There are, of course, a raft of answers: some from those who dismiss him, some from those who are vaguely interested in him or in religion, and some from those who have encountered his message and have followed him

in one way or another. It is this third group that are our concern. Jesus did not ask disciples an open question (e.g. what do you think people make of me? To which they might have replied: 'Well, the Romans think you are just another Jewish hot head; while the priests in the temple think you are another heretic; while the followers think you are great!'), but rather he asked them about who the followers – that is those who knew him as the Son of Man – thought he was. This is a question about the integrity of our belief and our preaching as his church.

4. The range of opinions (John the Baptist, Elijah, a prophet) held by Jesus's followers among those who first heard the gospel may be far closer to ways of viewing Jesus held in the average congregation today than you would expect!

5. The first position is that Jesus is another John the Baptist. Jesus was influenced by John; but while both proclaimed the closeness of the kingdom, they presented very different visions. John preached repentance, for the coming of the kingdom would be the great crunch when God would mete out his justice. Jesus came saying the kingdom was at hand when the Father would mete our forgiveness and mercy, and inaugurate the reign of peace and love. Jesus ate with prostitutes and tax collectors, and was criticised for this (Mt 9:10-11); John spent his time telling these people about the wickedness of their lives and warning them of the future retribution. Many then, and now, would prefer such a finger wagging, 'Tell it to them straight,' type of religious leader than the incarnation of the gentleness and forgiveness that is the Lord.

6. The second position is that Jesus is another Elijah. When we hear words like 'lord' we thing of a mighty leader who can march his men on to victory over opponents. If God is going to save his people, we sometimes imagine, the best way to do it would be with a great wonder-working person who can intervene, stop things happening, and get things moving. That was exactly how Elijah was remembered. When he took on the prophets of Ba'al, they were roundly shown to be frauds

through God's power, gathered up and slaughtered 'and not one escaped' (1 Kgs 18). This is a powerful type of saviour whom people must respect, and who shows who is really in charge. And, deep down, many of us would like Jesus, just now and then, to show the world just who is in charge. You may think this is not so; but consider the fact that the legend of St Patrick is based on him being another Elijah; while many private revelations (St Margaret Mary or Fatima) have elements of John the Baptist and Elijah bound up in them. But just as Matthew presents Jesus as very different to John, so also he presents him as very different to Elijah; at the moment of his arrest Jesus asks: 'Do you think that I cannot appeal to my Father, and he will at once send me more than twelve legions of angels?' Those who like an Elijah-style Christ would have had the twelve squadrons 'buzz' the scene, even if they do not go all the way and call in an air-strike!

7. The third position is that Jesus is just one more wise religious leader who calls or recalls people to the faith they already held. Jesus's work was not just a 're-heating' of the religious wisdom, but the establishment of a new community, a new covenant, a people intimate with the Father. Jesus is the 'new wine' (Mt 9:17) who has established the new relationship between us and the Father, and between us as sisters and brother.

8. This gentle, forgiving Christ offering us adoption by our loving Father – so unlike the expectations of religious people then or now – is revealed to us, not by flesh and blood, but by the Father himself.

Twenty-second Sunday of Ordinary Time

CELEBRANT'S GUIDE

Introduction to the Celebration

In today's gospel we hear the call of Jesus to become his followers. This is no easy invitation: 'If anyone wants to be a follower of mine, let him renounce himself and take up his cross and follow me.' We enter into the cross of Jesus, and begin our following of him, when we are baptised. It is at that moment that we become members of this body that can gather at the Lord's table, and it is the grace of baptism that sustains us on the difficult road of following the Lord of life, and goodness, and truth. So now let us recall the fact that we are a baptised people, and ask God to bless us and strengthen us to continue following his Son.

Now use the *Asperges* option, Missal, p 387.

Headings for Readings

First Reading

The prophet Jeremiah reflects on the suffering that has come his way as a result of answering the divine call to be a prophet.

Second Reading

St Paul reminds us that the way we live our lives is our offering to God.

Gospel

Jesus himself tells us that being his disciples is no easy task.

Profession of Faith

Use the Renewal of Baptismal Promises from the Liturgy for Easter Sunday (Missal, p 220) as a variation on the creed. In the introduction, change the sentence 'Now that we have completed our Lenten observance, let us renew the promises ...' to 'Now, let us renew the promises ...'

Prayer of the Faithful
President

Sisters and brothers, following the Way is the task we have taken upon ourselves. Let us pray now for ourselves, other members of this church, and all who call themselves Christians, that we may be given the strength to be disciples.

Reader(s)

1. Let us pray for whole church of God scattered across the world, that we may have the strength to take up our cross and be followers of Jesus. Lord hear us.

2. Let us pray for those Christians, our sisters and brothers in Christ, who are being persecuted for their faith, that their suffering will cease and that they may have the grace of perseverance. Lord hear us.

3. Let us pray for all who have been called to special ministries of leadership among God's people, that they may have the wisdom and strength to teach their sisters and brothers the way of discipleship. Lord hear us.

4. Let us pray for those who have joined the church recently or who are young members of the church, that they may be given the strength to continue in the path of discipleship they have set out upon. Lord hear us.

4. Let us pray for ourselves, gathered at this Eucharist, that we may have the strength to continue each day as disciples, taking up our crosses, remaining faithful in prayer, and constant in works of love. Lord hear us.

6. Specific local needs and topics of the day.

4. Let us pray for those who have gone before us as disciples marked with the sign of faith, that they may enjoy the harvest won by their faithfulness in bearing their crosses. Lord hear us.

President

Father, your Son taught us to follow the way that leads to you. Hear our prayers and grant these requests for we make them as the community baptised into union with Jesus Christ, your Son, our Lord. Amen.

Eucharistic Prayer

None of the prefaces for Sundays in Ordinary Time pick out the theme of discipleship or of the cross, but this theme of the sufferings of the Christ becoming the basis of the community of the baptised is expressed in the Preface of the Sacred Heart (P45, Missal, p 448) which is rarely heard by the average congregation. It works particularly well with Eucharistic Prayer II.

Invitation to the Our Father

It was immediately after our baptism that each of us first called on the Father in union with the community of the church. Let us now do so again:

Sign of Peace

In becoming disciples of the Lord we became sisters and brothers in the community of the church, people committed to acting together in peace and love. Let us express that faith now in offering each other a sign of peace.

Invitation to Communion

The Lord Jesus has gathered us around his table as disciples, and now wishes to offer us the food that will strengthen us for carrying our cross as his followers. Happy are we who are called to this supper.

Communion Reflection

The poem 'The Call' by George Herbert. The text can be found in the Breviary, Poem 78 (vol 3, p 786*).

Conclusion

Solemn Blessing 12 (Ordinary Time III), Missal, p 372.

Notes

The gospel today raises central issues about discipleship and a consumerist society not only finds these difficult (a phenomenon common to all societies including Matthew's audience) but risible. The essence of consumerism is that 'I will become happy by pleasing myself, doing as I choose' and it is a cultural assumption that includes the notion that any other approach is just downright silly. This sets up a complex tension in the liturgy: if one just 'lays down the law' and 'tells it as it is,' one simply is greeted by not being heard. So the task is to present the gospel's challenge in such a way that it is heard and so can be a cause of reflection. One strategy is to present the challenge within a larger context of teaching, and in these notes that context is a reflection on the meaning of baptism.

COMMENTARY

First Reading: Jer 20:7-9

Jeremiah reflects on how his own life is symbolic of the message God wants to impart to the people (18:1–20:18). His own experiences of being rejected and despairing of his work communicate something of what it is to be faithful. This section of the book reaches a climax in 20:7-18 and it is the opening verses of this section ('What am I and Israel to learn from my situation of despair?') that form today's reading. The prophet has been brought into the work of God by God, and yet now he is suffering: Why is this and how could this come about? The reflection does not give an answer, but shows us a pattern in God's dealings with his prophets. So the prophet complains to God of the cost of his discipleship, for being a bearer of the Lord's word has brought him insult and derision.

Psalm: 62 (63)

There is no obvious link between this psalm and either the first reading or the gospel.

Second Reading: Rom 12:1-2

These are the opening verses of a new section of the letter which contain exhortations to take up the demands of an upright Christian life. This first of these exhortations is that Christians can now engage in the true worship of the Father, and this involves the whole of their lives. So their sacrifices are not confined to specific offerings in a fixed temple, but that in the whole of their lives and in all that they do they can be praising God with even greater effect than those sacrifices which are offered in the temple of Jerusalem. Through Christ, the whole world has become a temple and every life's true work a sacrifice.

This is a major theme in early Christianity, famously summed up in the words of Minucius Felix (early third century): 'We Christians have neither altars nor sacrifices.' By this he meant that access to the holy was no longer circumscribed by places or people or specific acts, but all life could be brought into the presence of the Father through the entry of the Christ into the creation. This aspect of early Christian thought has been obscured, however, by the a tendency to identify any mention of 'altar' and 'sacrifice' with the Eucharist, while forgetting that this is a major strand of Christian faith covering the whole of life, and which can, indeed, be used as one of the ways by which we explain to ourselves our gathering around the Lord's table. So if you chose to preach on this text, then note that it is the whole of life that is capable of being brought into the presence of God, i.e. brought into his 'sanctuary'/'temple', i.e. 'sanctified', and anything that is brought into that holy place is, by being brought into the holy place, 'an offering', i.e. 'a sacrifice'. But it is the essence of our faith in the incarnation that the Word has entered the whole of the creation, and so in every place there is openness to the holy and every aspect of life can be 'brought' into that presence, i.e. made an offering. So the theme announced by Paul is the theology that would one day be captured in the slogan: 'Make your work-bench an altar.'

First Reading > Gospel Links
The relationship between the two readings today is most unusual. The gospel points out that anyone who is a follower of the way can expect to have to carry the cross in his or her life just as Jesus had to carry his cross. The first reading is an example of such sacrificial dedication by the prophet. So Jeremiah is a moral example of how Christians are called to live their lives.

Because the reading from Paul focuses on us becoming in our lives a sacrificial offering to God, this is one of the days on which it is easy to present all three readings as having a common theme. However, it is an easy option that one should resist for two reasons. First, this is merely an accidental alignment and by suggesting that the three readings today are linked, the false impression that this is true every Sunday is either implanted or reinforced. Second, the gospel's message is that discipleship involves sharing in the cross, but this is presented as fact: discipleship costs! It is not presented through the theological optic of 'sacrifice'. So by combining the readings one is creating a theological muddle of the sort 'pain equals cross equals sacrifice' (not found in either Paul or the gospel), rather than letting the readings be heard on their own.

Gospel: Mt 16:21-27
This is a far more complex piece of this gospel than it at first appears. Let us begin by not looking at it, but at Mk 8:27–9:1 which is the textual parallel of Mt 16:13-28. In Mark, Peter's confession of the identity of Jesus is followed directly by the first prediction of the passion, that is followed by the rebuke to Peter, and that, in turn, leads to sayings on the cost of discipleship. However, Matthew, while keeping all that material, adds a couple of items that shift the focus decisively. First, in 16:21 he adds 'from that time' which breaks the chain of events as found in Mark. The prediction of the passion stands alone, followed by the rebuke, followed by the sayings on the cost of discipleship. Matthew is making a key point: this warning is not a one-off moment in the life of Jesus, but an on-going aspect of discipleship. Discipleship and the cross are intimately and continually linked. It is this break in the sequence of thoughts in Matthew, in contrast to Mark and Luke, that makes the starting point of today's gospel a good starting point for a reading. In so far as we can tell, Matthew intended this portion of his gospel to be read as a unit of sense (alas, that unit ends with v 28, the fifth of five sayings, but for some reason it has been omitted in the lectionary which

means that today's reading has a less than ideal ending). Second, Matthew adds that Jesus is to suffer in Jerusalem, and is the only evangelist to identify the city. This presents Jesus within a tradition of prophets who have suffered there and presents his sufferings in the context of the temple: his suffering will be part of the life of God with his people.

Matthew presents 'the cost of discipleship' sayings as five distinct statements. The first three of these can be read as his commentary on the commands on how to love God as seen in the temptation scene in 4:1-11. Then follows two apocalyptic sayings (only one of which is included in today's reading) in which the central figure is 'the Son of Man'. In this combination we see an aspect of his christology which he shares with Mark while giving it added weight (Mark and Luke mention the Son of Man only once, Matthew repeats the title): Jesus is not only the teacher of disciples, but the one who leads his people into the presence of the Father and is their eschatological priest. His followers are not just another theologian's sectarians, but the community of the final (in every sense of the word) revelation of the Father.

HOMILY NOTES

1. Think about these statements:
    - Christianity is about discipleship.
    - Christianity is about community.
    - Christianity is about doing the heavenly Father's will.

    When we relate these statements to one another, we start to glimpse that Christianity is not a 'well-designed consumer product'.

2. Discipleship. This is never easy because we like to imagine that we know the best way to our own happiness without any guides. This is even more problematic for us because we are left in no doubt that following is a matter of the cross. 'From that time Jesus began to show his disciples that he must go to Jerusalem and suffer many things from the elders and chief priests and scribes, and be killed, and on the third day be raised.'

We do look forward to new life, but it is not something that just happens or to which there is an easy road. 'If anyone would come after me, let him deny himself and take up his cross and follow me. For whoever would save his life will lose it, and whoever loses his life for my sake will find it.'

3. Community. Community is problematic for us as we are convinced that others get in our way and limit our choices. Most contemporary visions of a happy 'society' are based on the notion that everyone will be happy if there is as little restraint on their activities as possible (and the only limit is that we should not get in the way of others doing their thing). At the same time, we are people who crave companionship, crave acceptance, and fear being alone. A pretty mixed up situation!

But Christianity is built on the notion of being gathered from being scattered and lost individuals into a community. We talk about the importance of caring for one another; loving self, indeed, but to the extent that we love others; acting as sisters and brothers in the family of the Father, and gathering each week as a community not because we as individuals like the idea, but because this is the will of the group.

Being disciples also involves community, for we are part of a group around our teacher and we become his body by working together.

4. The heavenly Father's will. This also is hard for us because while our society is very good at noting the affective side of religion (it gives people a sense of 'where they are') and the individual choice aspect of religion ('this religion suits me') we have problems with the notion that there are demands to act with justice, to bear witness to the truth, to oppose wickedness. This is where religion 'pinches.'

5. All these ideas come together in what we say about the formal act of becoming disciples: baptism.

• Baptism is about following Jesus by joining him in death and resurrection.

• Baptism is about joining the community and declaring that

we wish to belong to it.

- Baptism is about becoming daughters and sons of the Father and praying that his 'will be done on earth as it is in heaven.'

6. Are we ready now to declare that we wish to renew our baptismal promises?

Liturgy and Accountability

In every situation of social responsibility – and the duty of pre-
siding at the liturgy is one such – a key question to be asked is
who is responsible for what to whom. While any answer is never
clear-cut or wholly defined, in a successful group activity there
is normally considerable agreement among all parties about the
various regions and directions of responsibility. On the other
hand, when this question cannot be answered, chaos follows.
While in those areas where there are major divergences between
the various individuals or groups, each with a stake in a situation, the result is stress, poor cohesion, and often strife between
parties.

This sort of problem seems so much the stuff of industrial
relations that it is not usually discussed in works on liturgy or in
liturgy training. The result is that many priests are bewildered
by what is demanded of them by their congregations.
Furthermore, many are aware that somehow the whole situation
where questions of responsibility are raised seems 'wrong'.
While from the congregation's side there are very often feelings
of deep dissatisfaction with the performance of their priests.
Indeed, there seems to be a profound crisis in Catholic liturgy.
Anecdotal evidence of falling and greying congregations apart,
there are English and Welsh hierarchy figures for Mass attendance showing a fall of 130,000 between 2002 and 2005. Such an
obvious 'sign' that things are not working is demoralising. This
has then to be coupled with (1) the tensions of closing churches;
(2) the increased strains of getting to more places over
Saturday/Sunday; and (3) congregations ever more ready to
criticise a priest's perceived poor performance. The effect is that
already tired and stressed men become more disheartened and
disempowered by being unable to respond creatively. However,
this aspect of ministry receives almost no attention at meetings
of clergy among themselves, at diocesan level meetings, or in the

literature. My purpose is to draw attention to the problem to stimulate discussion among clergy themselves, and then between them and their congregations when they meet to discuss parish matters.

A rough comparison

Let us try to see where we are now by noting where we have come from. While we are now nearly forty years since the arrival of the new Rite and more than forty years since the vernacular was introduced, many priests active today were formed in the liturgy of the pre-conciliar period. The attitudes and culture of that liturgy did not disappear overnight on the First Sunday of Advent in 1969. Some are only now changing as generations have grown up, and have come with their children to Mass, for whom the pre-conciliar rite is 'history'. So while new attitudes are increasingly found among the key groups for handing on faith within a community, many priests are still having to change attitudes often formed before they entered a seminary.

Compare two groups in 1960: a Catholic parish and Congregationalist church. The Catholics expected that the priest alone was responsible for liturgy above the factual needs. He provided public Mass at pre-announced times in sufficient number – in accord with his legal abilities to binate – for parishioners to fulfil their duties on Sundays; (2) he provided an opportunity for any Catholic who wished to receive Communion; and (3) he preached on specified days. Parish Priests had the additional personal duty of offering the *Missa pro populo*. While many priests may have seen themselves as having other obligations, those tasks were supererogatory. The minimum standard was clearly defined and known. For their part the congregation had the duty – clearly spelled out – to 'hear Mass' on Sundays and other days appointed, and the Easter Duty. Hearing Mass was further defined as to duration and minimal presence. Everything above that minimum was voluntary, and unnecessary.

The priest's major responsibilities were not to the congregation as they were for virtually every Mass (i.e. Low Mass) an optional extra to the actual celebration, but to the law (on major issues), the rubrics (on performance issues), and to God (in terms of his own fitness to celebrate). Should any of these fail, there was a fall back position of 'valid, but illicit' celebration, which could still ensure that 'the job was done' (*opus operandum operatum*) and which were clearly defined in the Missal. This concern with the ritual was an individual responsibility to an abstraction – the whole corpus of ritual law. While this some-times caused stress to priests suffering from scrupulosity, there were no ritual police ensuring ritual details were being ob-served. Many priests, learning that the rubrics would not permit this or that, simply put the law to the test by saying 'watch me'. When the heavens did not fall, they knew that every law – un-less backed up by physical force – has only that binding force that people accord to it. So the priest had two wholly distinct sets of responsibilities. In terms of quantity, that to people was minimal, that to the law was maximal. Both were clearly separ-ate, and in each case were well defined. Moreover, everyone knew these boundaries. Hence, priests were interchangeable at a moment's notice, at least, in terms of saying Mass. For example, an English parish might not have liked having an Irishman as their 'PP', but that did not affect the actual celebration of Mass. While a visiting French priest who wanted to 'say Mass' was just slipped in to celebrate a public Mass without further ado if that allowed the local priest to avoid bination and to get his breakfast sooner!

The Congregational church situation could not be more dis-similar. The group would have seen itself as there by choice and personal decision, not out of obligation to law. It was their as-sembly; they collectively were responsible for the service; and would have shunned the idea of being part of a ritual. This min-ister was one of them, although acknowledging his/her skills due to training. There was no automatic right to preside due to status, independent of the congregation. The congregation, in-deed, was the minister's employer. They had interviewed him/her and checked to see if they liked the style. The prospective minister would have been initially invited to come and preach – the process called 'preaching with a view' – because preaching was the minister's personal bit in any service, and preaching performance was a key indicator of suitability. The rest was a free form made up and changed to suit the congregation. While this might often have been decided upon by the minister, it was clear that the congregation's wishes were paramount. Moreover, there were mechanisms to hold a minister to account and, if necessary, dismiss him/her. S/he was 'minister to them', i.e. the servant of the congregation and only for so long as they wanted and on their terms. Despite the differences with the Catholic parish, there was an equal, and probably more explicit, awareness of liturgical responsibility. The congregation was responsible collectively for their worship, 'their' minister facilitated this. There might be an awareness of maintaining patterns of worship with the larger denomination, but that was little more than an awareness that certain practices were 'too Romish' to be considered. The minister was wholly responsible for his, and by 1960 her, particular part in the liturgy to the group. Personal responsibility before God was a wholly private affair, and the key tasks upon which the minister had to perform were to communicate through the sermon, to co-ordinate the various groups through negotiation, and to an extent have a winning style that neither frightened the horses nor bored too many too often. The parallel situation of the visiting French priest would have seen a pastor from Zürich simply sitting as a visiting member of the congregation. There would be no need for any special consideration for him/her, and any idea of leading the service *ratione personae* would have been absurd.

Many priests today are stressed by being caught mid-way between these extremes: pulled in both directions with insufficient training, and often being unable to articulate this problem that has crept up upon them.

Obeying the Rubrics!

There is still the tension with regard to obedience to the general law and the rubrics. The liturgy is not a free form; it must be in accord with the permitted limits of adaptation. Rome has repeatedly pointed out the rights of people to have 'the authentic liturgy', has criticised 'abuses,' and has encouraged local ordinaries to police the celebrations in their charge. In effect, any departure from the rubrics, no matter how worthily demanded by a situation, can be considered an abuse.

However, there are three other complexities unknown when the rites were in Latin and when, the odd lay expert apart, they could not be followed by the congregation:

The first is the rising phenomenon of unpaid and self-appointed liturgical informants: the priest has broken the rubrics, therefore he should be reported. Every community seems to have one and they are functionally similar to biblical fundamentalists: the liturgy is given, frozen by text, it is approached by rejecting modern scholarship, and one always approaches those who work with it on the suspicious assumption that they are 'not sound.' Fundamentalism is a fact in all forms of modern Christianity, and is especially virulent in the Anglophone world; it is often reduced to its most plentiful form ('biblical fundamentalism') but is far more diffuse. Among Catholics one of its forms is liturgical fundamentalism: 'Father has been given a book, he should stick to it.' The simple answer is that the liturgy is worship, not a book; and that the books are only elaborate aids to the memory. But because Catholicism has patrolled the liturgy since 1570 through insistence on printed uniformity, this reply excites the fundamentalists' worst fears that the 'old time religion' is being sold out!

Second, often priests when 'following the book' find their actions are rejected by parts of their congregations as if he were acting on a personal whim. The foot washing on Holy Thursday provides an example. Recently, a zealous bishop pointed out that only twelve males' feet were acceptable. This may have seemed sensible when the rite was composed in an all male atmosphere, but experience showed that this was not a good idea in regions where Catholic women assumed their equality with men in the congregation. A priest following the zealous bishop's instruction is then torn between his duty to the law and pastoral common sense. Some priests just proclaim loudly: 'blame the bishop!'; others, unwilling to 'pass the buck,' are blamed personally as not being 'willing to listen'. These tensions derive from an adherence to responsibility to the law whose boundaries within the groups it affects are unclear.

Third, the focus of most training is still competence to perform the liturgy as a given, not as a set of skills on how to preside at the liturgy – an activity that assumes there is more free form in the liturgy than is commonly seen – so every departure from the training creates a tension over loyalty as well as uncertainty about what is best. However, given the richness of our liturgy, seminaries must concentrate on technical mastery in training.

What the liturgy demands
There is the tension that results for many priests through a sense of responsibility to 'ideal ritual form'. The restored liturgy of Vatican II presented an ideal of Eucharistic liturgy more excellent than anything seen before. This was the result of more than a century of scholarship and well-resourced piety going back to the time of Guéranger. The result has been that many priests have worked to renew the liturgy in their communities. Often there is incomprehension, disinterest and, at worse, open opposition – and this too is a factor in stress and low morale. Here is a case of someone recognising their basic responsibility as liturgical leader and teacher, but where there is often a rejection of responsibility by others in the community, primarily by those who perform functions in the liturgy such as sacristans and musicians, but this refusal to take responsibility as a genuine participant in a participation-based liturgy is a major failing among Catholic laity today. The resulting dissonance of expectations between the liturgy's president and the other participants often makes a shambles of the whole liturgy.

Whose celebration is it anyway?

There are the stresses that result over the boundaries between the priest's role and the congregation's being unclear. In the pre-1969 liturgy a priest had few matters on which he needed to consult anyone in the community about the Eucharistic liturgy. Now he is expected to be listening to the needs of the community and responding to their needs as a basic element of his functioning. The priest in a vernacular liturgy must also be a skilled communicator, and is judged by the congregation on this point against a benchmark of professional communicators. A priest who 'bores me' or, even worse, 'bores my children' is in the eyes of many only fit for the clerical scrapheap. That the Eucharist cannot be celebrated without him is seen as secondary: in the eyes of many, if he cannot communicate and meet 'my needs,' then either he or 'I' must go. The key responsibility here is seen to be in meeting the needs of those who see themselves in a quasi-employer role. The priest is expected to be the listener.

With this goes the further stress of co-ordinating the various liturgical interest groups, and arbitrating between them. Often in these processes no one is clear to whom they have responsibility except to their own role. That they might all have responsibility to the community, or the effective worship of the community, or 'the church's liturgy' or the virtue of religion is not part of their decision frame. In such situations, because the priest is one individual, and the focus of the listening and co-ordinating process, he is in a lose-lose situation. It is little wonder, therefore, that many priests have given up on the agenda of the renewed liturgy; which, in turn, exacerbates the fundamental problem of people seeing the liturgy as irrelevant.

Finally, we must not see this new line of responsibility for 'performance' to the congregation as a transient pathology. Within a vernacular and participative liturgy, as Vatican II recognised the Eucharistic liturgy should be, this line of responsibility of the president to the assembly is at least as important as his, or the group's, responsibility to the demands of the liturgy as expressed in our liturgical books.

Discussion

The effects of changes that began forty years ago are only now being felt. Celebrating liturgy is now more demanding that ever. It is informative to look back over the pre-1960s manuals on how to say Mass. They saw it as an individual's action needing technical skill and practice, but the tasks are clear and the lines of responsibility crisp. Today the skill-set needed is far more diverse, but often under-acknowledged. That there are new attitudes towards, and new lines of responsibility within, liturgy is something we tend to ignore, but should be discussing openly and widely. Moreover, since presidency at the Eucharist is something that is very closely linked with the whole notion of the identity of the ordained priest, that discussion will have ramifications well beyond the liturgical sphere.

Twenty-third Sunday of Ordinary Time

CELEBRANT'S GUIDE

Introduction to the Celebration

We have just declared that we have gathered here as the people who in the Spirit's power follow the way of the Son to the Father. However, we all know that following the way of the Lord is much easier said than done. Our own shortcomings lead us to stumble again and again, while the shortcomings of other Christians both hurt us directly and embarrass us. Yet we must continue our task of being disciples, we must be prepared to take the risk of pointing out the failings of others, and, what is even more difficult, we have to have the humility to hear and learn from those who point out our blind spots, weaknesses, and failings. Let us reflect on our need for forgiveness, our need to grow as disciples, and our need to have greater self-knowledge.

Rite of Penance

For those times when we have refused to admit our sinfulness. Lord have mercy.

For those times when we have denied our failings. Christ have mercy.

For those times when we have found the speck in another's eye but failed to see the plank in our own. Lord have mercy.

Headings for Readings

First Reading

The work of the prophet reminds us that a constant task for the People of God is to call people to repent and begin life afresh in a new way.

Second Reading

Love is the answer to every one of the commandments.

Gospel
The Lord reminds us that a constant task for the People of God is to call people to repent and begin life afresh in a new way.

Prayer of the Faithful
President
Brothers and sisters, let us stand before the Father and intercede as a priestly people for ourselves, for all our sisters and brothers in Christ, and all humanity.
Reader(s)
1. For ourselves and all our sisters and brothers in Christ, that we will have the courage to proclaim the Way of Life and Truth and Goodness. Lord hear us.
2. For all who hold positions of responsibility in the world, that they will act with justice, work for understanding, and pursue peace. Lord hear us.
3. For all those people of goodwill who are seeking the truth, that their quest will bear fruit in understanding and wisdom. Lord hear us.
4. For this church, that we will grow in our commitment to the way of discipleship and that our weekly gatherings will express our care for each other. Lord hear us.
5. For all who are suffering for bearing witness to the truth, for revealing falsehood, for calling attention to offences against human rights, that the Lord will sustain and help them. Lord hear us.
6. Specific local needs and topics of the day.
7. For all our sisters and brothers who have completed the long road of discipleship, that they may be fully reconciled with God and enter the fullness of the kingdom.
President
Father, we stand here as the brothers and sisters of your Son who we know as Jesus our brother and Lord. Hear our prayer and help us in our needs for we make them in union with Jesus, the Lord. Amen.

Eucharistic Prayer
Eucharistic Prayer for Masses of Reconciliation I fits the gospel well.

Invitation to the Our Father
Let us ask the Father to forgive our sins and lead us to forgive those who sin against us:

Sign of Peace
Let us ask forgiveness of our sisters and brothers and express our willingness to extend our forgiveness to them.

Invitation to Communion
We are here around the Lord's table because he has offered us his forgiveness; happy are we who have been able to offer thanks to the Father through sharing in the life of his Son. Lord I am not worthy …

Communion Reflection
The Lord has welcomed us to his table.
   Do we welcome others?
The Lord has offered us the kiss of peace.
   Do we offer the gift of peace to others?
The Lord has shared his banquet with us.
   Do we share our riches with those in need?
The Lord has made us into parts of his body.
   Do we behave as sisters and brothers?
The Lord has made us all his children.
   Do we act as if some are greater and some less?
The Lord has beckoned us towards his kingdom.
   Do we build that kingdom around us?

Conclusion
Solemn Blessing 4 from the Rite of for the Reconciliation of Several Penitents.

Notes

There is a theme of sinfulness, the need for forgiveness, and the challenge to be active in reconciliation found over several Sundays in Year A about this time. This presents the president with a particular set of difficulties with regard to the 'tone' of the celebration. The tone can all too easily become one of 'telling them they are sinners' which not only misses what was distinctive about Jesus's teaching, but which sits ill with the paschal joy that is an essential part of every Eucharist, where we are gathering in joy in the risen Lord to bless the Father for his goodness. It is worth reminding ourselves periodically that Jesus did not come to tell us we are sinners. The reality of sin and its effects in the human condition are 'the given', the 'normal' situation, underlying the work of the Christ and his church; then the preaching of the church is that that situation is not the last word: we can start over again, we can be reconciled. We can ask for divine help to grow as disciples, and we can live and act with hope.

COMMENTARY

First Reading: Ezek 33:7-9

At the beginning of his ministry as a prophet (see Ezek 3) Ezekiel had received the task of being to the people their watchman/sentry: he would warn them of impending danger. The image taken over by Ezekiel (and already used by earlier prophets such as Hosea, Habakkuk, and Isaiah) was that of the guards on a city's walls at night: they were to watch that no one was able to approach and attack the city without being spotted, then when an attacker was spotted they were to raise the alarm. The JB translation of 'sentry' – a distinctly military word – is better than the often-used 'watchman' which has more domestic overtones of caretaker. The prophets wanted their task to be understood as containing danger and urgency and so choose a rugged task as the metaphor by which their ministry could be understood.

However, when Ezekiel first took on this task Jerusalem was under threat from the Babylonians and the call to repent was framed in terms of averting the danger to the city and, above all, the temple. By Ezek 33, the city has fallen, but the task of sentry to Israel is still needed and so he received a new commission and the work is set out in 33:1-9. Even if the city has fallen, there is still hope: God is calling people to repentance; and there will be a new perfect temple (which is outlined in graphic detail in Ezek 40-48).

Psalm: 94 (95)
This is the great morning psalm of the liturgy of the temple and then of the church. Its imagery is of the people going into the Lord's presence as the People of God, rather than returning to his ways.

Second Reading: Rom 13:8-10
Paul continues his teaching on how the members of the community are to act towards one another. And here he presents his version of a common theme in the early teaching: what is the greatest commandment, to what can they be 'boiled down'? He then gives his answer: love is the answer to every one of the commandments. We are more familiar with this question in the various ways it surfaces in the gospels (e.g. Mk 12:28; Mt 22:36; Jn 13:34 or 15:12).

First Reading > Gospel Links
The choice is intended to show a continuity of (1) activity, and (2) teaching between the times of the two covenants. The prophet carries out a task given him by God, and the final prophet announces that this same activity is to be part of the life of his community. In both cases the effects of the task of warning have the same effect: you are to warn them, and then it is their responsibility.

Gospel: Mt 18:15-20
Given the role that these verses have played in the history of the church, and particularly in the development of its legal structures, it is amazing that they are confined, virtually, to Matthew, and within that gospel as among the more obscure passages.

    We have a passage today that has a unity in that it concerns the authority of a gathering of two or three of the male members of a church to act corporately and thereby exercise divine authority. The context appears to be the need to have a trial procedure (built on procedures already well attested in the synagogues) for dealing with problem individuals in the community. First, we have the regulations (vv 15-17); then we have a version (v 18) of the text on 'binding and loosing' which is also found in Mt 16:19 that is intended to show the authority of the group to carry out exclusions; and, finally, a verse (v 19) intended to indicate that the excluding group are not simple acting on their own, but that in addition to divine authority as displayed in v 18, they actually have the Lord as a member of their jury.

It is interesting that the final verse of this passage, which was intended to add weight to the power to excommunicate, has a distinct history within the life of the church: read as a single verse, i.e. without context, it is taken as the 'authority' for the claim that Christ is present in every gathering of the church for liturgy. However, it would be inappropriate to focus on this final verse in any comments made in the liturgy because the lectionary clearly wants it, on this occasion, to be read in its context as part of the correctional process that Matthew imagines being used in the churches where he preaches.

HOMILY NOTES

1. Do you like having your faults, limitations, weaknesses, or biases pointed out to you?
2. One of the few attitudes that one can safely assume is universal is that we do not like our faults pointed out, nor the faults of our children, nor the faults of our friends. When they are pointed out, we tend to become defensive (denying that the faults are real or that they are simply the produce of the biases and prejudices of the observer) or aggressive ('You are patronising me!'/'You are interfering with my rights'). The proof of this is that in any industry where there is on-going staff assessment, those assessing fellow workers usually have immediate access to lawyers while the workers carry

the emergency numbers of their union reps. Likewise, teachers know that even the most incompetent work has to be criticised only in the so-called 'praise sandwich': find something that is done well; then point out the blunders; then conclude with more commendations of the work!

3. It is clear from the gospel that the community of the Christ is to be a little more robust in its way of doing things: the community is called to point out where sisters or brothers are not acting with love towards the community or projecting the lifestyle of the New People called into existence by Jesus. This clash between the notion that the community can censure the behaviour of individual members and our inherent dislike of criticism is one of the reasons that many find Christianity distasteful. This is not a new objection to Christianity, but one that can be traced back across the centuries; and it has not been uncommon for people to accept Christianity but reject the notion that there is any place for 'fraternal correction' or an authority to excommunicate members. It is this text, after all, that has been cited for centuries as the 'authority' for a coercive canon law – and one does not have to be a sociologist to know that that is not a popular aspect of Christianity today!

4. Ironically, on the other hand, the fact that there is not enough fraternal correction by Christians is one of the main objections to Christianity, to the poor leadership of church leaders, and to Christians collectively. The church is condemned for not excommunicating dictators: witness the furore when an army chaplain was sent from Chile to Britain to celebrate midnight Christmas Mass for General Pinochet while detained there. This was seen as an example of church collusion with militarism and dictatorships. The churches are condemned for being chaplains to warlords and of glorifying warfare and 'baptising' nationalism and imperialism. The memory of Pius XII is vilified for not making statements about The Holocaust. The churches are condemned for having owned slaves and for not condemning slavery (and that

support for slavery goes all the way back: note that St Patrick stated that part of the wickedness of the Irish was that they stole his family's slaves – and they were a clerical family for at least three generations). Bishops are accused of covering up for, and not punishing, those clergy guilty of abusing children and vulnerable adults. And, part of the blame for the ecological crisis is usually laid at the way that Christians have interpreted Genesis 1:28: 'Fill the earth and subdue it; and have dominion over the fish of the sea and over the birds of the air and over every living thing that moves upon the earth.' And the list goes on and on. Moreover, in every one of these cases there is more than a grain of truth: people expect those who claim to know the mind of God, or to be disciples, to have a higher awareness of morality and a greater courage in speaking out against falsehood, deceit, and injustice in the world.

5. So when it comes to speaking out with a voice of 'fraternal' (no doubt this masculine language will be seen as another of the church's blind-spots) correction, Christians are 'damned if they do, and damned if they don't'.

6. What can we draw from today's gospel that will help us? Perhaps all we can do is highlight the dilemma: we want others corrected, but not ourselves. Part of our human condition is that we may want to grow and improve, but we also want to avoid correction. We want to know and highlight the problems with others, but not ourselves. But it is already an improvement, when we have heard about this in-built contradiction in our make-up that is a stumbling block in the path of each us.

Twenty-fourth Sunday of Ordinary Time

CELEBRANT'S GUIDE

Introduction to the Celebration

We often describe ourselves as 'the People of God' and as 'a people set apart'; and very often such names have been misinterpreted by Christians to mean that we are somehow 'God's elite' or that he has some special friendship for us and our doing that he does not show to others. Today's gospel confronts us with the reality of what it means to be 'a people set apart'. We are the ones who must reject the desires for vengeance and retaliation, and in the face of those who offend us must work for reconciliation. To start afresh, working for what is good, after one has been hurt is never easy; it goes against a deeply embedded instinct in our humanity that calls for retribution. But to be the group who seek to continue the reconciliation of the world that was accomplished in the Paschal Mystery of Jesus is what we are about. Now, as we begin to celebrate this mystery, let us remind ourselves that as 'a people set apart' we must be willing to be those who bring forgiveness and new hope into the world. Let us ask ourselves whether we are willing to be reconcilers.

Rite of Penance

> For those times when we have wronged one another. Lord have mercy.
>
> For those times when we have held grudges against one another. Christ have mercy.
>
> For those times when we have failed to forgive one another and work for reconciliation. Lord have mercy.

Headings for Readings

First Reading

Vengeance and hatred come easily to us, but they destroy both the one who seeks vengeance and the one from whom it sought.

Second Reading

Note: this reading as presented in the lectionary (as opposed to being one item within the chain of Paul's argument in the Letter) is really no more than a theological soundbite; to give it an introduction would swamp it.

Gospel

If we as a community wish to consider ourselves the People of God, then we must become the people who forgive.

Prayer of the Faithful

President

We have been called to forgive one another and be the bearers of forgiveness in our society. As such, let us put our prayers before the Father.

Reader(s)

1. That the whole church will be strengthened in its ministry of bringing God's pardon and peace. Lord hear us.

2. That groups who use violence or seek destruction to forward their aims may learn the ways of peace. Lord hear us.

3. That all the countries of the world and their leaders may learn to co-operate and act with justice. Lord hear us.

4. That the members of this church gathered here may learn to overcome divisions and learn to be able to forgive one another. Lord hear us.

5. Specific local needs and topics of the day.

6. That those who have died may know pardon and peace. Lord hear us.

President

Father of mercies, through the death and resurrection of your Son you reconciled the world to yourself. Hear our prayers we beg you for we make them in union with Christ Jesus, our Lord. Amen.

Eucharistic Prayer

Eucharistic Prayer for Masses of Reconciliation II fits the gospel well, and virtually quotes the first reading.

Invitation to the Our Father

Let us ask the Father to forgive us as we have forgiven those who have trespassed against us:

Sign of Peace

Recalling that we should forgive each other as brothers and sisters seventy times seven times, let us offer a sign of forgiveness and peace to those around us.

Invitation to Communion

We come to share in this banquet because we have been forgiven our sins and reconciled to the Father. Happy are we who share in this supper.

Communion Reflection

The second reading is often an intrusive element in its normal position on Sundays between the related First Reading and Gospel. This is exacerbated when the second reading itself is little more than a soundbite having neither a story element nor the structure of a well-formed piece of teaching; and regrettably, the Letter to the Romans has been so cut up into little bits in the lectionary for Year A that it is often very hard to make much use of it as it is presented in the liturgy. And, this is true of today's Second Reading. However, as a 'thought for the day' it can be used as a Communion Reflection thus:

> We have being celebrating the forgiveness we have received from the Lord in being made sharers of his table;
>
> we have affirmed anew our desire to be the people of forgiveness;
>
> now let us reflect, with St Paul, that none of us lives to himself, and none of us dies to himself.
>
> If we live, we live to the Lord, and if we die, we die to the Lord; so then, whether we live or whether we die, we are the Lord's.
>
> For to this end Christ died and lived again, that he might be Lord both of the dead and of the living. Amen. *(Rom 14:7-9)*

Conclusion

The Father of mercies has reconciled the world to himself in Jesus the Christ; may he fill you with his mercy during the coming week. Amen.

The Son has come among us and brought about our reconciliation to the Father in his death and resurrection; may that reconciliation give you hope and joy in the coming week. Amen.

The Holy Spirit has been sent among us to bring us pardon and peace; may his presence be our power to be agents of pardon and peace during the coming week. Amen.

Notes

Consider omitting the Second Reading (it is a good soundbite, but so short that it is simply an intrusion in the chain of readings: first, psalm, gospel. Use it instead as the Communion Reflection (see above).

COMMENTARY

First Reading: Sir 27:30-28:7

The book of 'the wisdom of Jesus the son of Sira' is one of the oldest and longest tracts of Jewish wisdom literature that has come down to us. The book was written about 180BC and proposes a way of living a holy and wise life before the Most High. Today this book has a somewhat shadowy existence as most churches of the Reformation do not consider it canonical, some even label it 'apocryphal', and most do not even print it in their bibles. This 'shadow' has now even begun to affect Catholics through the recent invention of the category of the 'deutero-canonical' (i.e. a second-rate canon) books. However, it is clear that all the early churches considered it fully canonical. Indeed everyone – Greeks, Latins, Syrians – until the 1540s, with the exception of St Jerome, considered it canonical, and so close in its teaching to that of the New Testament that it earned the name of 'the church's book' (*ecclesiasticus*) by which it is still known in the lectionary. That use in the early churches can be seen in today's gospel which echoes today's first reading.

Most of the reading's meaning is transparent. However, it is worth noting that this wisdom is not a species of philosophy nor an ethics: as the final verses make clear, the wise person is the one who remembers the Most High, and in the light of that act of memory, knows the way of wisdom.

Note: the numbering of the verses in the lectionary follows the modern critical edition of this work, so if you want to look it up in a bible you will find that this numbering corresponds exactly to translations such as the NRSV/JB; older translations (e.g. RSV) use a variety of numbering systems.

Psalm: 102 (103)

While the first reading focuses on the need for human beings to be truly forgiving (i.e. reconciling), this psalm is solely concerned with God as reconciling.

Second Reading: Rom 14:7-9

The context of this reading is that the strong and rich in the community owe a duty of love, welcome, and hospitality to those who are weak/poor in the community.

First Reading > Gospel Links

1. Continuity of teaching: the gospel opening is on the need for Christians to show reconciliation; the attitudes of reconciliation are outlined in the first reading.

2. Part of the first reading (28:3) lies directly being part of the gospel (18:23-35); so we see how the early preaching adopted and recycled the wisdom literature.

Gospel: Mt 18:21-35

This pericope from Matthew can be viewed as made up of two parts: first, a small question and answer dialogue (vv 21-22) on reconciliation, which has a parallel in Lk 17:4; and, second, the 'parable of the unmerciful servant' (vv 23-35) which is found only in this gospel. However, this way of viewing it destroys the unity of Matthew's thought on the topic of reconciliation, and obscures what is theologically distinctive about the passage.

The unity of today's text can be easily seen. The topic of forgiveness is introduced by Peter's question in v 21: how often must I forgive my brother? That the whole text, dialogue plus parable. form Matthew's answer can be seen in v 35: so will the Father behave 'if you do not forgive your brother'. What is theologically distinctive about this gospel can be seen by comparing the opening here with the same topic in Luke. In Luke, the forgiveness is dependent on the offending brother repenting and asking for forgiveness (Lk 17:4: 'And if he sins against you seven times in the day, and turns to you seven times, and says, "I repent," you must forgive him'). Here, the demand to forgive is unilateral and absolute: one must forgive whether or not the offender repents or asks for forgiveness. It is this stark demand that is illustrated by the parable: if we need absolute forgiveness from God (and have been given it in the coming of the Christ establishing a new covenant), then we too must be prepared to act in this way.

HOMILY NOTES

1. Reconciliation is a word that is bandied about in Christian discourse: we talk about it in relation to individual sinfulness; we talk about it in social situations of injustice; and we use it as the name of one of the sacraments: the Sacrament of Reconciliation. We use the word so often that it can become just a synonym for repentance, penance, the process of 'getting rid of sin', offering forgiveness, or a process for rebuilding harmony in society. It is all of these things, but it is also one of the key words by which we can understand (1) the role of the Christ in relation to church, (2) the role of the Christian body towards the larger society, and (3) the one of the central Christian attitudes towards life and how it should be lived.

2. It is easiest to begin by sketching the habit of being reconciliatory, being someone with the attitude of wanting reconciliation. It is worth noting the exact implications of Peter's question of Jesus: 'Lord, how often shall my brother sin against me, and I forgive him? As many as seven times?' There is no hint in the text that this brother has come and

asked for forgiveness. This is not a mutual process. The forgiveness in question is a unilateral act by the one who has been sinned against. Someone has been offended/attacked; that person now wants to forgive the offender without any hint of the offender seeking forgiveness or showing an awareness of their crime or showing contrition. The question is how often is this attitude of offering forgiveness unilaterally and unconditionally to last? Is it a one-off event, something that should be given a good trial (let's say 'seven times') or something that must be on-going ('seventy-times seven')? The Christian position is made abundantly clear.

But what is this attitude? The forgiveness in question consists in continuing to seek the way that builds up peace with those who offend one, rather than seeking either to get revenge for their offences or seeking to write them out of the script of one's own plans for right acting. The Christian must act rightly, despite how others behave, even when that behaviour is directed against them. Reconciliation is the steady willingness to build the universe aright in spite of, and in the aftermath of, those who would break down peace and goodness between people, or between people and the environment. One must not only seek to stop damage to individuals, society, the environment, but one must always be ready to start over, repair damage, and begin again. This beginning afresh, rather than pursuing a vendetta or engaging in recriminations, is at the heart of reconciliation.

3. The task of the Christian body, the church, is to act as an agent for reconciliation in a human situation where, after any offence has been felt, our instincts and 'gut reaction' is to find the culprit, extract redress (sometimes we are honest and openly call this 'vengeance' and admit that we like the idea of 'getting our own back'; sometimes we opt for spin and speak of 'restoring the status quo' or of 'condign justice'), and then have an extended period during which the offender suffers the effects of their crime whether this is imprisonment, isolation, being given the cold shoulder, or some other

kind of exclusion. However, reconciliation is focused not upon redress, but upon getting back on track, repairing the damage, and starting afresh. The past is past; we must get on with building the kingdom of justice, love, and peace. If we look back it is only to learn lessons, not to engage in the activity of retribution. This is a very different view of the way humans should act to that which most societies have pursued either now or in the past.

The church is the minister of reconciliation whose vocation it is to work to repair the damage done within the creation, material and human, from evil choices. And this ministry cannot be confused with wagging fingers at problems nor naming sins, nor should it be reduced to the individual reconciliation of penitents, (viewed in terms of an individual's relationship with God). This working for reconciliation is part of the priesthood of the whole people of God.

Wherever there is division, corruption, suffering or disruption in the order of things, there is a task of reconciliation to be addressed; and Christians make the claim that they are willing to adopt this task as their own. In a world where the pursuit of vengeance keeps conflicts running and multiplies the amount of suffering and misery, Christians are supposed to be taking a different tack.

4. Reconciliation is also a way of understanding the Christ-event: God in Jesus was reconciling the world to himself. The pattern for all Christian reconciliation is the way the Father has offered a new beginning to the creation in the Last Adam. This use of reconciliation as an overarching theme for the whole of the gospel is captured in the opening statement of the current formula of sacramental absolution: 'God, the Father of mercies, through the death and resurrection of his Son has reconciled the world to himself and sent the Holy Spirit among us for the forgiveness of sins ...' The Father allows us to begin afresh and to then grow to the fullness of life; we rejoice in this as the joy of faith. We must allow those who have harmed us/our creation to start afresh and help

them grow to the fullness of life; we accept this as the challenge of the life of faith.

5. Perhaps we are now in a better position to appreciate the wis-
    dom of Ben Sira: the homily could conclude by reading the
    first reading again as its various messages (e.g. 'stop hating')
    should now fit into a larger framework.

Lectionary Unit VI

This unit comprises Sundays 25-33, and the lectionary gives it the title of 'Authority and Invitation – the ministry ends.' However, it has far less unity of theme or focus than the other units.

Seven Sundays are presented as devoted to narrative: Sunday 25-31; then Sundays 32 and 33 are presented as discourse: the final sermon.

However, the narrative section begins with four Sundays on which parables are read (25-28), which are followed by three other elements which are located here as that is roughly where they fall in Matthew's gospel read continuously.

This unit's structure is an attempt to find a logic in Matthew's gospel, after the fact, and its rationale of 'narrative followed by discourse' is artificial.

Twenty-fifth Sunday of Ordinary Time

Introduction to the Celebration

When we assemble around the Lord's table we bless God for his forgiveness, mercy, generosity and love: he has sent us his Son to bring us pardon, to transform us from being isolated individuals into the community of his love, and he gives us the hope of everlasting life. So, as God's holy people, we recall that God is merciful and forgiving; God is life-giving and generous; and that God is love.

Rite of Penance

> Lord Jesus you are the Son of the Father calling us to enter your Father's vineyard. Lord have mercy.
> Lord Jesus you are the Son of the Father offering us the fullness of life. Christ have mercy.
> Lord Jesus you are the Son of the Father transforming us to become the kingdom of heaven. Lord have mercy.

Headings for Readings

First Reading

God's ways are far above our ways. We have to struggle to be generous and loving; God is wholly generous. Indeed, God is so generous that we cannot fathom such goodness and love.

Second Reading

St Paul tells what it means to him to have a relationship with Christ.

Gospel

God's generosity knows no bounds.

Prayer of the Faithful
President
God's love makes us his people, able to call on him in our needs confident that he will hear us and be generous to us with his gifts.

Reader(s)
1. For the whole People of God, that we will share with others the generosity and love we have received from the Father. Lord hear us.
2. For ourselves gathered here, that we might grow in understanding and wisdom as witnesses to God's love. Lord hear us.
3. For unity among the followers of Christ so that we can better share with others the love we have received from the Father. Lord hear us.
4. For those for whom any mention of 'God' brings fear or resentment, that they may be comforted and given new insight. Lord hear us.
5. For those for whom any mention of religion provokes anger, that they may glimpse God's generosity and love in the structures of creation. Lord hear us.
6. For those who have died, that in God's generosity they may be given the fullness of life. Lord hear us.

President
Father, we rejoice in your goodness and generosity. Hear us and answer our prayers for we make them as a priestly people in union with our Great High Priest, Jesus Christ, your Son, our Lord. Amen.

Eucharistic Prayer
If you gather people around the table, then use Eucharistic Prayer I which has a reference (albeit obscured in the translation) to those men (*famulorum*) and women (*famularumque*) standing around (*circumstantium*); otherwise, there is no preface or Eucharistic Prayer that picks up in a special way the themes of the readings.

Invitation to the Our Father
As workers in the Lord's vineyard, let us pray for the coming of the kingdom:

Sign of Peace
Gathered around this common table, let us express our willingness to love and work with one another in Christ.

Invitation to Communion
We are gathered here through the generosity of our loving Father who has sent Jesus among us to gather us into the kingdom; happy are we who are called to share in this supper.

Communion Reflection
Instead of a reflection, consider what is suggested in the notes for the actual celebration of the eucharistic meal.

Conclusion
Solemn Blessing 10: Ordinary Time I (Missal, p 372).

Notes
The Eucharist is the common meal of a gathering of disciples whereby they become united with the Lord and can bless the Father. In learning to have that common meal – and so all the sharing and willingness to be with others and work with others that such a meal entails – the community are supposed to learn the fundamentals of Christian love; and in sharing a common loaf and cup they are supposed to get a taste of the banquet of the kingdom. Unfortunately, this meal is usually reduced to a mere tokenism, the explanations take over from the activity, and words and more words bury the experience. So every so often it is important to try to re-set our values. So keep words (e.g. the homily) to a minimum and concentrate on the actual eating and drinking. Gather the assembly around the table (it was for this reason churches were re-ordered after Vatican II); use a single loaf or at the very least do what the rubrics 'earnestly desire' and

let people eat only from bread consecrated at this Eucharist, and share the common cup.

All such celebrations are messy; but if we cannot learn to live and work with each other in such situations, then talking about 'loving one another' is just noise.

One the other hand, many celebrants fear that these more participative forms upset people's expectations or 'take too long'. The answer to the first form is that in every congregation there are those who are just drifting away from the Eucharist: they are not up-set; they just do not seem to think this gathering worth caring about! Any practice that might help those people to see that it is not just watching a priest and hearing words is worth trying. As to those who think it 'takes too long' (there are still many who have inherited the culture of 'First Mass' when, including sermon but not communion, one could be 'out' in under twenty minutes) there is the reality to be faced that they may be viewing their presence not as participating in the community's activity in Christ, but as obtaining a commodity ('getting Mass'). However, most people expect the Eucharist to take place within the hour, and provided the Liturgy of the Word is not too lengthy, it is possible to have a more obviously meal-like celebration in that time.

COMMENTARY

First Reading: Isa 55:6-9
Second-Isaiah runs from 40:1 to 55:13 and is sometimes referred to as the 'The Book of Comfort'. The conclusion of that whole book is found in 55:1-13, and it is from that conclusion that today's lection has been extracted. As it appears in the lectionary, the text is intended to supply us with a single proposition: God's ways are infinitely above human ways, and this is seen in forgiveness. This idea is intended to be read as an absolute statement, whose authority is its prophetic source, of an element of belief; for this reason, dwelling on its larger relationship within Second-Isaiah is irrelevant.

Psalm: 144 (145)
This links the first reading and gospel in being another expression of the basic insight of faith: God is full of mercy and compassion to his creatures.

Second Reading: Phil 1:20-24; 27
The first church established in Europe by Paul was in Philippi. It was predominantly gentile and had caused him much suffering in its establishment. By the time he wrote to them (this letter cannot be dated except to note that it is later than 50AD, and it is unclear how many times Paul wrote to this church, and the letter as we have it may be a composite of those letters) it appears to be a vibrant community, and one with which he had very good links. In the snippet we read today we have Paul seeking to establish a bond with his audience prior to beginning an exhortation to them (which begins in v 27). This link of shared sympathy with his audience he sets up through pointing out to them that he is choosing their interests over his own. Paul is now in prison and he reflects on the meaning of the Christian vocation of living and dying for/in Christ. He then expresses this with the full force of a rhetorical dilemma: from his personal point of view it would be better it if he were dead and with Christ, but he is not. Why? Because he has chosen to live so that he can serve the Philippians! So (the Philippians are supposed now to respond) are we not a lucky church? Paul has chosen to stay with us rather than go to Christ just so that we can hear his preaching!

This sort of rhetoric is still used in some advertising displays (e.g. 'we work hard making widgets just so that you can have the opportunity to have one for yourself!') but it is not a trick that we find very convincing for we know that there was no real option behind the choice made (i.e. Jesus did not offer Paul an option: do you want to die and go to heaven or write a letter to the Philippians?/The widget factory stays open because it can sell widgets not out of consideration that if it closed, then someone might be without a widget). So this rhetorical flavour has to be conveyed, somehow, in the reading. This may seem a moot point, but if this text is read literally, it can be seen as a basis for opting for death as a deliberate act of service to God.

Once again, we have a lection that has been needlessly mutilated in the lectionary (presumably to save 30 seconds of reading) by cutting out verses. The obvious unit of sense runs from v 19 to v 26, with v 27 beginning a new unit of sense. Omitting vv 25-6 simply makes Paul's thought more opaque.

First Reading > Gospel Links

Continuity in the basic understanding of the divine nature between the time of the first and second covenants: in each case the mystery of God's love is beyond human comprehension. This combination of readings is a reminder that the implicit Marcionism that characterises many popular presentations of Christian belief and which take the form 'The Old Testament God was a God of law/fear; while the New Testament God is a God of grace/love' are both historically and theologically inept and should be countered whenever they are uttered.

Gospel: Mt 20:1-16

This parable, probably the most notorious of all the parables in the history of exegesis for its difficulties, is found only in Matthew; and many argue that because of its accurate rural details it could be one that goes right back to Jesus's own teaching in its format.

To me, two items seem clear within the story. First, the audience (be that the audience which heard it from Jesus's lips, from Matthew's lips, or your lips next Sunday) are expected to identify with those workers in the story who are said in verses 11-12 ('And on receiving it they grumbled at the householder, saying, "These last worked only one hour, and you have made them equal to us who have borne the burden of the day and the scorching heat."') to murmur and grumble. Such people are going to find that in the kingdom there is a reversal of places, and expectations.

Second, this change of fortune is due solely to the goodness and love of God: God alone can be totally generous, and his generosity knows no bounds. It is this aspect of the nature of God, his absolute generosity, that seems to be the point of the whole story (and, hence, it is the theme running through the resources for this Sunday).

HOMILY NOTES

1. Parables are little tales that are intended to shock the perception of an audience; they are not little moral stories that we are to learn from by decoding each element. Alas, we do this so often that we destroy them.

2. So [asking for a show of hands] how many people think that this parable is unjust? After all, surely if you have worked all day you deserve more than people who have only worked an hour! If you do not find it unjust then the whole basis of arguing for the rights of workers, that has been part of the church's social teaching for more than a century, is flawed.

   The simple fact is that if you have had to work all day, you deserve recompense *pro rata*.

3. The interesting thing is that we are all associating ourselves with the group who have laboured all day, not with the last group that have been indulged.

4. Yet, we are looking forward to the fullness of the kingdom not because we deserve it because we have worked so far and for long, but because God is forgiveness, mercy, generosity and love.

5. We are one-hour workers, but we are looking forward to the fullness of life.

Twenty-sixth Sunday of Ordinary Time

CELEBRANT'S GUIDE

Introduction to the Celebration

We are called by Jesus to follow the way of integrity: to match our deeds and our words; to humbly walk in the path of right-eousness; and to seek the Father's will. Now as we begin this celebration, let us ask pardon for our sins, and be conscious of the goodness of God who forgives us, makes us welcome here, and beckons us towards the kingdom.

Rite of Penance

Option c iv (Missal, p 393) is appropriate.

Headings for Readings

First Reading

We are called to act with integrity; we are called to repent and begin afresh.

Second Reading

Paul tells an early church, and us today, of the importance of the community being united in love and acting with a common purpose and a common mind.

Gospel

Who are those who have accepted the Father's invitation to enter the kingdom?

Prayer of the Faithful

President

Friends, standing before the Father as the People of the Way, let us pray:

Reader(s)

1. The Lord Jesus calls on us to act with integrity; that our actions towards one another may not betray the faith we have professed with our lips. Lord hear us.

2. The Lord Jesus presents us with the challenge of wholeness, that our lives may reflect the love we have received and profess. Lord hear us.

3. The Lord Jesus showed us how to be the people of the kingdom, that the church throughout the world may be a beacon of holiness. Lord hear us.

4. The Lord Jesus was reproved by the self-righteous for having the tax collectors and prostitutes at his table; may we be a welcoming community at our gathering for his supper. Lord hear us.

5. Specific local needs and topics of the day.

6. The Lord Jesus spoke to us about those entering the kingdom, that all our brothers and sisters who have died may be welcomed by the Father. Lord hear us.

President

Father, we seek to follow the way of the Lord Jesus. Grant that our deeds may be at one with our words and may show your glory to the world in Christ Jesus, our Lord. Amen.

Eucharistic Prayer

There is no Preface or Eucharistic Prayer that is particularly appropriate.

Invitation to the Our Father

We look forward to making our way into the kingdom of God as we pray:

Sign of Peace

We have declared that we will follow the Way of the Lord as disciples. Let us re-affirm our dedication to following his way of peace.

Invitation to Communion
The Lord came to seek out the lost and to welcome them to his table. His love has sought us out, gathered us, and now he invites us to share in his banquet.

Communion Reflection
The Philippians' Hymn, either repeating it now as a prayer, or use it for the first time now if the shorter form of the epistle has been read.

Conclusion
Prayer over the People 20 (Missal, p 383) can be used as a Solemn Blessing by pausing for 'Amen' after each of its three petitions.

Notes
'The Harvest Festival'
In many communities, part of the autumn's activities is a Harvest Festival. Such thanksgiving rituals arose in Christian communities where the Eucharist was not a weekly event and such rituals were seen as forming a bridge between worship and life. So it is also a ritual that is often not well integrated into Catholic practice, and it is certainly not an item that integrates well with the cycle of Sundays in Ordinary Time. So is it worth thinking about? Some reject such festivals as superfluous to the notion of thanksgiving inherent in the Eucharist itself (cf the Prayers over the Gifts); others reject them as mawkish sentimentality: most people buy their food in a supermarket, yet this sort of festival uses images of rustic baskets full of fruit; still others reject them as something that belongs to the school: and certainly they often become no more than classroom activities where the only direct participants are small children and others in the assembly are involved only in so far as a parent wants to photograph his/her child doing his/her part.

However, we do need to re-connect as Christians with our responsibilities to the creation and become more aware of our need to offer thanks for God's goodness in it. When environmentalists want us to become more aware of our dependence on nature, we as Christians have to see this also in terms of our dependence on God. We also need to reflect on where and how we obtain our foods: are they obtained by paying producers unjust wages or at excessive damage to the planet through 'food miles'? Moreover, we need to foster a sense of the liturgical year being in tune with other cycles in time such as that of the harvest, and to recall that without the grain harvest we would not have the loaf of bread we need for the eucharistic meal, and without the grape harvest we would not have the wine for the cup of blessing which we bless. And, lastly, we do need rituals that help children become aware of the rhythms of the liturgical year.

So such a festival can have many benefits in helping a community remember and celebrate, and because it is not a form prescribed in the liturgical books, one which can give scope to the creativity and imagination of the liturgical planning group as it is a theme rich in possibilities and connections.

COMMENTARY

First Reading: Ezek 18:25-28
The reading is extracted from a longer section (Ezek 18) which makes the case for the individual responsibility of each member of the community of Israel before God. The latter half of this argument (vv 21-32) deals with the reality of repentance and conversion on the human side, being met from the divine side with mercy and welcome.

Psalm: 24 (25)
Continues the theme of the first reading of the upright man who seeks forgiveness for past sins and asks help to act with integrity for the future.

Second Reading: Phil 2:1-11; shorter version: 2:1-5
This whole passage (1-11) forms a unit within this letter which Paul wrote to a vibrant, and apparently very well organised

church. The basic question concerns how a Christian community should live, and central to Paul's answer is that they should live and work in unity and harmony. If they are united in their discipleship, they will have the mind of the Christ and so act and live 'in him'. The latter half of the section (6-11) is, in all likelihood, an early liturgical hymn that has been woven into the text by Paul. Since it is a piece of a liturgical prayer, it is best used as prayer – for example it is ideal as a communion reflection today – rather than simple read as a 'reading'. So this is a good day to opt for the short version, if the hymn is used elsewhere in the liturgy; however, it was the mind of Paul that his audience should hear both his ideas and the hymn, so it would not be appropriate to use the shorter version if that meant that the hymn was not going to be heard at the same assembly.

First Reading > Gospel Links
Similarity of teaching: integrity must link words and deeds; the repentant sinner has more integrity than the 'upright man' (i.e. one with public respect) who commits unjust acts.

Gospel: Mt 21:28-32
This passage, found only in Matthew, can be seen as a commentary on the preceding verses (21:23-27) which are not read in the Sunday lectionary. However, it can stand alone as a piece of teaching drawing attention to a key aspect of discipleship for Matthew: everyone who follows Jesus is judged in their discipleship by obedient faith.

In the context of Matthew's preaching the ideal hearer is a disciple who is learning a key test of discipleship.However, within the historical framework of Matthew's narrative the question is not addressed to disciples but to highlight a group that opposed the ministry of Jesus. This group is not identified as a particular nameable faction, rather it is a contrast between two more extreme groups: the faithless leaders and the faithful outcasts.

Two other points are worthy of note. First, this is often referred to as the 'Parable of the Two Sons,' but this title is unhelpful as it is not really a parable in any sense, but a question which demands an answer (X or Y) from those to whom it is addressed. It is a hypothetical teaching question and, as such, is a much simpler text to read than a parable. Second, those chosen as exemplifying faithful outcasts, tax collectors and prostitutes, are not just any group. Jesus was condemned as a false prophet by his opponents for sharing his table with these groups of people (Lk 15:2), and so there is an implicit link between the sinners being welcomed into the kingdom and those who are welcomed to sit now at Jesus's table.

HOMILY NOTES

1. The question posed by Jesus touches a fundamental human dilemma: the gap between words and deeds, between intention and decision, between desires expressed in the calm of reflection and the quick fixes of lived life. This is a gap we all know, primarily in others whose deeds often fail to match their high-minded words!
2. This lesson is an important reality check in our practice of discipleship: it is easy to prattle, practice is more problematic. However, the gospel also raises more profound questions for us than simply reminding us to practice what we preach. The gospel poses us a series of interconnected challenges.
3. First. There is the challenge to act with integrity: bring the inward person and the outward person into harmony. This is not simply the moral and the psychological challenge of integrity, but is at the heart of right living and faith. This quest for harmony takes place in the presence of God: we need to have integrity not just in ourselves, but to have integrity in the divine presence before whom we are transparent.
4. Second. We know that integrity is a quest for wholeness: that the various parts of our lives will be connected up to one another. Wholeness involves us as individuals, as members of families and communities, and its links keep spreading out.
5. Third. We are called by God to be people of obedient faith,

and that means that we are not just dealing with a religion of ideas or warm feelings. Anything declared as believed is tested in so far as it informs our commitment to the creation.

6. Fourth. The obedient son first rebelled and then recognised the path that he should follow. Being disciples involves taking this second look at our actions. We all like to declare our independence and to state boldly that 'We will not serve!' It is part of our human nature to be aware of our independence and freedom. Yet, we as disciples have to balance this with our appreciation of the limitations of our knowledge and of the Wisdom that created us. Integrating awareness of our freedom with our acknowledgment of the Christ as our teacher is an essential part of completeness and wholeness. It is part of the wisdom and integrity of holiness.

7. Fifth and finally. There is a challenge to each of us to acknowledge the generosity of God. We all tend to think of ourselves as models of humanity, and as Christians we even tend to think of ourselves as model disciples. But here lies a great illusion! Those whom Jesus met that were self-satisfied, he challenged with questions. Those whom the self-satisfied automatically excluded, the tax collectors and prostitutes, he sat and ate with that they might come to know the goodness and forgiveness of God.

Twenty-seventh Sunday of Ordinary Time

Introduction to the Celebration
Christ Jesus came among us to invite us to become part of a new people, to gather scattered individuals and transform them into his new community, the kingdom. Let us pause and reflect that we are members of this community, this communion, this body, this priestly people, this kingdom. And, as such, we have now assembled to celebrate with one another and with the Lord.

Rite of Penance
Option c i (Missal, p 391-2) is appropriate.

Headings for Readings
First Reading
A vineyard is something that needs constant care if it is to produce fruit. We are God's vineyard, he lavishes care on us, and we are called by his love to respond with love to him and towards one another.

Second Reading
We Christians, Paul reminds us, are to be a cheerful lot and we are not to be afraid to praise every good and noble part of the creation we encounter.

Gospel
Jesus strengthens his followers by reminding them that even though the Christian life seems to make little difference in the world, in the end God will bring our work to fruition.

Prayer of the Faithful
Use Sample Formula 1 (Missal, p 995).

Eucharistic Prayer
There is no Preface or Eucharistic Prayer that is particularly appropriate.

Invitation to the Our Father
We pray that we will be found worthy to be part of the kingdom of God as we say:

Sign of Peace
We have gathered here, not as collection of individuals but as sisters and brothers around the table of the Christ. Let us express that unity to one another in the sign of peace.

Invitation to Communion
He has gathered us as his family around his table. Happy are we who are called to his supper.

Communion Reflection
If we are thankful for the generosity of God in making us one in the eucharistic banquet – and remember most people still think of this as 'getting Holy Communion' – then part of our thankfulness must spill over into care for others who, materially, are not so lucky. So invite a member of a group in the community which works to alleviate poverty to explore this link between the Eucharist and their work in helping the poor. Then give people a chance to collaborate in that work, i.e. a collection. It is always worth remembering that the origin of collections at Eucharist is the need for the community to express its care for the poor. How can we tolerate earthly poverty when we have just been rejoicing in our surfeit of celestial riches?

Conclusion
Solemn Blessing 13 (Ordinary Time IV) (Missal, p 373) is suitable.

Notes

It is good to vary the forms of profession of faith so that they do not simply become a recitation of words; the homily notes given below work well with the question-and-answer form of the Renewal of Baptismal promises; see Missal, p 220-1.

COMMENTARY

First Reading: Isa 5:1-7

This is the Song of the Lord's Vineyard. The vineyard becomes a metaphor for the further image of the love and care of God not finding an appropriate response. Love is not met by love but by sin and social crimes; and the song ends with the intimation that this situation will end in a judgement against the unresponsive people.

Psalm: 79 (80)

This continues the theme that God's work is the formation of his people, and they are compared to a vineyard.

Second Reading: Phil 4:6-9

These are final words of encouragement to continue in the way of discipleship.

First Reading > Gospel Links

The link is based on the similarity of the range of images used for God's work on earth: both readings use the image of the vineyard.

Gospel: Mt 21:33-43

The vineyard image for the People of God as the result of the divine handiwork was already an ancient one (see the first reading and psalm) before it was taken up by Jesus as an image that related to Israel and the New Israel. We see it in this story (which is common to all three synoptics) and we find it again in John 15.

The common form of today's parable is contained in vv 21-42 (which is virtually identical to Mk 12:1-12 and Lk 20:9-19) and ends with a quotation from Ps 117:22-23. The force of the parable is contained in the psalm verse: despite the fact that Jesus is rejected and his work seems to be fruitless, yet God will vindicate him. As such this parable can be seen as offering hope in the face of the fact of the suffering and death of Jesus, and the suffering of his community. Although the work of the Anointed One seems futile, yet he shall be exalted by God and eventually all will see his glory. This message is wholly altered by Matthew by the addition of vv 43-5: now the parable is not about the Christ and his church, but about the Jews: they are the ones who are rejecting the messengers, then the Son, and so they will be disinherited. There will be a transfer of divine favour from one group to another.

Quite apart from the fact that Matthew's theology of the succession of groups 'in favour' with the Lord is not shared by other early Christian preachers (e.g. Paul or Luke), and displays a certain anti-Jewish attitude common to many Christian writers in the late first century (e.g. John and the author of the Letter of Barnabas), it has a more profound failing: it makes the actual parable (which we can establish from the common triple tradition) far more obscure. Yet, this Matthaean form is the form which is most remembered. Since the lectionary often shows no hesitation at sheering off a verse here or there that it considers as either obscuring meaning or giving out a confusing message, it is a great pity that these last two verses (although this means omitting vv 43-45 it is only two verses as the modern editions, on which the lectionary in English is based, omit v 44 as an interpolation) of this unit of text were not cropped. In actual use there is a strong case for concluding with 'marvellous in our eyes'.

HOMILY NOTES

1. How do we learn to be Christians? Listen carefully to this question: how do we learn to be Christians? A stock answer might be: 'What's with this WE stuff?' I might want to learn to be a Christian, to find out what it means to live as a

Christian, I might want to build up the habits of thought and action that would mean my life would have a Christian character, but that is *my* concern – I do not want others interfering with me, and I do not want to interfere with others! This is not only a possible answer to the question, it is one that is consistent with the dominant social trend in contemporary Western society: we are individual consumers. I take from any heap just what I want, leave the rest; and in everything to do with religion there must be a strict code of non-interference – *it* (religion) is my business and no one else's!

2. The unfortunate thing about the notion of isolated individual unit is that it just does not fit the facts of humanity!

3. First, if we lived consistently on this isolationist model of having a meaningful life we would have to abandon love, the notion of family, the notion of caring for others, and become Robinson Crusoe figures (except that we would not welcome the arrival of man Friday!). Indeed, many who do live lives that are truly individualistic, do find having stable relationships a problem, they fear love as commitment and their first thought about others is that they are potential threats.

4. Second, Jesus did not come to offer ideas to individuals which they might pick up or reject; rather he came to form a community. This was to be a new type of community that would live with love towards one another, they would view everyone (men/women; masters/slaves; Jews/Gentiles; rich/poor; posh people/'not our sort' people; neighbours/foreigners) in the community as 'brothers' and 'sisters'. This community would be an expression on earth of the love of the Father and the Son in the Spirit; and the love that community would show to others who do not belong to the Christian community would be an expression of the love that God has for all humans. You can only learn to be a Christian by belonging to a Christian community. And you cannot be an isolated individual and be part of a community.

5. You can only learn to be a Christian when you live and collaborate as a Christian with others in a community; then *we*

all learn to be Christians together. We are not always very successful in becoming Christians, and it is difficult to share the life of a community, but that is the only way we will grow as disciples and move along our pilgrimage of faith.

6. So how is this community working together? What are we doing to break down the individualism that keeps us from growing more like Jesus? How are we collectively expressing care and love for the larger society, thereby manifesting the love of God for humanity? These are painful questions.

    Are poor people being helped by our work?

    Do people caring for the planet know that they have support from us as a group?

    Would people suffering from injustice realise that we will be their allies?

    Would people who are victimised or excluded in our society know that Christians will stand up for them?

    Have we become so individualistic and so consumerist in our attitudes that we imagine we can be Christians and ignore such questions?

7. If we are failing in our answers to this question, then we are the wretched and corrupt tenants who have rejected God's servants, the prophets, and, indeed, the Son.

8. We should pause and consider this before we decide to stand and profess our faith.

Twenty-eighth Sunday of Ordinary Time

Introduction to the Celebration

Whenever Christians assemble to celebrate there must be a spirit of joyfulness and thanksgiving in our gathering. This is not some jolly optimism that things just might 'look up' or that 'we might be lucky' or that maybe 'the worst won't happen'. Our joyfulness is founded on the most basic of our beliefs: God is good, God is generous, and God is love. God is greater than our suffering, our wickedness, and he bestows his love with largesse. We experience meanness and limitation, we often act with bitterness and without thought; but God's mercy is greater than this, and his goodness stands as a beacon at the end of all human existence. Today in the readings we are reminded of this unconditional generosity, this goodness underpinning the universe, this love that forgives us and gathers us here at the Lord's banquet.

Rite of Penance

Lord Jesus, you came among us proclaiming the kingdom of love and peace. Lord have mercy.

Lord Jesus, you came to show us the way to the Father. Christ have mercy.

Lord Jesus, you came to call us to the banquet of the kingdom. Lord have mercy.

Headings for Readings

First Reading

The Lord calls us to him and our meeting is like a great banquet: and it is this banquet of heaven that we anticipate every time we gather for this banquet of the Eucharist.

Second Reading
Paul says farewell at the end of a letter and blesses God for all his goodness both to himself and the little community he has been addressing.

Gospel
We are about to read a gospel that shocks many people. But from it we can take this message: the banquet of heaven is within the reach of every human being. It is God's gift, it is not bounded by our boundaries of party or group or church, and his forgiveness is greater than all we can imagine.

Prayer of the Faithful
Sample Formula 10 (Ordinary Time II), (Missal, p 1002) is appropriate for today.

Eucharistic Prayer
There is no Preface or Eucharistic Prayer that is particularly appropriate.

Invitation to the Our Father
The Father bids us to journey towards and look forward to the great banquet of heaven; in the meantime, we pray:

Sign of Peace
We have been gathered by the Lord to his feast and made one in him, let us express that unity that exists among us by offering each other the sign of peace.

Invitation to Communion
We are gathered at the wedding feast of the Lamb; happy are we who have been called and accepted the invitation to this dinner of the Lord.

Communion Reflection
Have a short structured silence after using the time to make the actual eating and drinking more like a wonderful banquet.

Conclusion
As we have gathered to listen to God's word today, may we take it with us into our world during the coming week. Amen.

As we have gathered to thank the Father today, may our thankfulness for his goodness inspire us with hope and joy in our daily lives. Amen.

As we have gathered at this feast today, may we look forward to being re-united one day at the Father's heavenly banquet. Amen.

Notes
Given the problems today's gospel causes the average listener, it is much better to use the shorter version. This removes an additional problem in vv 11-14; and, because the rest of the text is what is common with Luke (14:16-24), this shorter version probably represents the parable in as close a form to that which was used by Jesus as we can establish.

COMMENTARY

First Reading: Isa 25:6-10
This is the classic text introducing life in God's presence as a banquet. It is this text that stands directly behind today's gospel; just as it ultimately stands behind the notion that the Eucharist is the sacrament of the future (*convivium ... futurae gloriae*).

Psalm: 22 (23)
This continues the banquet prepared for us theme.

Second Reading: Phil 4:12-14, 19-20
This is the conclusion of the letter whereby Paul expresses his dependence on God as the source of his energy, and then, using a liturgical formula, invokes a blessing on himself and on his

readers. The omitted verses link the letter to its original audience and give it a sense of place; omitting these verses (as is done here) has the effect of turning the reading into an abstract assertion. It is as well to restore the omitted verses as they remind us that the whole church is not an abstraction but a mystery encompassing space and time made up of physical groups of named people, in particular places and cultures.

First Reading > Gospel Links
The first reading is the classic expression of heaven as the Lord's banquet prepared for us; it is this imagery that stands behind the gospel.

Gospel: Mt 22:1-14 (shorter version: 1-11)
This gospel, the Parable of the Marriage Feast, is one of the most awkward parts of the whole gospel tradition to interpret adequately, and one of the most difficult passages to use as the basis for preaching. The main text (i.e. the shorter version) is common to Matthew and Luke, and the last verses in Matthew may represent an attempt by him to make sense of it.

See the homily notes on the difficulties it presents.

HOMILY NOTES

1. The first thing to say in any homily is to acknowledge that this gospel (and this assumes that you have read the shorter version) presents us with a series of shocking images. A peeved and angry despot sets out on a spree of murder and mayhem just because he has suffered an insult. It is the behaviour we find shocking when we read of such happenings with dictators today. Why on earth is this being held up to us in the scriptures with the implication that the murderous king is to be equated with God?

    There is no easy answer. The most popular solution for most of the twentieth century was to say that there is a fundamental difference between a fable (where every detail is there to be decoded) and a Jewish teacher's parable: here is a deliberately shocking story designed to draw out just one point: everyone that can be found is invited to the wedding feast. This distinction is not, however, anything like as clear-cut as many popular books declare; and, moreover, it is any-thing but clear that the early churches interpreted these stories in this way. We have to start with this fact (one which is awk-ward for many): there are parts of the early preaching, as recorded in writing, which we do not understand and which may represent positions that were later excised from the kerygma. This passage is one such case: what it means is a guess, and the task, once it has been read in the liturgy, is to reconcile it with the overall thrust of the gospel.

2. So, assuming that you have explained that we simply have to guess our way here, let us use this distinction between a fable and a parable. What is 'the bottom line'? It is this: everyone that can be found is invited to the wedding feast. Why is this such an important message? This is the question that we must focus on, not the details of the parable.

3. First, the feast is not just for a select group, an exclusive group that are 'in favour' with God. God loves everyone.

4. Second, the feast is not just for those who know about it: many will arrive at the feast at the End without realising that they 'were heading in that direction'. God's love is greater than groupings.

5. And, third, they are there at the wedding feast because God wants them there, not because we could recognise them as 'good or bad'. God's love is infinitely forgiving. We often think of the call to eternal life backwards. We do not think of it primarily as God sharing his love with us, but as God met-ing out retribution to those who 'should not be let in' such as Hitler or Stalin or Mao.

6. The banquet of heaven is within the reach of every human being, it is God's gift, it is not bounded by our boundaries of party or group or church, and his forgiveness is greater than all we can imagine. This is a message that is just as shocking for many as the images of the despot in today's gospel.

Twenty-ninth Sunday of Ordinary Time

CELEBRANT'S GUIDE

Introduction to the Celebration

The Holy Spirit has gathered us here to offer thanks and praise to the Father through our union with Jesus. But in discovering our relationship with God, we also discover our relationship with other human beings, and our place within God's creation. So we are called to love and serve God and we are called to love and serve others. We often think that it is enough to serve either God or humanity: serve one and ignore the other. But life just isn't that simple: we have to give back to Caesar what belongs to Caesar and give back to God what belongs to God. Part of our mission as Christians is to negotiate and balance these responsibilities. It is this mission we are going to reflect on today.

Rite of Penance

> For those times when we have ignored our duties to the things of the Lord, Lord have mercy.
>
> For those times when we have ignored our duties to the things of this world, Christ have mercy.
>
> For those times when we have played off one dimension of our duties against the other, Lord have mercy.

Headings for Readings

First Reading

Cyrus is a great king, but the Lord is greater than all.

Second Reading

Paul offers a blessing for the community in Thessalonica, and it is the same blessing he wishes every church – including our own gathered here today.

Gospel

This gospel reminds us that there is no simple answer to what are our responsibilities as God's people.

Prayer of the Faithful
President

Our mission as Christians is a complex one: serving God and serving his creation. Standing in his presence as a priestly people, let us ask the Father that we be given the strengths we need to respond to his calling.

Reader(s)

1. That this gathering may become a community which serves God with minds and hearts and souls. Lord hear us.

2. That this gathering may become a community which serves our society with minds and hearts and souls. Lord hear us.

3. That this gathering may become a community which serves the human family with minds and hearts and souls. Lord hear us.

4. That this gathering may become a community which serves the needy with minds and hearts and souls. Lord hear us.

5. That this gathering may become a community which serves the care of the creation with minds and hearts and souls. Lord hear us.

President

Father, your Son called us to render our duties to Caesar and to render our duties to you, hear us as we seek to offer you our thanks and praise and grant our prayers in Christ Jesus, our Lord. Amen.

Eucharistic Prayer

There is no Preface or Eucharistic Prayer that is particularly appropriate.

Invitation to the Our Father

Let us pray for the coming of the kingdom as we say:

Sign of Peace
God is the reconciler and the giver of peace; let us be reconcilers and givers of peace to one another.

Invitation to Communion
Jesus gathers us here and invites us to share in his life, happy are we who are called to this supper.

Communion Reflection
Poem 103, Gerard Manley Hopkins's 'Pied Beauty,' from the Breviary, vol 3, p 803*.

Conclusion
Solemn Blessing 12, Ordinary Time III (Missal, p 372) is appropriate.

COMMENTARY

First Reading: Isa 45:1, 4-6
In Deutero-Isaiah, it is a foreign king, Cyrus of Persia, who is presented as the Lord's chosen means to bring liberation to the Lord's own people (44:24-47:15). We read today from the 'commissioning' section (45:1-8) of this narrative. The implication is that the whole earth, even its greatest king, is under the control of Israel's God: nothing on earth is outside his power. The Lord is using these forces to effect his will on earth.

Second Reading: 1 Thess 1:1-5
This is the opening blessing of the letter.

First Reading > Gospel Links
Similarity of situation: in Isaiah, the foreign king Cyrus is presented as having a place in the Lord's plan; in the gospel, the emperor is presented as having a place in Lord's plan.

Gospel: Mt 22:15-21

This incident, most probably one that is a memory of a distinct event in the life of Jesus, is found in all three synoptics. The background is that of the various sectarian groups within Palestinian Judaism at the time: should they 'collaborate' or cut themselves off entirely from the Romans and their allies? It was, indeed is, a 'no win' question for once someone is asked about 'collaborating with the enemy', the answer is a foregone conclusion. Jesus sidesteps the question by pointing out that the range of duties of any individual in a society is always complex, and attempts to reduce them to a single dimension are false.

This text has been used down the centuries to show that the structures of civil society cannot be seen as simply 'this worldly' or wicked, and which could be ignored in the light of an all-embracing theocracy. The creation has a genuine autonomy which must be respected by those who believe, meanwhile, that it does not have within it the basis of its existence.

HOMILY NOTES

1. The phrase 'rendering to Caesar the things of Caesar, and to God the things of God' is one of the bits of scripture that people often use without recognising its origin. But it is a phrase that we can do well to keep with us.

2. We all know that we have a variety of duties and responsibilities:

   • To those immediately around us who love us and whom we love: care, respect, and tenderness are not optional extras in our relationships;

   • We have responsibilities to those we work with and those who employ us – honesty and integrity are supposed to be hallmarks of Christians;

   • We have responsibilities to the larger society: we are called to be responsible citizens;

• We have responsibilities toward the whole of humanity in that we must work for peace and development – this is something that we are conscious of today but which it would hardly having been worth mentioning a century ago;

• We have responsibilities toward the environment and the care of the planet, indeed because we believe we are all creatures and that God has made us stewards of creation we have an interest in this that is far more demanding than that of an environmentalist who would not recognise the divine origin of the creation – again this is not something that would have been given prominence even a few decades ago and some who call themselves Christians still think environmental concerns are not really 'religious' issues despite saying each week ' we believe in one God ... maker of all that is, seen and unseen'.

• And we are called in the Spirit to follow the Christ, to become part of his body the church, and offer praise and thanks to our heavenly Father – prayer and praise and an awareness of the mystery that surrounds us is part of our humanity.

3. If we had a little score card of all those duties with this question before each of them: 'Do you think this is part of the duties of a member of the People of God?', then virtually every one of us would tick the 'yes' box for each question.

4. However, just as at the time of Jesus, we try to play one off against the other.

5. Some Christians try to argue that it can be an 'either ... or' situation. Some people who are opposed to religion argue that religious people are only concerned with 'spiritual' things. Others opposed to religion argue that they should be only concerned with 'spiritual' things. Many, for various reasons, argue that 'religion has no place' in this or that sphere of human living. Thus they imply that we should not consider ourselves as having any responsibilities in this or that concern.

6. In the face of this we must remember that God is the Lord of all creation. In his love God has given the creation a freedom and integrity, and given humanity responsibilities within it. We are called to live lives of prudence, always keeping in mind the variety of our duties to self, others, the world, and God. It is in taking care of this variety of responsibilities that

we fulfill the command to render Caesar's things to Caesar, and God's things to God.

Thirtieth Sunday of Ordinary Time

CELEBRANT'S GUIDE

Introduction to the Celebration

Why have we gathered here? One answer is to assemble together to show our love for God and for one another – because the whole of the Christian way can be summed up in these two commandments. But let us pause and recall that we do not always love God with our whole hearts nor our neighbours as ourselves.

Rite of Penance

> For those occasions when we have put other concerns before loving God with all our heart, and with all our soul, and with all our minds. Lord have mercy.
>
> For those occasions when we have put other concerns before loving our neighbours as ourselves. Christ have mercy.
>
> For those occasions when we have put other laws or desires before loving God and our neighbour, Lord have mercy.

Headings for Readings

First Reading

To be part of God's people means we must act with love of our neighbour; and this means acting with care, with justice, and with gentleness.

Second Reading

Paul praises a young church for their exemplary behaviour and the joy in the Holy Spirit with which they embraced the good news.

Gospel

If we wish to live as members of the kingdom, then we must love God and our neighbour.

Prayer of the Faithful
Sample Formula for Ordinary Time II (Missal, p 1002)

Eucharistic Prayer
No preface or Eucharistic Prayer is particularly appropriate.

Invitation to the Our Father
The greatest and first commandment is 'You shall love the Lord
your God with all your heart, and with all your soul, and with
all your mind.' Let us express that love as we pray:

Sign of Peace
The second commandment is 'You shall love your neighbour as
yourself.' Let us express that love as we exchange the kiss of
peace.

Invitation to Communion
The Lord has gathered us through his love to this table. We have
gathered here through love of him and one another. Happy are
we who are called here today.

Communion Reflection
Care for one another is at the heart of the Eucharist, so invite an-
other group from the community to speak about their work (see
Resources for Sunday 27, above).

Conclusion
Solemn Blessing 10, Ordinary Time I (Missal, p 372) is appropriate.

COMMENTARY

First Reading: Ex 22:20-26
The Book of Exodus presents Israel as receiving the Law, whole
and entire, in a great revelatory event on Sinai (19:1-40:38). The
Law itself begins with the 'Ten Commandments' (20:1-21) and
this is then followed by the Covenant Code that specified how

the ideal people should act (20:22-23:33). This reading comes from the final section of this Code and outlines the blessings that are presented as following from keeping the Law.

Psalm: 17 (18)
The first reading having highlighted the second commandment mentioned in today's gospel, in this psalm the commandment to love God is stressed. This psalm is a complement to the first reading rather than a reflection upon it.

Second Reading: 1 Thess 1:5-10
This is part of Paul's opening praise of this community in one of his early letters. They are praised for how they have behaved up till now, and that now they are waiting and ready for the return of the Lord – an event which at this time in his life Paul believed (or at least presented) as taking place in the very near future. It is this nearness of the End that has made this letter a favourite with millenarians.

First Reading > Gospel Links
Continuity of teaching: the first reading stresses that the law involves love of neighbour, and this is confirmed in the gospel.

Gospel: Mt 22:34-40
This passage is found in all three synoptic gospels. It is not clear whether the questioner was asking for a summary of the Law in a nutshell or whether he was seeking its 'centre' and driving force, but there is a hint in Matthew (as distinct from the others) that this was not simply a desire for an answer but to test Jesus. In any case, Jesus responds by combining two quotations from the Law and asserting that in this combination we have the key to the whole way of following the Lord. The first quotation is on loving God and comes from Deut 6:5 – a text at the very heart of Jewish liturgy; while the second comes from Lev 19:18. However, what is crucial is the combination of the two as inseparable.

HOMILY NOTES

1. How do we learn to be Christians? The answer is that we have to learn to behave in a particular way: the way of love. It was to establish the community that would live in this way that Jesus was sent to us by the Father; and it is to be the people who live in this way that we are called to belong to the church today.

2. You shall love the Lord your God with all your heart, and with all your soul, and with all your mind; and you shall love your neighbor as yourself.

3. This is what is commanded to each of us; but it is given as the greatest commandment of 'The Law' – and The Law was the most valuable possession of a community, a people. We are each called to love God and neighbour, but we do this not as loners but as part of a community. Then, with each practising love of God and neighbour, the community will be like a transmitter showing the love of God and the new way of life he calls us to live to all around us.

4. People should be able to spot us as Christians by the way we live long before they have found out what beliefs distinguish us.

Thirty-first Sunday of Ordinary Time

CELEBRANT'S GUIDE

Introduction to the Celebration

One of the great gaps in each of our lives is between intentions and actions; we often have only the best intentions but what we actually do is a lot less wholesome. We have noble words and ignoble deeds. We make professions of faith with our lips, but not with our deeds or our wallets; we say we are willing to be disciples of the master, but we often find easier paths and other guides. We claim the enlightenment of the gospel and to be the people of love and peace, yet our behaviour often brings the very name of Christ into disrepute. It is this gap that is the focus of our thoughts and prayers in this assembly. Let us reflect now on this chasm that opens up between our public religious identity and our ways of living.

Rite of Penance

For all those times when our words have spoken of love, but we have acted with malice and hate. Lord have mercy.

For those times when we have claimed the truth, but have acted with cynicism and selfishness. Christ have mercy.

For those times when we have spoken of peace, harmony and humility, but have acted with pride, carelessness, and arrogance. Lord have mercy.

Headings for Readings

First Reading

The prophet warns the religious leaders that God is far greater than the petty concerns to which they attach so much importance.

Second Reading

Paul wants the church in Thessalonica to appreciate how hard

he has worked for them, and so to appreciate just how wonderful a gift is the good news.

Gospel
This gospel invites us as a community to pose to ourselves this
question: We may know what we preach and assert with our
lips; but do our lifestyles and actions belong to a different
teacher?

Prayer of the Faithful
President
Sisters and brothers, Jesus calls us to examine our behaviour as
his followers and to re-focus our activity on what is truly important for servants of God; let us ask the Father's help in this on-
going task of conversion.
Reader(s)
1. That we assembled here for the eucharistic meal will be given
the wisdom to take stock of our discipleship and receive the
strength to re-align ourselves with Christ. Lord hear us.
2. That all God's people, scattered across the globe, may seek the
way of the Lord and have the courage to leave behind any religious pre-occupations that distract from following Christ. Lord
hear us.
3. That those who are scandalised by our behaviour as Christians
may find other ways to come to know the Father's goodness.
Lord hear us.
4. That those who do not believe in God, or think that all religion
is harmful, may discover the wonder within the creation and the
mystery beyond it. Lord hear us.
5. That all those who have suffered through actions done in the
name of the church may receive healing and comfort. Lord hear us.
6. Specific local needs and topics of the day.
7. That those who have died may be fully conformed to the mind
of Christ, and enter the inheritance he has shared with us. Lord
hear us.

President

Father, we stand before you as your holy priestly people, but also as a group in need of your mercy for our failings and your help towards growing more perfect in your service. Hear us now, and come to our aid in Christ Jesus, our Lord. Amen.

Eucharistic Prayer

Preface of Sundays in Ordinary Time I (P29) makes very clear the dignity of the community as the church; none of the Eucharistic Prayers is particularly appropriate.

Invitation to the Our Father

As a people who seek to witness to the Father's love and forgiveness, and who are aware of their need to love and forgive their sisters and brothers, we pray:

Sign of Peace

The Lord has united us as his people, and established peace among us, let us express that gift to one another as brothers and sisters in Christ.

Invitation to Communion

We have been called to the place of honour at the feast, we gather as disciples sharing at the table of our master. Happy are we who are called to be here.

Communion Reflection

Lord,
around your table
there is none who is greater
there is none who is less
you are our one teacher,
and we are all sisters and brothers.

Lord,
around your table

we know that anyone who exalts himself will be humbled,
and anyone humbles himself will be exalted
you are our one master, the Christ
we seek to be servants of one another.

Lord,
around your table
we offer our thanksgiving to the Father
we praise him for his goodness in creating us
we praise him for his goodness in sending you to be our master
and teacher
we adore him as our beginning and our end
in union with you and the Holy Spirit
God forever and ever. Amen.

Conclusion
Solemn Blessing 12: Ordinary Time III (Missal, p 372) is appropriate.

Notes
Given the gospel's warning of pride in earthly adornments and
the need for humility, take care that you do not appear to contradict it with references by honorific titles rather than ministry description in any notices that are read out! Likewise, if you use incense, this is not a day to have one's self incensed or to incense
other clergy by rank. Rather simply incense the gifts on the table,
and then the whole community, and thus the smoke forms the
link between the offerings, the table, and all the participants
who are equal and brothers and sisters in baptism at our common meal with the Lord.

COMMENTARY

First Reading: Mal 1:14-2:2, 8-10
This book was written, probably, in the aftermath of the construction of the Second Temple in 515BC. It is made up of six
criticisms of the people and their leaders that show them to be

less than faithful to the covenant that makes them who they are. The second of these criticisms (1:6-2:9) concerns the priesthood and its rituals: they are allowing imperfect animals to be sacrificed, they are leading the people astray, they are failing as teachers – and this interest in the ritual of the temple probably indicates that the author comes from a priestly family. In the section we read, this criticism is coming to a climax. The priesthood has not been true to the covenant, they have not been true to the knowledge of God imparted to them; so now they and their children will be punished (the more graphic elements of this have been omitted) because they have led the people to stumble. The closest gospel text to this theme is not, however, today's gospel but Mk 9:42 and parallels.

One of the themes running through the whole book is that of the people not bearing adequate witness to the sovereign nature of God's activity (this can be seen in 1:14 and 2:10). It is against this background of the holiness of God, that the people, or particular groups among them, are judged.

Psalm: 130 (131)
This is the classic psalm of humble trust, and it is presented as a preparation for the theme of humility in the gospel reading.

Second Reading: 1 Thess 2:7-9, 13
In the church in Thessalonika, at the time of this letter, we have probably the earliest reference to what we would recognise as professional clergy: they claim the support of the community for religious assistance they provide for the community. Paul refuses them any other name than the *ataktoi*: 'the idle ones'. How we know that these people were offering ministry to the community, and were not just loafers, is that their behaviour is condemned by Paul's, and his companions', apostolic example: they did not claim any support for their preaching of the gospel, they financed their ministry by working, and they spread the light of the gospel solely for the glory of God (this last point is made explicitly in one of the omitted verses). This apostolic example is

for Paul seen in the paradigm on loving service: a mother feeding her child. So what drives the *ataktoi* to labour: the exact opposite emotion to that of a mother, greed. The church is to reject
these ministers as driven by greed, untrue to the pattern of apostolic work, and untrue to the pattern of loving service. In being
the fruit of that genuine ministry, this church is the cause of
Paul's thanksgiving.

If you read this text, then make the snippet flow a little better
than it does in the lectionary by reading from verse 7 to verse 13
(which is still far less than a coherent unit of text). If you do offer
an exegesis of the context of this passage, then own up to the
irony that there will also be a collection today that will go toward clergy salaries which is the very idea that Paul is rejecting!

First Reading > Gospel Links
The link is common teaching within the prophetic tradition.

Gospel: Mt 23:1-12
Although elements of this passage are found in Mark and Luke,
this is by far the longest treatment of this theme; and in Matthew
this criticism of Jesus's opponents forms a unit running from
23:1-39. Its context was the increasingly bitter separation disputes, in the aftermath of the destruction of the Temple in 70AD,
between those who will soon be known simple as 'Christians'
and those who will soon be known simply as 'Jews'. In this context, mutual recrimination became the style of the day with each
side accusing the other of being untrue to the tradition of Moses.
However, Matthew is also critical of developments he sees taking place among those who are following Jesus. They are adopting the styles and structures of social hierarchy that were endemic in ancient society where people related to one another in
terms of one being higher and one being lower, with these rungs
indicated by titles. This was not to be the case among the alternative social structures imagined by Jesus. This alternative paradigm was to be one of equality and mutual service, with only
God being treated as above the community; in this paradigm,

humility was the indicator of the person who understood status. The curious list of titles mentioned (rabbi, master/teacher, father) gives us a clue to both the date and background of Matthew's preaching. Rabbi was a title that emerged after the destruction of the temple and literally means 'The Great One' (Jn 1:38 is inaccurate); this is opposed by Matthew to the relationship of the community to God, only God is great, humans are servants. The other titles 'Master' (somewhat similar to our use of the term 'guru') refers to someone who acts as a teacher and social guide, while 'father' was used of the founders of particular groups, perhaps even churches. All such titles, for Matthew, only serve to confuse Christians about the social inter-relationships that should characterise the churches.

This text has caused much difficulty down the centuries because the church has evolved elaborate social hierarchies, indeed some of these very titles have continued in use. Some people hearing this gospel will notice this, even if they do not express their disquiet. The older tactic was to defend the use of honorifics such as 'Fr' with spurious arguments and complicated logic or to point out that one papal title is 'servant of the servants of God' (but ignoring all the others!). Such special pleading is historically bankrupt and dishonest. The real problem is an ongoing one that is not confined to titles, or indeed to those churches that use such titles, and is this: we become members of the church and bring our human social attitudes with us – and notions of social hierarchy are endemic in human societies. Entering the church is to enter a community that has a radically different vision of the universe, and adapting to it is a challenge we do only partially. It affects us all. However, that still does not explain why we continue to promote such titles of distinction officially!

HOMILY NOTES

1. If one asks Christians, and especially clergy, whether or not the world benefits from their presence as religious people, one gets a clear affirmative: we point out that our religion is

peace-making and loving, that it promotes humility and the care for the underdog, we point out our work for society in areas such as education, and for the world at large giving examples of help offered to poor countries or in the wake of disasters. Clearly, religion is a good thing!

If, on the other hand, one asks people who have no formal connection with religion whether they think that religions, or organised groups of religious people, are a good thing or not, the overwhelming answer is not one of neutrality (e.g. 'each to their own so long as the horses are not frightened') but one of positive fear. Religion, they say, promotes discord, its organisations promote fragmentation within society, it only gets involved in social structures so as to enforce its own practices or ideas within society, it is pompous and arrogant, and can lead to backwardness, coercion, and hatred. Religion as a private sentiment may be fine in a consumerist society ('you want it, you can have it'); but when religion is organised, it is subversive and divisive.

2. This attack upon religion may be the major threat that faces us as Christians during the next century. Its power comes partially from the fact that one can express most conflicts across the globe in terms of religious divides; and having done so, can imagine that this distinction between conflicting groups is the cause of the conflict between the groups. However, its power as a critique of religion (and the reason I do not believe it will go away any time soon) also comes from the fact that it tunes in with a dominant theme in our culture: individualist consumerism – there should be no limits on my personal desires and any external authority regarding my choices is inherently a threat to my freedom. However, rather than tilt at such giant ideas – a policy of questionable value in the context of short homily at a Eucharist – one can note that some of the criticisms offered are strikingly similar to the criticisms of the religious establishment in today's gospel.

3. But even if there were no external criticisms of religion (and

the presence of such criticism should call us to self-reflection as a first reaction), we need to take stock of ourselves and see whether or not we are 'fit for purpose'. This is even more pressing for any religious group, such as the local community assembling for the Eucharist, than for other groups which may gather for some good purpose, because of the nature of the claims we make as a group. We call ourselves 'the people of God,' we say that we are disciples of Jesus, we claim publicly to be followers of the 'The Way,' and we propose a message that we will announce to all. Making such claims means that we acknowledge that other people can have higher expectations of us and so can castigate us even more trenchantly when we fail to meet our own proclaimed standards. Sometimes church leaders claim that such an added standard is unfair, arguing that church people should not be expected to be more responsible than any other group; but such apologies are perceived as deceitful for they fly in the face of the wisdom contained in the proverb: people in glass houses should not throw stones.

4. The fact is that while we say that we are following Jesus, we continually 'lose the plot'. It is this losing of the plot, failing 'to see the big picture,' 'failing to see the wood for the trees' that is the criticism of Jesus of the religious structures of his day. 'The scribes and the Pharisees sit on Moses' seat; so practise and observe whatever they tell you, but not what they do; for they preach, but do not practise.'

So, since we are the people of God, how to we assess ourselves that we are living up to the claims? We need some pointed questions that can provoke our thinking.

5. Such questions really belonging to each actual group: each parish, community, group within the community, each eucharistic assembly. One way to form those questions is to note that there are three endemic fallacies that lull Christians into indolence and self-satisfaction:

First, the fact that the organisation is running smoothly indicates that it is helping people to grow as disciples. For example, the Eucharist has been celebrated at 10.30am for years and everyone who comes is happy with this, no one is complaining, and the music group always has the sheets ready and loves what they sing. Maybe the larger community's profile has changed and no one inside this parish circle has noticed? Maybe those times or that music is very much at variance with what others can cope with or expect?

Second, the fact that we have many achievements of which we can be proud indicates that we are attentive to the voice of the Spirit. The parish may run a very successful school and put great efforts into raising money for this school, but is it putting forth a vision of Christian education or just a good consumer product? Would those who work for it be willing for it to relinquish its ability to produce students who 'can get on in the world' if that were the price of it having a more person-centred education?

Third, the fact that there was a genuine listening and response to the call of God at one time means that we can keep repeating that activity with confidence that that is what is called for from us. Built into religions is the need for repetition: we repeat stories, we repeat rituals, and we have structures for this such as the lectionary and the liturgical year. But repetition can easily become a love of the past; how willing is the community to change in order to proclaim the Word in each new situation? As Picasso is reported to have said: 'Tradition is about having a baby, not wearing your grandfather's hat.'

6. These are, of course, big questions; and so we usually hear them asked at the big structural level: we hear them at 'national pastoral conferences', at 'diocesan renewal events', and the like. But the call of Jesus was not originally heard in such large structures: the gospel was preached in small gatherings for the eucharistic meal that probably never had more that fifty people present. So Matthew imagined that this piece of gospel would be provocative at the small level at a Sunday assembly, indeed at a much smaller gathering than most of

the assemblies we now have! It is the actual eucharistic group that this gospel expects will have to come to grips with this challenge, not some greater and more remote structure.

Thirty-second Sunday of Ordinary Time

CELEBRANT'S GUIDE

Introduction to the Celebration

Sisters and brothers, each week when we assemble for the Eucharist we enter into the presence of the Father, and offer him the sacrifice of praise in union with Christ Jesus. We enter into the presence of Christ, and through him into the presence of the Father. Today we reflect that as the people of the Lord Jesus we are called to be always awake and ready to bring his wisdom to our world and to be his presence among all the people we encounter.

Rite of Penance

> For those times when we have not been ready to welcome the Lord Jesus into our lives. Lord have mercy.
>
> For those times when we have not stayed awake as the Lord Jesus commanded us. Christ have mercy.
>
> For those times when we have not looked forward to the coming of the Lord Jesus into our lives. Lord have mercy.

Headings for Readings

First Reading

God's wisdom is bright and it can transform how we see life and the situations we find ourselves in. The divine wisdom must be like a beautiful and constant companion in our lives.

Second Reading

Use the shorter version of this reading.

Our hope as the community of Christ is that if we die in Christ, so we shall rise with him in glory. This is what we proclaim as the mystery of faith when we say: Dying you destroyed our death; rising you restored our life; Lord Jesus, come in glory.

Gospel
The people that make up the kingdom must be people who live in accordance with the divine wisdom, and who are alert to its demands and ready to accept its prompts.

Prayer of the Faithful
President
Sisters and brothers, let us pray that we can live our lives with wisdom as our constant companion.
Reader(s)
1. For the whole church of God, that we shall live by wisdom. Lord hear us.
2. For this church gathered here, awake and ready to encounter the Lord. Lord hear us.
3. For everyone who holds a position of responsibility, that the divine wisdom may give them light to see the true nature of the creation. Lord hear us.
4. For all who have difficult decisions to make, that God's wisdom may be their companion in their judgement. Lord hear us.
5. Specific local needs and topics of the day.
6. For those who have died, that they may have the reward of lives wisely lived. Lord hear us.
President
Father, we gather here in union with your Wisdom, Jesus the Anointed. Hear us because we are his priestly people and grant our petitions made through him. Amen.

Eucharistic Prayer
There is no Preface or Eucharistic Prayer that is especially compatible with today's readings.

Invitation to the Our Father
Jesus, the Wisdom of God, has shown us how to pray to the Father; so we pray:

Sign of Peace
Peace is the fruit of the wisdom of reconciliation, let us express
forgiveness and peace to one another.

Invitation to Communion
Behold the Lamb of God who bid us to join him in his great wedding feast. Happy are we who are called to the banquet.

Communion Reflection
Have a structured silence.

Conclusion
That the Lord may bless us with his wisdom during the coming
week. Amen.
That the Lord may bless us with the strength to act wisely during the coming week. Amen.
That the Lord may bless us with his mercy and love during the
coming week. Amen.

COMMENTARY

First Reading: Wis 6:12-16
This is one of the great poetic praises of wisdom that has come
down to us. Wisdom is personified as a beautiful woman and
seen as intrinsically related to God as his gift, rather than being
seen simply as a human quality or rational prowess. In the face
of materialist notions of intelligence as simply technology, this
reading has an important role in our recognition that such tech-
nology-driven notions of understanding (e.g. 'we know how to
make a complicated computer, so we must be intelligent' or 'we
invented a gadget that makes things quickly and cheaply, so we
must be brilliant') are incompatible with a belief in the Creator.

Second Reading: 1 Thess 4:13-18 (shorter form: 4:13-14)
This is one of Paul's earliest letters and in it he sets out an eschatology that imagined the return of the Christ in the very near
future and this would be announced by a cosmic resurrection. It

is an eschatology that Paul himself quietly abandoned and what became the churches' fundamental teaching on resurrection was seen to be contained in its opening verses (today's shorter form). However, the graphic nature of the cosmic resurrection, with its archangels and trumpets and clouds, has meant that it has been retained in Christian imagery and imagination.

This imagery was combined with that of the end of 1 Cor to produce the notion of the bodily resurrection at the end of time that became a normal part of the tradition, and the more bizarre features of this text (such as meeting Christ 'in the air') were swept into the background. Alas, they did not stay there! Several strands of American fundamentalism in the later nineteenth century made these verses the core of their doctrine of 'The Rapture' that holds that the End-times are upon sinful humanity, but the chosen ones will be suddenly whisked off to safety with Jesus. This notion may seem just a curiosity of a rather nutty group, but it is very widespread among American protestant churches. It often stands behind (1) unwillingness to acknowledge an ecological crisis because 'Jesus is in charge', or (2) to assume that the crisis is just God's plan to punish sinners and, therefore, there is nothing that can be done to stop it (and anyway God will rescue 'the saints'). It would, moreover, be a mistake to assume that no one in your congregation will have heard of this sort of thing: it is a message increasingly disseminated through satellite TV and the web. The simplest way to deal with it is to simply not use the longer version. While exegetes point out that 'The Rapture' theory has no basis in Paul, we still have the fact that this is a way of imagining the eschaton that Paul himself abandoned.

First Reading > Gospel Links
The first reading praises wisdom, the gospel links wisdom with being willing to act as members of the kingdom. The former is presented as a preparation for the latter.

Gospel: Mt 25:1-13

This parable is found only in Matthew and expresses his interest in the notion that the judgement will be sudden and unexpected. Wisdom is being ready for the *Parousia* at any moment.

HOMILY NOTES

1. How do we learn to be Christians? This question assumes that we already have a clear sense of who we are when we gather here.

2. Let's think of some groups that we are all familiar with. The first is a group of people on a plane: they all want to go to the same place at the same time, so they have something distinctive in common; but would you call them a community? They are really a collection of individuals who just happen to have something in common, and it is easier to get a service if the costs are distributed. Imagine someone offered that group a free lottery: ten lucky people could win a chance to travel in a private jet to the same destination at the same time: there would be them (either on her/his own, or if they are travelling as a couple or a family, then just the couple or family on the private jet). How many would want his/her name in the draw? I suspect, virtually everyone. The group travelling together is only a collection with little that matters in common.

   Now imagine a long-distance train or bus journey: the train/bus goes along a fixed route each day from A to Z, and there are a few who are on it for the whole journey. Others get on at C and off at K, while others get on at K and go on to X; still more get on somewhere else and get off at yet another stop. It is a friendly train, the conductor reminds people that they are approaching a station and warns them to be ready to get off, if that is their stop and reminds them to check that each has all personal belongings with them. Sometimes those who take a train often, recognise other travellers by sight, sometimes they might even speak, sometimes not a word is uttered. And, while they all go along the same journey together, each has individual interests: some are reading, some chatting to friends, others listening to music on headphones, others texting on their mobiles, and here and there you can see people with a look of deep concentration: they are doing Sudoku.

3. Now shift your imagination to a birthday party. Again, lots of people in the same place at the same time with a common interest. But the dynamics are completely different: they all have a sensed of being there because of something that unites them. There would be no sense in asking if they wanted to eat separately or go off on their own: their whole purpose is to be together. This is what celebration means. People are doing different things, but it is the whole group that makes the party.

4. Now consider this: is gathering today for this Eucharist just people together in the sense of the plane (all want the same thing and cannot get 'it' individually) or the bus (people just joining in for the bits they need) or is it a celebration: all invited to be the party at the banquet?

5. Jesus came to form a community. We say that we are called to his supper, and he wants the way we behave here at his table to be a model for how we treat one another and all people.

6. But is this our attitude? We offer a sign of peace, but are we ready to make common cause with those around us? Do we seek to get to know them? This is the great open meal, so if someone has just joined us today, would they feel welcome?

7. We have to learn to be Christians by learning to live and work together; but Jesus realised that a primary first step was to learn how to share with one another at this meal. Here we learn how to be Christians; here we learn how we must communicate the welcoming love of the Father; here we are acclimatised as a group for the banquet prepared for us in heaven.

Thirty-third Sunday of Ordinary Time

CELEBRANT'S GUIDE

Introduction to the Celebration

Friends in Jesus Christ, we are all called to build the kingdom of God, but no two people have exactly the same task in this divine project which we call 'creation'. Each of us is called to bring God's love, presence, light and peace into a particular world in which we are the centres. This is our vocation; this is the unique set of talents that has been entrusted to each of us by God. Today our thanksgiving focuses on these sets of talents that each of us has been given; and repentance is for those times when we as individuals have hidden our talents and failed to build the kingdom, and our prayer is that we will each follow our unique vocation more closely in future.

Rite of Penance

Option c vii (Missal, p 394-5) is appropriate.

Headings for Readings

First Reading

This reading is an ancient man's description of the perfect woman: she is a wife, who uses all her gifts and skills wisely. We read this passage today because it is a reminder that if we are to be the people God wants us to become, each of us must use all our individual skills for the common good.

Second Reading

Paul warns the Thessalonians not to be trying to predict the end of the world: the Day of the Lord can come up upon us like a thief. This moment is 'the hour of our death' which can come all of a sudden. Then our individual worlds will come to an end; and so we are to stay awake.

Gospel

Each person in this story receives a different commission. Each of us has been given a different set of talents which we must use to the full to build the kingdom of God.

Prayer of the Faithful

President

My sisters and brothers, let us stand before the Father and ask him for the gifts we, and the whole church scattered across the globe, need to become good and faithful servants responding to our individual vocations.

Reader(s)

1.That we might use our skills to build the kingdom of God. Lord hear us.

2. That we might use our skills to build the kingdom of justice and peace. Lord hear us.

3. That we might have the courage to walk the path of faith. Lord hear us.

4. That we might have the courage to use our skills to the fullest. Lord hear us.

5. Specific local needs and topics of the day.

6. Let us pray for the dead that they may hear the Lord's voice calling: 'Well done, good and faithful servant; you have been faithful over a little, I will set you over much; enter into the joy of your master.' Lord hear us.

President

Father, you have sent us your Son to open the way to you; hear us and help us to know, love and serve you with all our talents in Christ Jesus, our Lord. Amen.

Eucharistic Prayer

The focus of the Parable of the Talents is upon the building of the kingdom, but this is not a theme that is picked up in a notable way in any of the prefaces or Eucharistic Prayers. However, the church is empowered to build the kingdom through the gift of the Spirit and so the Preface of the Holy Spirit II (P55) does fit with the theme of the kingdom, providence, and vocation. Eucharistic Prayer II's theology of the Spirit then links flawlessly with that of this preface.

Invitation to the Our Father
Let us ask the Father to give us that food so that in our everyday lives we may be his good and faithful servants:

Sign of Peace
We are each called to play our distinctive parts in building the kingdom of love and peace. Let us now express our commitment to help one another in this aspect of our vocations.

Invitation to Communion
The Lord has called us to establish his kingdom, and has called us to share in his supper.

Communion Reflection
A solemn silence, possibly with a note given: 'Let us reflect for just one minute on the talents we have been given, and be thankful for the vocations we have been given'; then conclude the silence with 'Amen' before standing for the concluding prayer.

Conclusion
Solemn Blessing 13 (Ordinary Time IV), Missal p 373, is appropriate.

Notes
1. The first reading is one of those texts that cause maximum irritation today. It generates such comments as 'How dare men decide that an ideal wife is someone who works for them!' or 'So a woman can only be ideal if she is a wife!' or 'Where is the biblical text on an ideal husband?' Moreover, the notion that there are divinely allotted tasks based on sex is a notion that few western women will consider today. There is no smart answer to such questions: these texts – all those found in the canonical

scriptures – were written in a male-centred society where women were seen as inferior and were seen in relation to what service they provided for men (and such societies are still to be found!). So either replace the reading if such texts usually generate reaction, or else try to neutralise the reading by pointing out that the key point is that this woman used all her individual skills. The point of this reading is to provide a backdrop to today's gospel, and if reading Proverbs makes many in the assembly only think of questions relating to the equality of the sexes it has not only failed in its task, but actually obscured the gospel. If you want to replace it, then 1 Sam 3:1-10 would be an alternative. This is the story of the vocation of Samuel and his three-stage process of discernment that the Lord was specially calling him.

2. First Thessalonians is the text that has been responsible for much of the millenarianism that afflicts many Christians today. Many people, in any gathering, will have heard these ideas and it is important to note the difficulty and try to allay it before people start raising useless questions about it. Hence the approach taken in the above Heading for the reading: identify the end of the world with the moment when an individual's world ends, i.e. the moment of death. Trying to explain that Paul abandoned the notion of a fairly imminent *parousia* usually only confuses further those people who are worried by texts like this.

3. If there has not been some sort of 'Harvest Thanksgiving' (see notes, above, for the Twenty-sixth Sunday) which is, in effect, a way of highlighting our thanks for the goodness of God's creation and our dependence upon, and stewardship of, that creation; then this is the last Sunday on which some sort of attention to this theme can be paid. A very simple form is to bring food, other than the loaf and the wine, in the procession of gifts, lay them at the base of the table, and remind people that this food is a token reminding us of our dependence on God for our needs.

First Reading: Prov 31:10-13, 19-20, 30-31

With this beautiful piece of poetry the Book of Proverbs ends. It
is an acrostic poem of 22 verses; each beginning with the next
letter of the 22 letters of the Hebrew alphabet – look at how it is
laid out in the Jerusalem Bible. Therefore, the first point to note
is that if this had to be used in the lectionary, then omitting verses,
as is done here, is really to despise the text.

Many contemporary hearers of this passage reject the notion
that the ideal woman is to be viewed in terms of a mother/
housewife. But this is a positively glowing account of women in
comparison with most of the wisdom handed on in Proverbs:
women are threats to a man's integrity, they are the cause of sexual temptation, and they undermine the household and the family. Here, by contrast, there is an ideal woman, but she is married, looks after her husband's children and estate, and even can
carry out business on his behalf (this is no ordinary woman but
the wife of a member of a ruling elite).

However, even here there is a note of warning: charm de-
ceives, so goodness must be based in the fear of the Lord.

Psalm: 127 (128)

This text has nothing to do with the gospel; its presence here is a
consequence of the choice of Prov 31 to go with the gospel. That
choice of a first reading having been made, then this psalm
seemed to complement it because of its second verse on the
fruitful wife.

This text does nothing for the liturgy today except highlight
an aspect of the first reading that is accidental to its use today! So
replace the psalm with another (e.g. Ps 150 with 'Praise God for
his surpassing greatness') or a musical item.

Second Reading: 1 Thess 5:1-6

This is part of Paul's attempt to correct views about the eschaton
that were causing difficulties. There were those who believed
the end was just about to come, others that thought they could

predict the end, and probably other confusions besides. Paul does not want to place the *parousia* in the distant future, but at the same time wants to condemn the ideas of it being imminent. It cannot be predicted, so the community must be marked by is seriousness and its being ready for the Lord whenever he chooses to return.

First Reading > Gospel Links
One suspects that Prov 31 was chosen either in a nodding moment or else because no other text could be thought of! As the readings stand, the gospel shows people who use their several gifts to the full, this reading presents an abstraction, but this 'Woman' uses her skills to the full. So the link is similarity of activity in fulfilling their allotted tasks.

Gospel: Mt 25:14-30 (shorter form: 25:14-15, 19-20)
This parable-story evidently was in widespread use (it is found in virtually identical form in Lk 19) in the early communities as a way of viewing the time between the resurrection and the return of the Son of Man, Jesus, in glory. The master is to be identified as Jesus, and the events of the judgement of the three servants is at the end of time.

At this judgement there will be both rewards and punishments, and mere non-violation of the commandments (the third servant) will not be found to be sufficient to fulfill the demands of discipleship. Given that we are to think of the parable as pointing to the future time, the hearer has to react to it primarily in terms of its implications for what one does before the time of judgement. If one is to be rewarded then, one must act with wisdom now. But in what does wisdom consist? It seems to lie in the action of proclaiming and making present the kingdom, so that it will be found fully grown at the return of the Lord in glory.

This parable is one of the basic nuggets in our collective memory of the content of the preaching of Jesus as it is remembered in the churches, and has its classic form in Matthew as it is read today. Moreover, the Lukan form of this parable is not read in Year C, so this is the only occasion in the three-year cycle that this story is recalled in the liturgy.

The Shorter Form

One cannot overstate how the unity of the church, not just among its living members but over centuries and cultures, is maintained by having common stories that are known and owned by all and each in memory. The Parable of the Talents is one such story, and as such it is one of the building blocks of our common memory that makes us one people. Chopping the story – and one can always find a valid reason if one wants to – is, in effect, damaging that process of memory. It is by re-membering, literally re-calling stories time and time again, that our common identity is established, a common language and system of symbols established, and our apostolic links secured. It is by repeating these stories that the tradition becomes active and is formed for another generation. So the story should be read in its complete form, and anything less should be seen as damaging the ecclesial memory and not simply as meaningless saving of 'time' viewed as a commodity. But if time is so short that there is no time to hear a whole gospel story then ask the congregation whether they are there to celebrate as a community or 'to get something' before enjoying the rest of the day – if it is the latter, then why give yourself any trouble: hold a collection, give them 'Communion' from the tabernacle, and then go and relax with the Sunday paper.

HOMILY NOTES

1. 'Vocation' is a word that always conjures up churchy images: we know somehow it belongs to the sphere of religion more than the world of 'career choices'. We also know that it is a word that is intensely personal and individual: it affects me and my living of my life.

2. However, many Christians – and this is true especially of Catholics – have become very confused (since the early nineteenth century) about what is referred to when we talk about

the theology of vocation. For Catholics, in particular, it is ironic that the traditional theology of vocation has been retained for studies of Mary, but has been largely abandoned in practical spirituality. The problem is that 'a religious vocation' has become almost identical to 'a vocation to be a religious'; and, as a result, 'vocation' is now linked with having sufficient personnel for church offices. An example of this confusion is that recruiting men for the presbyterate is never referred to as 'recruitment and training' but is called 'fostering vocations'. If a homily can try to break the link between 'vocation' and ecclesiastical offices, then it may have created a space where members of the community might be able to reflect on their individual vocations – remembering that each person's vocation is unique.

3. When we speak of bishops or priests or deacons (or any other ministry) we are essentially speaking of people the community (not just this community but every local church) needs if it is to live its corporate life within Christ. One must have someone who has oversight of the practice of being disciples, one must have those who preside over the Eucharist, and one must have those who assist the community in various defined ways. These are publicly recognisable tasks and so common roles within the community. But a vocation relates to each person in the world, however small or large it is, at which that person is the centre. It could be the need to care for a sick relative. It might be that someone is the only person who can mediate and act as reconciler between those in a family dispute. It might be the need to bear witness to the demands of acting ethically in a boardroom meeting. It might be that someone has to put his/her comfort on hold as he/she is the only person who can provide a service to the community such as clearing blocked drains on a miserable day or it might be learning to sing a difficult psalm for the liturgy. It might be a parent teaching a child to know our prayers. It might be giving resources (money, time, skill) to some project that advances the kingdom of peace. Vocation is

about the call each of us has to build the kingdom in that precise part of the whole creation where we are located.

4. A vocation is common to all the baptised, but what it calls on us to do is different for each of us: in the gospel no two people got the same number of talents. We all must build the kingdom, but the demands that commission makes are never the same for any two individuals. Church ministries are essentially similar – this is the very presupposition of ordination; while vocations are essentially different as no two individuals occupy the same position in time/space, and within a set of relationships and skills, in the creation. This vocation is essentially religious: it involves God's providence and our loving co-operation by which we move along our individual pilgrim's path while at the same time the whole church moves along its pilgrim route as the People of God. This uniqueness of vocation is now almost exclusively only spoken of by Catholics in relation to the vocation of Mary; but each Christian's vocation is similarly unique: only that individual can bring the kingdom of God into existence in her/his situation.

5. Obviously there are overlaps between ministries and vocations: there are some whose vocation includes a formal ministry; but even then the way that ministry is used for the glory of God will be individual to the person, his strengths and weaknesses, his skills and native genius, the place, the culture, the time, and the assortment of people who make up the community in which he uses his ministry. But if when you hear the word 'vocation' you think of someone wearing religious garb: then you have a problem in your understanding of what it is to be a Christian!

6. Here are a few slogans that can help clarify the situation:

(i) A religious vocation is not the same as a vocation to be a religious.

(ii) Ministerial tasks are common to many people; vocations are unique to individuals.

(iii) Ministerial tasks are visible to the group; a vocation is only visible to the individual.

(iv) All Christians have a vocation; only some will be given ministerial tasks.

(v) All have received talents; only you know what they are and how best to use them.

Lectionary Unit VII

The Son of Man coming in glory is king. This unit consists of just one Sunday: Sunday 34, the Last Sunday of the Year; and the lectionary describes its focus as 'God's kingdom fulfilled.'

The theme of the Sunday is the Matthaean presentation of Jesus as the King in judgement at the end of time.

In this unit all three readings form a thematic unity; indeed in Year A the second reading and gospel supply, together, all the basic imagery that underpins the Feast of Christ the King

The Feast of Christ the King

Introduction to the Celebration

Way back in January we began the year by celebrating the Baptism of Jesus when a voice was heard calling him 'the beloved Son'. During the year we have greeted Jesus under all the views of him we find in the gospels. Now today, at the end of the year, we greet him with the all-embracing title: Jesus Christ, Universal King.

The Christ is the one who will gather us all together at the end of time, the one who will judge the living and the dead, and then present his kingdom to the Father. In our pilgrimage of faith that kingdom of justice, truth, and peace is to be our beacon, and Christ our guide. But before we join Christ in his banquet, we must ask pardon for the times when we followed other paths and other ways, when we listened to false prophets of greed and materialism, and for when we have failed to work for the coming of the kingdom.

Rite of Penance

Lord Jesus, you are the king of all creation and our light. Lord have mercy.
Lord Jesus, you are the king of all creation and our guide. Christ have mercy.
Lord Jesus, you are the king of all creation and our peace. Lord have mercy.

Opening Prayer

The alternative prayer is a very rich text focused on the Christ as the One who brings the universe to its perfection.

Headings for Readings
First Reading
The promised king is one who will shepherd his people, make sure that none is lost, the wounded are bandaged, the weak made strong.

Second Reading
Christ, our king, will gather all the parts of the kingdom together in his hands at the end of time and present them to the Father. Paul in this reading echoes our own prayer today: 'As king, Jesus claims dominion over all creation, that he may present to you, his almighty Father, an eternal and universal kingdom.'

Gospel
The Lord Jesus will come again in glory, as King, to judge the living and the dead; and he will call to himself all those whom the Father has blessed. Matthew in this gospel pictures the finale of the creation, the event we are bringing to mind in this feast.

Prayer of the Faithful
President
Friends, our thoughts are on 'endings' this week: the end of the cycle of celebrations we began a year ago with Advent, the end of the cycle of reading when we have focused on St Matthew's gospel, and today on Christ as our Lord who will come again to judge the living and the dead at the end of time. Conscious of this time of 'endings,' let us put our needs before the Father.
Reader(s)
1. We have gathered here as a priestly people, so let us intercede for the whole church on earth, that it may be worthy of the kingdom. Lord hear us.
2. We have gathered here as a priestly people, so let us intercede for all peoples, that they may receive the gift of peace, and discover a kingdom beyond the powers of this world. Lord hear us.
3. We have gathered here as a priestly people, so let us intercede

for those who have positions of power in this world, that they recognise that there is an order in the creation, and respect it. Lord hear us.

4. We have gathered here as a priestly people, so let us intercede for those who have lost hope, lost faith, or lost courage. Lord hear us.

5. We have gathered here as a priestly people, so let us intercede for all in this community, that we may be found in the kingdom of Christ at the end. Lord hear us.

President

Father, you sent us your Son as our prophet, our priest and our king, and so made us your holy people. Hear our prayers and grant our needs through that same Christ, our Lord. Amen.

Eucharistic Prayer

Today has a proper preface (P51), Missal, p 454.

Invitation to the Our Father

Christ our king stands at the end of history gathering us together as the kingdom he presents to the Father; now, in union with Christ, let us pray to the Father:

Sign of Peace

We look forward to the time when Christ will be the universal king and bring the age of peace; until then we must be peace-makers and remind each other of this calling. So now we wish peace and forgiveness to our brothers and sisters.

Invitation to Communion

The Lord has prepared a banquet for his people, he bids us look towards the banquet of heaven. Behold he now bids us to share in his life at this table, Lord I am not worthy ...

Communion Reflection
As we sit around your table O Lord,
We recall that the Father anointed you,
With the oil of gladness,
As the universal King.
You claim dominion over all creation,
Yours is a kingdom of truth and life,
Yours is a kingdom of holiness and peace,
Yours is a kingdom of justice, love, and peace.
(Adapted from today's Preface)

Conclusion
May Christ the universal king guide your steps in the way of justice, guide your words with his wisdom, and guide your hearts towards his holiness. Amen.
May Christ the universal king be your leader, your light, and your peace both now and always. Amen.
May Christ the universal king grant this church a place in the kingdom he presents to the Father. Amen.

Notes
Today's feast is a celebration. Today we preach about the mystery of Christ and about the End-times, but this is for orthodox Christians the full realisation of the divine plan, it is the joy of a harvest, the quiet moment when a great work of art is completed, the advent of the rest and fullness of the life implanted in all human hearts. Alas, 'the End' has always provoked another strand of thinking by Christians: the end is the great reckoning, the great crunch, the vengeance of God. This is especially the case this year when we read the Matthaean judgement scene. This is a crucial challenge to all preaching: the reality of the call to build the kingdom, yet the reality that God is to be thought of in terms of loving generosity not those of vengeance. This dilemma in preaching is not new today – indeed it is visible in Matthew's own theology – but, while it has been resolved in various great theological systems, no one has found a simple way to

present it in preaching. However, being conscious of the dilemma at least prevents us from just opting for one side as if the other were irrelevant.

Dourness and eschatology seem, in the popular imagination, to go together! But the good news is that they do not. The End is not the great crunch, but the presentation of the kingdom to Father. The moment of return, the *parousia*, is not the image of the angry teacher returning to the noisy classroom, but of the entry of a king in splendour. So this is a day when the ceremonial tone, plenty of incense and lights, banners and fanfares, can play an important part in creating the sense that 'The End' is completion and consummation, not the Armageddon of apocalypticism. The ritual should set the note of a glorious finale.

COMMENTARY

First Reading: Ezek 34:11-12, 15-17
This is part of invective against Israel's religious leaders, those who were supposed to be 'the shepherds' of the people. In the ideal future time they will be replaced not by better versions of themselves, but by the Lord himself. And just as the scattering among the nations (v 12) is symbolic of all the suffering and evils that have befallen the people, so when the Lord comes they will be re-gathered to the perfect country, the New Land, and there they will be cared for by God. This event is, however, linked to the sorting of the good and the bad in the land, for the Final Shepherd will not only judge the shepherds but the sheep (v 17). In the present lection vv 13-14 have been inexplicably omitted, although they function as a gloss on v 12 and were the source of some of the earliest Christian imagery for the Eucharist as an anticipation of the eschatological banquet. Clearly, someone was nodding, scissors in hand!

Psalm: 22 (23)
This is the best-known expression of the shepherd-king motif. Today it is read eschatologically in the liturgy rather than in its usual reference frame of abiding caring presence. As an expres-

sion of eschatology it is a very valuable counter to the apocalyp-
ticist notions because it is such an approachable text; moreover,
it imagines the future in terms of the final banquet whose anticipation is, for us, the Eucharist.

Second Reading: 1 Cor 15:20-26, 28
See the comments on the gospel.

First Reading > Gospel Links
Continuity of theological imagery, especially between Ezek 34:
17 and Mt 25:32 which employs it. However, the parallel in imagery would have been more perfect if Ezek 34:13-14 had not
been excised.

Gospel: Mt 25:31-46
It is clear from even the briefest glance at early Christian literature that there was a profound interest in eschatology. There is a
common, and completely false, impression of how that interest
can be summed up: initially they expected the return of the Lord
to be very soon, then when that did not happen they re-assessed
their position and decided it was going to be a great judgement
at the end of time which would sort the sheep from the goats.
Like all great confusions, it has enough points of contact with
the facts to make it seem credible. However, reading Paul and
Matthew today should be enough to show that the scene is more
complex and much richer.

The first Christians had inherited a wide range of views from
the various Judaisms of the time: the end would be a new em-
pire, a great tribulation, a great judgement, a transformation, a
re-gathering, a consummation. In particular, there was a very
vocal stream within the churches who were devotees of apocalyptic teachings; and there were ex-followers of John the Baptist
who saw the end as the punishing recompense for the sinners.
Among Christians from a gentile background there were those
who thought of the future as a 'golden age,' those who expected
an end in 'the katastrophe,' and those who imagined 'The End'

as simply a code for a parallel perfect, celestial, universe (Plato's World of Forms with God as king). Alongside these views was the fact that Jesus had rejected both apocalypticism and 'the great crunch,' and the knowledge that his teaching spoke of the love and forgiveness of the Father, of the end as the banquet, the harvest, and the marriage feast. The challenge that faced the first Christian preachers – and the task is still incomplete – was to bear witness to the teaching of Jesus while coping with their own deepest imaginings and feelings about the future. None managed wholly successfully, and some failed miserably in facing this challenge. The result was a wide variety of eschatologies ranging from the brimstone imagery of the Apocalypse to that of Paul in today's second reading. And, each strand has had its devotees ever since: the fire and brimstone preachers seem to revel in every bit of bad news that comes their way as being an indicator that 'the end is nigh', while today we celebrate the end of the liturgical cycle with a celebration of eschatology based very much on this reading from Paul. What became the dominant Christian position was that there would be the glorious return of the king, then the return of the universe transformed through the Logos, to the Father, which would coincide with the tombs giving up their inhabitants and then the judgement between the two ways. And we should read both Paul and Matthew today as two distinct eschatologies, but founded in similar circumstances and cultures, and coping with the same range of problems (though Paul would not have approved of Matthew's apocalypticism). Both of today's texts are without parallel among the canonical texts (Mt 25:31-46 forms a unit that is proper to Matthew) and illustrate the variety of teaching in the early church and both contributed to the later common position. Our task as readers is to note how they subtly differ, while at the same time noting the similarity in original situations, while at the same time noting their contribution to the common memory, while remembering also that every generation must live in creative tension with the tradition so as to come to know as well as it can the mind of Christ.

HOMILY NOTES

1. One of the most lyrical passages in the whole liturgy is the
   preface for this day. It was produced in the immediate aftermath of the First World War, and appeared with the institution of this feast in 1925. It is a masterpiece of theology that,
   in many respects, anticipated the theology of the liturgy of
   the Second Vatican Council. However, it is rarely heard, and
   when it is heard each year on this feast it can be lost, as many
   prefaces are, as it is just a brief interlude between the bustle
   of the 'offertory' and the more serious-minded tone of the
   prayer after the Sanctus.

   At the end of the liturgical cycle there is a note of reflection, on what has happened and on the End-times, in today's
   liturgy and this can be fostered by replacing a preached
   homily with a reflection on this preface.

2. The simplest way is just to draw it to the assembly's attention, and then just read through it slowly, line-by-line.

3. One can add a commentary, but care has to be exercised that
   commentary does not take over from reflection. There is a
   thin line between the helpful comment aiding reflection and
   the series of glosses on the way towards the lecture.

4. Such a reflection, given the nature of the text, has an additional effect: it produces a nice, quiet way to end the Year –
   next week the liturgy will be all agog as everyone starts
   thinking of Christmas.